D1143178

THE MODERN BALKANS

THE MODERN BALKANS

A History

RICHARD C. HALL

REAKTION BOOKS

L 202, 712

For Audrey, as ever

Published by Reaktion Books Ltd
33 Great Sutton Street
London EC1V 0DX, UK
www.reaktionbooks.co.uk

First published 2011
Copyright © Richard C. Hall 2011

All rights reserved
No part of this publication may be reproduced, stored in a retrieval system,
or transmitted, in any form or by any means, electronic, mechanical, photocopying,
recording or otherwise, without the prior permission of the publishers.

Printed and bound in Great Britain by
MPG Books Group

British Library Cataloguing in Publication Data

Hall, Richard C. (Richard Cooper), 1950–
The modern Balkans : a history.
1. Balkan Peninsula – History – 19th century.
2. Balkan Peninsula – History – 20th century.
1. Title
949.6-DC22

ISBN: 978 1 86189 810 4

Contents

Introduction

The Balkan Peninsula of Southeastern Europe was the first part of the continent to achieve civilization. In ancient times it formed an important link between eastern Mediterranean and European civilizations. After the Middle Ages, however, the region seemed to fade into itself. First Orthodox culture and then Ottoman rule isolated the region from the rest of Europe.

Only at the end of the eighteenth and the beginning of the nineteenth centuries did the region again come into contact with the outside world. Especially important were contacts with Western Europe. As a result of these contacts the peoples of Southeastern Europe struggled to emulate the more economically and politically developed Western European states. These efforts led to much instability and war during the twentieth century. The Communist interlude also isolated the region from the rest of Europe to a degree, but imposed peace. Cold War concerns, however, increased Western interest in the region.

The end of Communism brought to the region the hope of restoration of its European identity. It also brought violence. Romania underwent a short but bloody revolution. The situations in Albania and in Yugoslavia compelled the European Union, the United Nations and NATO to intervene in order to establish stability. Only Bulgaria escaped bloodshed during this transition.

With the onset of the nineteenth century, Southeastern Europe began to achieve recognition as a distinct region of the continent. This recognition was based on the singularities of the area. Its geography was more complicated, its peoples more exotic and its politics more arcane than the rest of Europe. It seemed to have a penchant for mystery and violence.

Southeastern Europe appeared to be a part of another world, often referred to as 'The Balkans'. The association of the name Balkan with obscurity and violence became a cliché.

A variety of works on the region appeared in English at the beginning of the twentieth century. Most of these emphasized the distinct characteristics of the Balkans. A good example is the American historian Ferdinand Schevill's *History of the Balkans from the Earliest Times to the Present Day*.[1] During the Cold War the region came under scrutiny because of the Soviet shadow. Among the works to address the region as having a distinct identity was Robert Lee Wolff's *The Balkans in Our Time*.[2] This was followed by Stavos Stavrianos's *The Balkans since 1453*.[3] Both of these works offered thoughtful introductions to the complexities of the region. Another excellent introduction to the region is Mark Mazower's *The Balkans: A Short History*.[4] It is particularly good on the interaction of the region with the rest of Europe.

Southeastern Europe is now undergoing a process of integration with the rest of Europe. For this reason the terms Balkans and Southeastern Europe will be used interchangeably to refer to the region throughout this book. Recent studies of the region, such as John R. Lampe's *Balkans into Southeastern Europe* and Andrew Baruch Wachtel's *The Balkans in World History*, emphasize that the region is now integrating with the rest of Europe.[5] Now, with most of the countries members of NATO and the European Union, integration offers the region another opportunity for peace and prosperity.

one

Geography

The natural setting of any region is a significant factor in understanding the course of human events over time. Natural setting has played a particularly important role in the history of Southeastern Europe.[1] Southeastern Europe is a peninsula, often termed the Balkan Peninsula. Wide in the north, it tapers down to the Peloponnese, itself a peninsula, and from there to a series of rocky islands off its western, southern and eastern coasts. The main groups of these islands are the Ionian Islands in the Adriatic and Crete and the Cyclades in the Aegean. Rocky fragments of the Dinaric Mountain chain span the entire coastline of the Adriatic Sea from Istria to the Peloponnese. The construction of the Corinth Canal across the narrow isthmus which links the Peloponnese to the rest of mainland Greece in 1893 provided a direct water link between the Aegean and Ionian Seas. There are significant bodies of water on three sides of Southeastern Europe. In the west is the Adriatic Sea and to the south is the Aegean Sea; these two bodies of water are arms of the much larger Mediterranean Sea. To the east is the Black Sea, a self-contained body of water, accessible to the Mediterranean only through the narrow passage way of the Dardanelles, Sea of Marmara and the Bosporus. The two large islands in the eastern Mediterranean, Crete and Cyprus, although located at some distance from the mainland, have both played important roles in the political history of the region.

Mountains are another defining characteristic of Southeastern Europe. Almost 70 per cent of the region is mountainous.[2] The mountains impose an irregular and rugged topography over the entire region. Two main mountain systems dominate the region. The first is a generally barren limestone alpine system often called *karst*. These mountains generally run

Balkan geography.

from northwest to southeast along the entire length of the western portion of the peninsula. They are known as the Dinaric Alps in Croatia and Bosnia, the Albanian Alps in Albania and the Pindus Mountains in Greece. These mountains often run right down to the Adriatic Sea. Along the Dalmatian and Greek coasts there are many islands resulting from the continuation of the mountain system under sea. Crests of this system generally reach 1,800 m (6,000 feet). In some areas, notably the Albanian Alps in northern Albania and the Pindus Mountains in northwestern Greece, the peaks reach as high as 2,400 m (8,000 feet). Along the easterly edge of these mountains in Albania, Macedonia and Greece there are a number of freshwater lakes. These include Lake Scutari, which lies between Albania and Montenegro, Lake Ohrid between Albania and Macedonia, and Lakes Prespa and Doiran between Greece and Macedonia.

The other mountain system is more easterly. In Romania, the thickly forested Carpathians impose a reverse S-shape on the northeastern region of the peninsula. The peaks of the Carpathians in Romania can exceed 2,400 m (8,000 feet). Nevertheless numerous passes enable relatively easy access between hilly Transylvania and the plains of Moldavia and Wallachia. This mountain system crosses the Danube at a narrow defile called in modern times the Iron Gates. The range then extends through Serbia, where it is called the Northeast Serbian Mountains. It expands to the southeast and when it reaches Bulgaria forks into two separate systems. The northern portion is known as the Balkan Mountains, generally running west to east through Bulgaria. These mountains were known in ancient times as the Haemus. The term Balkan is a colloquial Turkish word meaning mountain chain. This is the origin of the popular name of the region.[3] The Bulgarians themselves call the Balkan Mountains the *Stara Planina*, or Old Mountains. There are numerous points of access across these mountains. The best known of these is Shipka Pass, which was the scene of an important battle in the nineteenth century. A smaller range, the *Sredna Gora* (Middle Mountains), parallels the Balkan Mountains to the south. This is really just a line of hills arising from the Thracian Plain. Often the forest cover is absent in the Balkans and Sredna Gora. The southern Bulgarian mountain system is known as the Rhodope Mountains. Peaks there, such as 2,289 m (7,510 foot) Vitosha, located directly south of Sofia, and Rila, the highest of these mountains at 2,925 m (9,596 feet), can retain some snow all year round. Parts of the mountain forests remain in the Balkan Mountains. The Carpathians, the highest of the southeastern mountains and the Rhodopes still retain most of their forest cover.

All of the Southeastern European mountains are crossable, yet by their very ubiquity they impose transportation and communication difficulties on the region. The Dinaric Alps in particular isolate the hinterland from the Adriatic. All of these mountains have provided havens for herdsmen, outlaws and guerillas throughout the history of the region. Only in modern times have these mountain regions come firmly under the control of a central government invariably located in lowland areas.

Nevertheless there is little flat land in the region. The main relatively level areas are the Vojvodina, northern Bulgaria and in Wallachia, Moldavia and Romania along the Danube, the Prut and Dniester Rivers. Another level area is the Thracian plain, which extends from a point in western Bulgaria near and spreads out into European Turkey. Smaller areas include Kosovo Polje and the fertile region between the abrupt northern turn of the Danube River in its lower reaches and the Black Sea, Dobrudja, called Dobrudzha by the Bulgarians and Dobrodgea by the Romanians. This agricultural region is an extension of the Eurasian steppe. Finally the coastal area of Albania is largely flat. It extends some distance inland. Towards the sea it is often marshy, and until recently has been malarial. Most of the rest of the region is either dramatically mountainous or picturesquely hilly. The lack of large areas of arable land has tended to limit the size of agricultural holdings in the region. While agriculture in the Byzantine and later Ottoman and Habsburg times was based on the manorial system, few really large estates ever developed, except in Vojvodina and the Romanian lands. Consequently the Balkans was never a region that provided great agricultural wealth to a landholding class. The difficult topography correspondingly made the accumulation of wealth unlikely. It also promoted local identity and political disunity.

The difficult topography of the region makes overland transportation problematic. The Dinaric Alps tend to cut the hinterland off from the Adriatic. The main gateway to the Adriatic Sea and the west across the Dinarics historically has been the city of Dubrovnik (Ragusa). The major river of the region is the Danube, which rises in southwestern Germany and empties into the Black Sea in a marshy delta. Most of the other rivers in the region are part of the Danubian system. These include the Sava, the Drina and the previously mentioned Prut. While the Danube is by far the most important river system in the region, its utility as a means of transportation is limited. One problem that hinders its utility is its outflow into the Black Sea. With only one outlet in its southwestern corner, the Black Sea is not a body of water affording wide global access. Another problem was that until 1896 the Iron Gates, the rock formations in the river where the Carpathian system crosses the Danube into Serbia, blocked river traffic further east. Ships had to be offloaded and goods transported by land for several miles before they were loaded again onto other ships for their transport further east. Only the invention of dynamite enabled the Danube to become open for river traffic all the way to the Black Sea. Even so, navigation through the swift waters of this passage often required assistance from a land-based locomotive.

Except for those in the Danubian system, no rivers in the region have much utility for navigation. Balkan rivers flow out of the relatively dry interior of the region. They often vary seasonally in depth. Few rivers flow westerly to the Adriatic and the Aegean. The only significant river in Bosnia to flow in this direction is the Neretva. Several others flow through Albania, including the Drin, the Shkumbin and the Vjosë. Further east the Vardar, the Struma and the Maritsa flow south from Bulgaria into the Aegean. The courses of the Vardar and Struma cut through the mountains and form narrow defiles or gorges formed as the rivers pass through the mountains. These defiles have served historically as pressure points and in modern times as passages for roads and railways. In Serbia, there is a relatively short gap in northern Macedonia between the Vardar River, flowing south, and the Morava River, flowing north to the Danube. This Vardar–Morava link forms an important transit corridor between the Danube and the Aegean and in a larger context between Central Europe and the Balkans.

Roads and railways generally follow the river systems through the difficult Balkan topography. The Morava–Vardar route is particularly important because it connects Central Europe at Belgrade to the Aegean Sea at Thessaloniki (Salonika). At Niš another important transportation corridor separates from this one and proceeds to Sofia and then through the Thracian plain to Istanbul. One important exception to roads and railways following river systems is the Belgrade–Bar Railroad, opened by the Yugoslav government in 1973, which links the Adriatic Sea with the Danube. It replaced an older narrow-gauge railway built from Sarajevo to Dubrovnik by Austro-Hungarian authorities in the nineteenth century. Although the Italians first built a railway from the Adriatic port of Durrës (Durrazo) to Tirana in the 1930s, Albania was not linked to the European rail system until 1986, when a line from Shkodër (Scutari) to Podgorica (Titograd) opened. Another important transportation corridor that does not follow a river system is the ancient *Via Egentia*. This road, constructed by the Romans, stretched from the Adriatic Sea at Durrës in Albania across the mountains to Thessalonika, and from there along the Thracian littoral of the Aegean Sea to Istanbul. It functioned as a land route from Rome to Constantinople. Modern roads and railways only approximate the route from Thessaloniki to Istanbul. Regional development plans, however, now contemplate the restoration of the entire route.

There are two main types of climate in the region. In Greece and the Adriatic and Black Sea coasts the climate is Mediterranean. This means warm, dry winters and summers and rainy autumns. Citrus and olive cultivation is possible in this region. The other climate zone, in the remainder of the peninsula, is continental. Although it has precipitation at all times of year, it is generally drier than the coastal region. The interior endures long, cold winters. Higher elevations in both zones experience more severe conditions.

There are some natural resources in the region. The most important was oil, found in considerably quantity in Wallachia. Gold, silver, copper and other metal ores such as bauxite have also been found in Bosnia, Serbia and Transylvania. Coal in the region is generally of poor quality. Most of the natural resources of the region had been exhausted by the beginning of the twenty-first century.

The entire Balkan region is earthquake-prone. Major seismic events have occurred throughout its history. A massive earthquake destroyed Corinth, Greece in 856 CE. More modern major occurrences were in Skopje (Skopie, Skoplje, Üsküb), Macedonia in 1963, in southern Romania in 1977 and in Athens in 1999. All of these events caused significant loss of life and property damage.

The difficult topography has facilitated a complex ethnographic development in the Balkan region. Because of this few clear ethnic and cultural borders exist. Peoples and cultures blend together. Absolutes in this context are rare. Some areas, such as Dobrudja and Macedonia, are particularly diverse.

The Albanians and the Greeks are the modern two groups with the longest sustained presence in the Balkan Peninsula. The Albanians (in their own language *Shqiptaria*: Sons of the Eagle) may be descended from the ancient Illyrians. The Albanian language is singular, and is remotely related to Greek. Albanian has an important dialectical divide. The rural and tribal northern areas, including Kosovo, speak the Gheg variant of Albanian, while the southern regions and urban areas speak Tosk. The language is written in Latin characters using a system developed at the end of the nineteenth century. The Tosk dialect is the basis for the modern written language.

Religion and culture is quite mixed in Albania. Most Albanians accepted Islam after the Ottoman invasion, but Orthodox Christians remain in the south and a Roman Catholic community resides in the north of the country. The breakdown traditionally is given at 70 per cent Muslim, 20 per cent Orthodox and 10 per cent Roman Catholic. The divisions among these faiths and cultures are not strong. Religion has not become a basis for conflict among the Albanians as it has in modern times among the South Slavs of Bulgaria and Yugoslavia. The ruggedness of the topography in the western Balkan Peninsula and its remoteness from major population centres have kept the Albanians relatively isolated throughout much of their history.

The Greeks (Greek: *Hellenes*) have occupied their southern part of the Balkan Peninsula and the Aegean islands since historic times. They were the vector for the transmission of civilization from the eastern Mediterranean regions to Europe. Undoubtedly over the centuries successive waves of invaders, settlers and refugees have greatly diluted the genetic material of the original Hellenes; the most recent of these were Anatolian Christians after the Treaty of Lausanne in 1923. The Greeks are overwhelmingly Orthodox Christian in religion. They write their language in an alphabet derived from that developed by the original Hellenes in the eighth century BCE.

The Romanians are something of an ethnic and cultural anomaly in the region. They are the only Latin-speaking people with Orthodox culture. Even though the Romanian language is clearly related to the other Romance languages, it has strong Slavic influences. Until the eighteenth century, Romanians used the Cyrillic alphabet to write their language. Since then they have used a modified version of the Latin alphabet. The Romanians assert that they are the descendants of Roman colonists who probably mixed with the indigenous Dacians, that part of the Thracian people living north of the Danube, and that these Latin speakers have maintained an uninterrupted presence in this region. Other sources suggest that the Romanians are in fact descended from Romanized peoples from elsewhere in the Balkans, who eventually sought refuge from waves of invaders in the safety of the Carpathians. There remain Latin-speaking peoples, traditionally shepherds, in Bulgaria, Macedonia, Greece and Albania, known as Vlachs. Traditionally these people were transhumant, and often stayed in the higher elevations with their flocks. Many of the Vlachs are now gradually assimilating into the peoples they live among. The controversy over the origin of the Romanians assumes a political tone, mainly in the case of Transylvania. Hungarians claim they were the first settlers of the region; Romanians assert that their presence in the region goes back to Roman times.

The Slavs are the largest and most diverse people in the Balkan Peninsula. They migrated south into the area in the sixth and seventh centuries CE. They came not just as conquerors but as agriculturists seeking permanent settlements. The Slavs gradually overwhelmed the efforts of the Roman authorities in Constantinople to interdict them along the Danubian frontier. Slavic settlements appeared as far south as the Peloponnese. Wherever they settled they undoubtedly intermingled with the partially Romanized and partially Hellenized Illyrian and Thracian populations they encountered. Gradually they differentiated into separate groups of extended families. The Bulgarians were the first to develop a distinct identity. This was largely due to the arrival of Turkic-speaking Bulgars in the Danube valley during the seventh century. These peoples, who originated further east on the Volga, imposed themselves as a military aristocracy on the Slavic peoples living along the Danube. Eventually the Slavic-speaking majority absorbed the ruling Turkic minority, establishing a pattern that would be replicated later in Russia and in Normandy, among other areas. The Slavs further to the northwest of the Bulgarians eventually coalesced into the Orthodox Serbs.

The Montenegrins are Serbian-speaking and Orthodox. Although they had enjoyed a separate political identity since at least the eighteenth century, a cultural identity distinct from other Serbs is not yet firmly established. The distinctiveness of the Macedonians is a matter of much dispute. Greeks have asserted that Macedonians are the descendants of the people whom Alexander the Great (356–323 BCE) led to conquer much of the known world. The Serbs have claimed that the Macedonians are South Serbs. The Bulgarians assert that the Macedonians are Bulgarians whom war and politics have divided from their fellow nationals living to the east. In any event, since Tito established a Macedonian Republic in 1945 with its distinct Cyrillic alphabet and with its own Orthodox church administration in Skopje, the Macedonians have assumed a singular Slavic identity. Croats and Slovenes received their Christianity from Rome. Politically and culturally these peoples were oriented towards Central Europe. The Croats had a long political association with Hungary, and the Slovenes with Austria.

Several other groups played an important role in the area. Turks under the command of the Ottoman dynasty settled into some of the more level and fertile regions of Southeastern Europe, and also along the approaches to Constantinople. While the rise of national states in the nineteenth century resulted in the expulsion or removal of some of the Turkish population from Greece and Serbia, many Turks remain in the Dobrudja, Macedonia and especially in eastern Bulgaria.

The Roma (Gypsies) arrived in Southeastern Europe at about the same time as the Turks. Although they have at times adopted Orthodox Christianity or Islam, the Roma have not assimilated into the larger societies in Southeastern Europe. Often pursing a transient lifestyle until modern times, they retain their distinct culture. Their numbers remain unclear. Despite efforts by Communist authorities to educate and settle them, the Roma never have been able to achieve significant economic or political success in the region.

While Jews have had a presence in Southeastern Europe since ancient times, they arrived in significant numbers in two distinct waves. The first to settle were refugees from Christian persecution in the Iberian Peninsula. These are known as the Sephardim. They speak a variant of medieval Spanish called Ladino. After moving into the Ottoman Empire in the sixteenth and seventeenth centuries, the Sephardim settled along the communication routes in the Balkan Peninsula. Salonika, with a Jewish population plurality in the early twentieth century, became a particular centre for Ladino culture. Yiddish-speaking Ashkenazi Jews moved into Moldavia and Wallachia from Galicia after enlightened Habsburg rulers lifted restrictions on their movements at the end of the eighteenth century. While the Romanian lands remained home to the largest Ashkenazi population in Southeastern Europe, other Ashkenazi Jews settled elsewhere along the Danube.

Significant Hungarian populations are found in Vojvodina and Transylvania. Habsburg rule in the western Balkans also brought smaller numbers of Czechs, Slovaks and Ukrainians into the region, especially in Bosnia, Croatia and Vojvodina. Germans have lived in Transylvania, Dobrudja and Vojvodina since the Middle Ages. Italians lived along the Adriatic coast. Most cities on the eastern shore of the Adriatic have Italian variants of their names. The mountains, however, prevented Italian influence from penetrating very far inland.

Twentieth-century conflicts somewhat simplified the ethnic diversity of the region. Population exchanges between Greece and Turkey in 1923 virtually eliminated the Greek-speaking and Turkish-speaking Islamic population in Greece. The German population of Vojvodina left or was expelled after the Second World War. The German-induced Holocaust victimized Ashkenazi and Sephardim alike. Much of the Jewish population who managed to survive the Second World War left the region after the war for Israel, the United States or Australia. The Yugoslav Wars of the 1990s concentrated the populations living there, especially in Bosnia. Before this catastrophe, Bosniaks (Serbo-Croat-speaking Muslims), Croats and Serbs had all lived in proximity to each other, if not actually together, for centuries. Afterwards they existed in mainly ethnic enclaves. Much of the Serbian population living in the Krajina region of Croatia and in Kosovo before 1991 also fled or was compelled to leave. Finally the German population of Transylvania, which had arrived during the Middle Ages and had managed to endure the tribulations of war and dictatorship, had largely moved to Germany by the beginning of the twenty-first century. Even so, at the beginning of the twenty-first century a German major of Sibiu (Hermannstadt) in Transylvania, Klaus Iohannis (1959–), attracted national political interest in Romania because of his 'Germanic' qualities of efficiency and diligence.[4] The Italian populations of the Adriatic coast and the Italian settlers in Albania for the most part left after the Second World War.

Geography does not explain the entire region. The northern extent of the Balkan Peninsula lacks clear definition. In the east it might be the Danube River, but that would exclude the Romanian lands, especially Wallachia and Moldavia. It might be the Carpathian Mountains, but that would omit Transylvania, with its Romanian Orthodox majority. The

L202,712

northeastern limit is equally problematic, because of the extension of Romanian-speaking people along the northwestern littoral of the Black Sea. There the limit of Southeastern Europe might best be the Dniester River, which is the functional eastern frontier of Moldova.[5] Romanian-speaking people do live east of the Dniester, but as a minority among the Ukrainians there. In the west the frontier might be the Sava River. Also there is the problem of Dalmatia, along the Adriatic coast. Although in the past there were Italians and Orthodox Slavs in Dalmatia, today the population is mainly Croatian and Roman Catholic. The Italians were derived from the Latin-speaking peoples of the Adriatic coast, who maintained this identity largely through connections to the traditional Adriatic powers of Venice and Dubrovnik. By the end of the twentieth century, most of the Italian-speaking population of Dalmatia either assimilated into the Slavic majority or left the region. Some Serbian Orthodox remain in Dalmatia. Because of these issues, the question of definition also requires a cultural context.

Most of the peoples of the region belong to the Orthodox or *Pravoslav* cultural sphere. These peoples – Greeks, Slavs and the Romanians as well as a minority of Albanians – derived their Christian culture from the norms established in the eastern part of the Roman Empire, centred at Constantinople. Their liturgies were in Greek or Slavic, not Latin. Their alphabets are Greek or Cyrillic, itself derived from Greek. Only in the eighteenth century did the Romanian peoples adopt the Latin alphabet. Before that they used Cyrillic to write their Latin-based language. All of the major peoples of the Balkans have an Orthodox component in their culture. The churches maintain a distinct ritual, with the use of religious images or icons accorded a prominent role. Priests, the 'black' clergy, wear specific garb and must marry. Monks, the 'white' clergy, live lives of austerity and celibacy, and often provide the leadership for the church. The concept of *Caesaropapism*, where the church accepts a subordinate position to the civil authority, remains strong in the region. Although all of the Orthodox churches in Southeastern Europe acknowledge the supremacy of the patriarch in Constantinople, they all retain local administrative authority.

In more modern times, the Sunni variant of Islam gained a foothold among all of the peoples in the Balkan Peninsula, except the Romanians. Most Albanians are Sunni Muslims. The Islamic Greek population had left the country by the 1920s in a population exchange with Turkey. Otherwise the Balkan Islamic populations remain intact. The South Slavic peoples converted to Islam in varying numbers. In Bulgaria these converts became known as *Pomaks*. Further west there were converts, especially in Bosnia. Christian Bosnians often refer to their Muslim neighbours as 'Turks', even though they all speak Serbo-Croat. The term to describe the Muslims of Bosnia is now Bosniaks. Other South Slavic Muslims, such as those remaining in the former Sandjak of Novi Pazar, lack a precise descriptive term. The process of conversion from Roman Catholic and Orthodox Christianity to Islam throughout the region was gradual and often without coercion.

While Roman Catholic minorities exist in Southeastern Europe, especially among the Albanians, their numbers are not large. There are also a few Uniates in the Balkans. Uniate churches follow Orthodox ritual and practices but acknowledge the administrative and theological superiority of the Roman pontiff. They are found in western Ukraine and western Belarus, but also in Transylvania. Protestants rarely succeeded in reaching many of the Balkan peoples, despite the efforts of many American missionaries in the nineteenth and twentieth centuries. This geographic and cultural definition for the Balkans excludes the Croats, whose Catholicism oriented them towards Central Europe and the Habsburgs. It also leaves out Transylvania, which despite having a Romanian Orthodox majority was likewise oriented towards Hungary and Central Europe. These regions, as well as the Central European Slovenia, can only be considered as Balkan when they are ruled by Balkan states. By this criterion Transylvania remains 'Balkan', while Slovenia was only 'Balkan' from 1918 until 1991 during its association with the two incarnations of the Yugoslav state. Because of its fighting against Serbia from 1991–5 and its ongoing involvement in Bosnia, Roman Catholic Central European Croatia continues to be 'Balkan' to some degree. The status of Moldova also is unclear. Until the nineteenth century, the princes of Moldovia ruled the region. From 1918–40 and again from 1941–4 it was ruled by Romania and known as Bessarabia (Basarabia). As an independent, largely Orthodox state, it is very similar culturally and economically to the other states west of the Prut River. In the end a comprehensive geographic and cultural definition of the Balkans remains elusive.

Contemporary trends often avoid the term Balkan to describe the region because of its association with backwardness and complexity. Instead, the term Southeastern Europe is preferred. This emphasizes the connection of the region with the more developed regions of the continent.[6] It is especially more appropriate since the amalgamation of much of the region into the European Union, and the anticipated joining of the remainder in the next twenty years. The process is by no means complete, and some regions, such as Albania, Bosnia, Macedonia and Moldova, remain far behind the rest of Europe in terms of economic and social indexes. Nevertheless, the very fact of the initiation of the integration process for this region is cause for optimism.

two

The Legacy of Empire:
The Middle Ages to 1804

Civilization spread into Southeastern Europe from across the eastern Mediterranean Sea. The first peoples to develop the rudiments of civilization, such as writing and urban living, were the inhabitants of Crete and the Cyclades islands. Heavily influenced by the Egyptians and Mesopotamians, the Minoan Civilization flourished on the Crete from around 2000 BCE to around 1100 BCE. The details of the Minoan Civilization and its written language, Linear A, remain obscure. From Crete the ideas of civilization spread to additional Aegean islands and on to the European mainland. The ensuing development in the Peloponnese and Attica was the Mycenean Civilization. The written language used there, Linear B, demonstrates a clear correlation with Greek. After several centuries from 1400 to 1100 BCE, an invasion of Dorians from the north snuffed this civilization out. These Dorians were related to the Myceneans linguistically, but they had not achieved the cultural progress that the Myceneans had. As a result a 'Dark Age' without the overt trappings of civilization descended upon the Aegean islands and the European mainland. Around 800 BCE, civilization gradually returned to these regions and the co-mingled Mycenean and Dorian peoples living there. This was the classic age of Greek accomplishment. The reinvigorated Greek city-state civilization, beset by the need for greater resources, expanded into the Black Sea in the east and the Ionian and Adriatic Seas in the west. In particular these Greeks sought grain and slaves from the peoples living along the shores of the Black Sea and to some extent those in the interior of Southeastern Europe. These Greeks founded colonies at such locations as Constanța and Nesebŭr (Mesembria) on the Black Sea and Durrës and Split on the Adriatic Sea. Probably the most famous of these colonies was

Byzantion, founded in the seventh century BCE by the Greeks from the city of Megara in Attica. Their leader was the legendary Byzas, from whom the name of the colony was derived. Small coastal settlements interacted commercially and culturally with the peoples of the interior. These included the Thracians in the east and the Illyrians in the west. The Thracians had achieved some level of political organization by the time of their first contact with the Greeks; the Illyrians, by contrast, were less developed.

Political unity was slow to emerge in Southeastern Europe. The Macedonians, whose origins remain obscure, imposed a brief control over the Greek states and the southern part of the Balkan Peninsula. These Macedonians were probably a mixture of non-Greeks and Greek colonists who had moved into the area.[1] In any event, they were Greek in terms of culture by the time they first appeared in history in the fourth century BCE. Under King Philip II (382–336 BCE) and his son Alexander the Great (356–323 BCE), Macedonian rule spread the Greek language and culture throughout the region.

Only with the advent of the Romans during the third and second centuries BCE, however, did the entire area become a single political and cultural entity. Roman power extended throughout Southeastern Europe. As they expanded, the Romans built cities and roads throughout the region. They founded or greatly expanded such cities as Belgrade, Sofia and Adrianople (Edirne). They also constructed an important road across the waist of Southeastern Europe. This *Via Egnatia* began at Durrës, and led to Salonika and then Constantinople. Roman control and influence were by no means uniform throughout Southeastern Europe. The more difficult the terrain, the less authority the Romans could exert. This was especially true in the case of the mountainous regions, such as Albania and Bosnia. The Illyrian hill tribes in these regions fought against the Romans more or less constantly, establishing a pattern that would continue through Byzantine and Ottoman eras. In 107 CE the Romans, led by Emperor Trajan (53–117), crossed the Danube River frontier and conquered the Dacians, a Thracian people. Roman rule there lasted until 275 CE, when Emperor Aurelian (214/15–275) ordered the legions back across the Danube. Goth attacks had pressured these forces for some time. The duration of Roman language and culture survival north of the Danube after the retreat of Roman military power remains uncertain. Romanian historians assert that the presence of Latin speakers, the direct ancestors of Romanians, remained north of the Danube up to the present.[2] Others insist that the contemporary Latin speakers in this region are derived from the Vlachs, who were probably the descendants of Latin speakers who persevered south of the Danube. These Latin speakers presumably moved north across the Danube at some later point, perhaps during the time of the Slavic invasions or even as late as the tenth century.

By the third century CE the Roman Empire had undergone a series of political and economic problems. The empire struggled through a series of civil wars. At the same time the population was in decline and the tax revenues available to the state shrivelled. Some of these problems were the consequence of the failure of the Roman system to develop a standard protocol for political succession. Others accompanied the movement of peoples into the empire from the east, bringing with them epidemic disease and economic collapse. Successive waves of Goth, Avar and Slav invaders beset the empire's Southeastern European frontiers for the next four hundred years.

In an effort to deal with these problems, the Emperor Diocletian (244–311), himself born in Illyria, divided his empire into four administrative areas called prefectures: Gaul, Italy, Illyricum and the Prefecture of the East. Southeastern Europe was divided between the Prefecture of Illyricum, which included modern Greece, Albania, Serbia, Macedonia, Montenegro and Kosovo, and the Prefecture of the East, which included modern Bulgaria. The overly complicated system Diocletian initiated failed to take hold. By the time of his death in 311, the empire once again plunged into a period of civil disorder. Another Illyrian, Constantine (272–337), known as the Great, succeeded in imposing his rule on the entire empire. He established his capital in 324 on the site of the ancient Megarian colony of Byzantion.[3] The new capital was initially called New Rome (Nova Roma), but soon came to be known as Constantinople, the city of Constantine. In 312 Constantine agreed to end the official persecutions of Christianity that had sporadically harassed its adherents since the first century CE. The barbarian invasions of Southeastern Europe continued throughout the fourth century, mainly by Germanic tribes coming across the Danube. In 378 a large force of Goths defeated and slew Emperor Valens (328–378) at Adrianople, the main Thracian city astride the approaches to Constantinople. In 392 the emperor Theodocius I (347–395) made Christianity the state religion of Rome. After his death Theodocius' two sons divided the empire. Honorius (384–423) took the western portion. This Western Roman Empire lasted only until 476, when the German general Odoacer (435–493) extinguished it. Arcadius (377/78 –408) obtained the eastern part of his father's empire. It endured as the Roman Empire until 1453.

Historians dispute the precise dates of the transition between the ancient world and the medieval world in Southeastern Europe. They also dispute the name for the political and religious entity, based upon its administrative and economic centre, Constantinople, that dominated the region for the next thousand years. Was it simply Rome? This was what the inhabitants called it. But unlike the original inhabitants of the bearer of that proud name, the people of this state were Christians by law, and the educated and upper classes mainly spoke and wrote in Greek. Other names for this entity are the Later Roman Empire, the Medieval Greek Empire and Byzantium. The last is probably the most popular. It is based on an anachronistic reference to the original Athenian colony that occupied the site of Constantinople. The inhabitants of the civilization that developed in this entity would not have recognized the term Byzantium. They always referred to themselves as Romans but usually in the Greek language, *Rhomaioi*. The modern Greek state regards Byzantium as its direct predecessor.

The city of Constantinople was one of the major factors in the long duration of this empire. It lay at the land and water crossroads of Europe and Asia. Only a narrow body of water, the Bosporus, separated the land mass of Europe from that of Asia. This same body of water, together with the wider Sea of Marmara and the equally narrow Dardanelles, connected the Black Sea with the Aegean Sea. This site brought goods from all over the world to Constantinople. It became one of the largest cities in the world in terms of population, and a major world economic centre.

The location of the city also provided defensive advantages. The city itself was surrounded on three sides by water.[4] To the east was a natural harbour known as the Golden Horn. To the south was the fast-flowing Bosporus. The currents of this body of water, which ran west from the Black Sea into the Sea of Marmara, made the Golden Horn the only viable seaward approach to the city. It was itself heavily fortified. A great chain extended across this harbour, anchored in the city itself and on the other side of the Golden Horn, in the fortified suburb of Galata. To the west was the Sea of Marmara. Sea walls protected the city from attack from this direction. To the north were the only land walls. Emperor Theodocius II (401–450) constructed strong fortifications that extended from the Golden Horn to the Sea of Marmara. Emperor Anastasius I (430–518) built a weaker wall extending from the Black Sea to the Sea of Marmara. This location and its fortifications were almost impregnable. They were so formidable that only once during a thousand years did the city fall to direct assault. This was during the Fourth Crusade in 1204. Even then, some elements within the city facilitated the attack. Only by hurling gunpowder-driven cannonballs into the city's fortifications in 1453 did the Ottomans succeed in collapsing the ancient walls.

Another important factor in the perseverance of the empire was the power of the emperor. He, and on at least three occasions she, ruled with absolute authority over a powerful state. A centralized bureaucracy carried out his commands. A powerful army and navy protected his realm. A sophisticated diplomacy extended his policies to areas not under his direct control. Furthermore, his power was based upon divine sanction and the subservience of the church.

The support of the church was extremely important to the position of the emperor. The church organization was based upon the administrative model of the Roman Empire. Christianity was the universal religion for the universal empire. Ultimate administrative authority resided in the five patriarchs, located in the major Christian centres of the ancient world: Alexandria, Antioch, Constantinople, Jerusalem and Rome. Of these, the patriarch in Constantinople enjoyed the status of first among equals. A series of councils, including those at Nicea in 326, Ephesus in 431 and Chalcedon in 451, established a rigid Trinitarian doctrine. While occasionally the church challenged individual emperors because of some doctrinal transgression, it by and large subordinated itself to the divine sanction of the position of the emperor. This domination by the political authority over the religious authority is called *Caeseropapism*.

By the time of the reign of Justinian I (483–565) the transition from ancient Rome to medieval Byzantium was largely complete. By then a new people had intruded into Southeastern Europe. These were the Slavs, who had first appeared between the Baltic Sea and the Carpathian Mountains and migrated down to and across the Danube beginning in the fifth century. During the later part of the sixth century, the Slavs moving into Southeastern Europe seem to have been associated with the Turkic/Mongol Avars, who possibly assumed some kind of command position over them. The Avar–Slavic association engaged in violence wherever it appeared. After the Avar–Slavic failure to take Constantinople in 626, however, the Avars lost their dominant position and dispersed. The Slavs continued to move into Southeastern Europe, even establishing settlements in the Peloponnese. They abandoned violence for the most part, and adopted agriculture. Imperial efforts to interdict these migrations failed because of the large numbers of Slavs. Like their Slavic counterparts to the northwest and to the east, the Slavs who entered the Balkan Peninsula came as settlers. They assimilated at least some of the indigenous Illyrian and Thracian peoples, as well as some of the Latin- and Greek-speaking portion of the population in the region. As a result of these migrations large areas passed out of the control of the imperial authorities in Constantinople. The empire remained in contact with the Aegean, Black Sea and Adriatic coastal areas, including the important cities of Athens, Corinth and Salonika. Salonika itself underwent several Slavic sieges. The Danubian frontier was irreparably breached. Important inland cities such as Belgrade, Niš, Sofia and Adrianople were lost to the empire. In the regions overrun by the Slavs, Roman Christian culture withered. Slavic animistic paganism prevailed. In a sense a 'Dark Age' prevailed over much of Southeastern Europe, as during the Dorian invasion of Greece some twelve hundred years earlier.

The first Slavs in Southeastern Europe to develop a state organization lived along the Danube. During the seventh century the Bulgars, a horde of Turkic-speaking people originally from the upper Volga region, moved into the Danube valley and established themselves as a military aristocracy over the Slavs already living there. The Bulgar leadership intermarried with the Slavic leadership to form an upper class of landholders, in Bulgaria called *boyars*.[5] The peasantry remained in a state of obligation to the landholder. The political entity resulting from this combination of Slavic and Turkic elements was the first Bulgaria. The Byzantines made some effort to eradicate this potential threat. They did not succeed. In a treaty of 681 Emperor Constantine IV (652–685) recognized the Bulgarian state north of the Balkan Mountains.[6] Bulgaria became the first Balkan state. Its proximity to the Byzantine Empire dictated its subsequent development. Bulgaria provided agricultural production to the empire. At times the relationship between Byzantium and Bulgaria was good. In 706 as a reward for his assistance, Emperor Justinian II (r. 685–95, 705–11) awarded the Bulgarian Khan Tervel (r. 702–18) the title *Tsar* (Caesar). Nevertheless conflicts continued between the two neighbours. At the beginning of the ninth century the Byzantines made a determined effort to eradicate Bulgaria. The emperor Nicephorus I (r. 802–11) invaded Bulgaria with a large force and burned the capital at Pliska. In 811 Khan Krum (r. *c.* 803–14) trapped Nicephorus and his army. The Bulgarians destroyed the army and slew the emperor. Nicephorus I became the first Roman emperor to die in battle since the Goths had killed Valens in nearby Adrianople in 378. Although he wanted to take the fight to Byzantium, Krum lacked the technology and logistical ability to maintain a siege of Constantinople.

Despite the defeat at the hands of the Bulgarians, the Byzantines increased their power in the Balkans during the ninth century. They did so not merely through a strong military establishment, but also by promoting the spread of their religion and culture among the Slavic peoples. In doing so the Byzantines sought to impose upon the Slavs and others the Byzantine political and religious world view. According to this concept the emperor was the universal emperor of the universal state supported by the universal religion. Conversion to Christianity implicitly meant acceptance of this ideology, if always not acquiescence to direct Byzantine political control. The resulting world view is described convincingly as the Byzantine Commonwealth.[7] This grew to include not only the Balkan Peninsula but also Asia Minor, the Caucasus region and the north shore of the Black Sea, including the Kievan State.

Emblematic of this religious and cultural effort were Cyril (Constantine) (827?–869) and his elder brother Methodius (815?–882). They were from Salonika, although whether they were Greek or Slavic in origin remains in doubt; they were comfortable with both languages. As part of an effort to establish contact with the Moravian Slavs, they devised a Slavic alphabet based upon Greek and Hebrew characters. This became known as *Glagolithic*. Although used in some monasteries in Dalmatia as late as the nineteenth century, it never achieved widespread acceptance. Nor did Cyril and Methodius' effort in Moravia succeed. A Slavic disciple of Cyril and Methodius, Kliment of Ohrid (840–916) is the probable inventor of the Cyrillic alphabet. Through this alphabet the Slavic language of the Balkans became a written language, known as Old Church Slavonic, and a means of pursing the Byzantine political and cultural agenda.

In 864 these efforts achieved a significant success when Khan Boris of Bulgaria (r. 852–89) converted to Christianity. Upon his conversion, he assumed the name Michael from his Byzantine sponsor Emperor Michael III (r. 842–67) and the title Tsar. Under Boris's son Symeon (r. 893–927), the First Bulgarian Empire reached the apogee of its power in Southeastern Europe. During his rule Bulgaria included most of the Balkans south of the Danube, including Serbia, Macedonia and northern Greece. After his death Bulgaria moved closer into the Byzantine orbit. During the tenth century Bulgaria became a client state of Byzantium. In 969 Byzantium annexed Bulgaria. Strong opposition to Byzantine rule arose in western Bulgaria and Macedonia.[8] The leader of this anti-Byzantine resistance was Samuel (r. 997–1014). The son of a former Byzantine official, Samuel established his administration in the city of Ohrid. Prolonged fighting between Samuel and the Byzantine emperor Basil II (958–1025) resulted finally in a Byzantine victory in 1018, with the seizure of Ohrid. Based upon this success, Basil later became known as the 'Bulgar Slayer'.[9] Much later this victory assumed an importance similar to that of Kosovo for the Serbs. For the first time since the reign of Justinian I, all of the Balkans south of the Danube came under Byzantine rule. Byzantine power was again paramount in the Balkans.

During this acme of Byzantine rule in the Balkans, the European Christian Church underwent a change. Up until the middle of the eleventh century, all European churches acknowledged a frail unity based on the authority of the patriarchs of Alexandria, Antioch, Constantinople, Jerusalem and Rome. These locations were the original administrative centres of the Christian Church. By the eighth century the patriarchs of Alexandria, Antioch and Jerusalem had come under Islamic political control, and lost much of their relevance. Gradually the relative administrative independence of the Roman patriarch, together with differences in dogma and alternative practices in ritual that arose in the regions of Roman authority, brought about a split in the Church. In 1054 the Roman Church and the Constantinople Church excommunicated each other. From then on the Western European and Eastern European churches developed separately. The Eastern Churches (Orthodox) continued to maintain Greek and Slavic ritual, permit priests to marry and to insist that the Holy Spirit emanated solely from God the Father, and not also from God the Son, as the Western Church (Catholic) maintained. Also the Eastern Church denied the special authority of primacy among the patriarchs claimed by the leader of the Roman church. The schism of 1054 has remained intact into modern times.

One important aspect of Eastern Christianity was its emphasis on monasticism. Monastic communities developed throughout the Balkans beginning with the acceptance of Christianity in the region. Among these were Rila in Bulgaria, Dečani in Kosovo and especially the large communities at Mt Athos in northeastern Greece. These monasteries became repositories for artefacts and manuscripts. Later they played an important role in the formation of Bulgarian, Serbian and Greek national ideas.

The Byzantine victory in the Balkans did not provide the empire with much security for long. In 1071, a little over fifty years later, the Byzantine state suffered twin disasters. In Apulia the Normans took Bari, the last Byzantine-controlled city on the Italian Peninsula. With the fall of Bari, the Greek presence in southern Italy ended. It had begun in classical times. Far more portentous was the catastrophe that occurred at the other end of the empire, in Asia Minor. At Manzikert that same year Turkish tribes under Alp Arslan (1029–1072) defeated the Byzantine army led by the emperor Romanus IV Diogenes (r. 1068–71). This defeat opened up the interior of Asia Minor (Anatolia) to permanent Turkish settlement. Thereafter Byzantine rule in Asia Minor was mainly confined to the coastal regions. The Manzikert defeat seriously damaged the empire, which had depended on the interior of Asia Minor for taxes, military recruits and agriculture production.

The weakened position on the periphery inevitably undermined the power of the empire in the Balkans. As early as the ninth century, Serbian states were forming in the western Balkans. Their exact parameters remain unclear. Initially they remained under strong Byzantine and Bulgarian influence. By the beginning of the twelfth century a viable Serbian state had emerged in Duklja, a region roughly coinciding with contemporary Montenegro. Christianity apparently seeped into the western Balkans through Bulgaria. The translation of the Gospels into Slavic undoubtedly facilitated this process. In these Serbian states leadership came from the patriarchs of extended families. The peasantry, as elsewhere in the Balkans, existed in a condition of obligation to the landholder.

Towards the end of the twelfth century both Bulgaria and Serbia were able to assert themselves against waning Byzantine power. In Bulgaria two brothers of Vlach origin, Asen (r. 1186–96) and Peter (r. 1196–7) revolted against Byzantine power. By 1187 they succeeded in re-establishing the Bulgarian state. It maintained Bulgarian authority south of the Danube and east of the Vardar Rivers. The question of its connection across the Danube to the Latin-speaking peoples living there remains open.[10] This Second Bulgarian Empire was centred on the northern Bulgarian city of Veliko Tŭrnovo. It reached its high point during the reign of Ivan Asen II (r. 1218–41), though it did not dominate the entire region to the extent that the First Bulgarian Empire had under Tsar Symeon.

Meanwhile for the first time, a single viable state arose in the Serbian lands under the Nemanja Dynasty. Its first important ruler was Stephen Nemanja I (1109–1196). He combined Raška, roughly equivalent with modern Serbia, with Zeta, roughly equivalent with modern Montenegro. His son Stephen II (r. 1196–1227) was the first Serbian ruler to assume the title of king.

While the Bulgarians were reasserting their independence and the Serbs were developing political cohesion, the Byzantine Empire was undergoing yet another major crisis. In 1204 a group of Western Crusaders became involved in a Byzantine political struggle. With Venetian help, they took Constantinople, where they installed one of their own as emperor, Baldwin I of Flanders (r. 1204–5). For the next 57 years a Western European ruled in Constantinople during the period known as the Latin Empire, or sometimes – confusingly – as Romania. These crusaders attempted to impose Western-style feudal regimes on the territory of the Byzantine Empire through the kingdom of Salonika, the duchy of Athens and the principality of Achaia. This was similar to the feudal system they established in Palestine in the twelfth century. Venice, the Crusader's ally, seized many of the Aegean islands. The looting and destruction caused by the Crusaders in 1204, combined with the presence of a Latin church authority in Constantinople oriented towards Rome, widened the gap between the Western and Eastern branches of the Christian Church.

Most of the rest of the empire, however, rejected Latin rule. Greek states arose in Europe in Epirus and in Asia Minor in Nicea and Trebizond. In 1261 the Nicean Michael Palaeologus (1223–1282) ousted the last Latin ruler, Baldwin II (r. 1228–61), from Constantinople and restored Byzantine power. The patriarch of Constantinople resumed his position in the city. This final incarnation of the Roman Empire was never able to assert great authority in the region. After 1261 the Byzantine Empire functioned as just another Balkan state, vying for control of Thrace and Macedonia with Bulgaria and Serbia. The restored empire never managed to reassert control over much of Greece. A number of independent entities, including the Duchy of Athens, contested control there. These complicated struggles were reminiscent of those that took place among the city states during classical times. Further complicating the situation were a group of Catalan mercenaries who originally came to Byzantium to help fight the Ottomans but quickly established themselves as independent rulers in Attica. Byzantine authority was centred in the Peloponnese around the city of Mistra. The Venetians also intervened in these struggles to take control of the islands of Crete, Euboea and Naxos, and the cities Coron (Koroni) and Modon in the Peloponnese. This confused situation endured until the Ottoman conquest in the fifteenth century.

Amidst the jumble of political jurisdictions in the Balkans, the Serbs under Stephen Uroš III (r. 1321–31) and then his son Stephen Dušan (r. 1331–55), who assumed the title Tsar, managed to establish a strong state that dominated the region and included modern Serbia and Montenegro as well as Albania, Macedonia and Thessaly. It did not endure. After Dušan's death, Serbia, like Bulgaria and Byzantium previously, disintegrated into small, mutually antagonistic states.

The fragmented political situation in the Balkans in the fourteenth century belied a religious and cultural unity in the region. Nevertheless, the emergence of a serious threat in the form of the Ottoman Turks failed to motivate the various Bulgarian, Byzantine and Serbian states to adopt a unified response. After Manzikert, Sunni Muslim Turkish tribes were free to migrate from the steppes of Central Asia into the interior of Asia Minor without Byzantine opposition. They formed small political units, which soon came under the control of the Seljuks. This Turkish dynasty controlled most of Asia Minor in the twelfth and thirteenth centuries until the Mongol invasion of 1243. Thereafter it lost most of its power and much of the region fragmented into mainly Turkish states. A Turkish leader named Osman established a small emirate in northwestern Asia Minor at the end of the thirteenth century. Osman I (1258–1324) founded what would become the Ottoman Empire. With a feeble Byzantine Empire to the west and a declining Seljuk state in the east, Osman was able to expand his holdings in Asia Minor quickly. His son and successor Orhan I (1281–1359?) institutionalized the expansion of the state through the *gazi* system in which Islamic Turkic warriors achieved fame and wealth in fighting against the infidel.[11] This practice enabled Orhan to gain the loyalty of warriors from other Turkish emirates throughout Asia Minor, and to use them to take over the remnants of the Byzantine Empire there. By 1345 Ottoman forces had not only eliminated Byzantine authority throughout most of Asia Minor, but had crossed the Dardanelles into Europe, where they rapidly achieved new conquests.

The Orthodox Christian states in the Balkans at this time were too fractious to offer much resistance to the Ottoman onslaught. Many of the local leaders quickly submitted to Ottoman authority in order to retain their lands. An attempt by various Serbian leaders to stop the Ottomans ended in disaster on the Maritsa River in 1371. This opened up Serbia and Bulgaria to Ottoman exploitation.[12] Better known, but probably less decisive, was the Battle of Kosovo in 1389. There the Ottomans – including Albanian, Bulgarian and Serbian vassals – and Serbs inflicted heavy casualties on each other. Both sides withdrew after the battle. This battle, like the victory of the Byzantine emperor Basil II over the Bulgarians, became a touchstone for modern nationalists. Both commanders, Sultan Murad I (1326–1389), perhaps through treachery, and Prince Lazar (1329–1389) by execution, perished. In the aftermath of the Kosovo battle the Ottomans overran all of Bulgaria by 1393, and continued to dominate Serbia. Serbian nationalist interpretation of this battle as a sacrificial defeat later became an important pillar of Serbian identity.

The appearance of the Ottomans in the Balkans was an important factor in the development of new political entities. One of these was Bosnia. Originally under Byzantine rule, Bosnia developed as an autonomous entity in the frontier region between the Orthodox (Serb) and the Roman Catholic (Croat) Slavs of the remote region east of the Adriatic Sea. After 1102 Croatia became linked to the Hungarian monarchy. Thereafter the Hungarian kings began to play a growing role in Bosnian politics, often exercising a loose suzerainty over local leaders. During the rule of Stephan II Kortromanić (r. *c.* 1318–53) a distinctly Bosnian church emerged that in its administration at least was neither Orthodox nor Roman Catholic.[13] Both the Orthodox and the Roman Catholics regarded the doctrines of the Bosnian church as heretical. The nominally Roman Catholic Stephen Tvrtko (1338–1391) ruled Bosnia during the high point of its independent political existence. Three forms of Christianity – Bosnian, Orthodox and Roman Catholic – coexisted there. The Hungarians attempted to defend Bosnia against the Ottoman onslaught, but to no avail. By the beginning of the fifteenth century the entire region had come under Ottoman rule.

Two other political entities emerged across the Danube River on much of the same territory as the ancient Roman province of Dacia. These were Wallachia, which lay between the Carpathian Mountains and the northern shore of the lower Danube, and Moldavia, which extended north from the Danube between the Carpathians and the Prut River valley. As in the case of Bosnia, both of these states coalesced under considerable pressure from the Hungarians, who were ensconced across the Carpathians in Transylvania. Orthodox Christianity had spread north of the Danube earlier, in a process that remains obscure. By the thirteenth century it seems to have taken hold, bringing with it Church Slavonic and the Cyrillic alphabet. Basarb (r. *c.* 1310–52) founded a Wallachia independent of Hungarian suzerainty. His successor Nicolae Alexandru (r. 1352–64) established religious ties with the patriarchate in Constantinople.

The emergence of a Moldavian state took a little longer, because of its proximity to the nomad dominated grasslands north of the Black Sea and its remoteness from Balkan centres of civilization. A local vassal, Bogdan of Cuhea (r. 1359–65), broke away from Hungarian control and achieved a shaky independence for Moldavia around 1365. Not only did

Hungary remain powerful across the Carpathians, but the Mongols dominated the steppes to the east, and a strong Polish-Lithuanian state loomed to the north. Another threat developed to the south for both Wallachia and Moldavia. Having emerged in the frontier region between Roman Catholic Hungary and Orthodox Byzantium, Wallachia and Moldavia found their independence challenged by the advance of the Ottoman Turks.

The Ottomans secured their domination of Southeastern Europe when they finally took Constantinople on 29 May 1453 after a siege lasting 54 days. Sultan Mohammed II (1432–1481), thereafter known as 'the Conqueror', achieved this victory. With Mohammed II's triumph, the Roman Empire ended in its Christian form. After allowing four days of looting, the Ottoman sultan took measures to protect the surviving Christian population. To gain support of the Orthodox Church, he appointed as patriarch Gennadios II (r. 1453–9), a strong critic of the Roman church. Soon after taking Constantinople, Mohammed's forces overran Attica and the Peloponnese, which had for a long time been divided between the Byzantines and a bewildering assortment of Spanish mercenary companies. Mistra held out until 1460. Venice continued for a time to control Crete, the Cyclades and the Ionian islands; Genoa, Chios and Samos; and the Knights of St John, Rhodes and the Dodecanese.

Most of the remainder of the Balkans soon came under direct Ottoman rule after the fall of Constantinople. While the Hungarians continued to hold on to Belgrade, the rest of Serbia came under direct Ottoman rule by 1459. Bosnia fell by 1463, except for the southwestern area (Hercegovina), which the Ottomans took in 1483. To further solidify their control, the Ottomans settled Turkic peoples from Anatolia in level areas of Bulgaria, Macedonia and Thessaly.[14] These peoples diluted the Orthodox culture of these regions to a degree.

As the Ottomans consolidated their control over Southeastern Europe, another peripheral region began to develop its own identity. This was Albania, which previously had been a remote part of the Roman, Byzantine, Bulgarian and Serbian Empires. In 1443 a former Ottoman hostage named George Kastriotis (1405–1468) united the Albanian tribes against the Ottoman occupation. He became known as Skanderbeg (Lord Alexander). This is the first time in history that the Albanians had developed a distinct political character. Skanderbeg, occasionally with Venetian help, continued his resistance to the Ottomans in the rugged Albanian Mountains until his death. Afterwards the Ottomans were able to subjugate the Albanian lands. Gradually after the Ottoman conquest, a majority of Albanians converted to Islam.

Similar resistance to the Ottomans persisted in the neighbouring mountains to the north in the old region of Zeta that would become Montenegro. After 1490 the Ottomans exercised a remote suzerainty over this region, which the Montenegrins themselves periodically challenged.[15] The local Ottoman authority in Shkodër Albania often had to decide whether the suppression of the remote Montenegrins was worth the effort.

The Romanian lands north of the Danube also came under Ottoman suzerainty towards the end of the fifteenth century. Unlike elsewhere in the Balkans, the Ottomans allowed the native nobility to remain in place under a leader, the prince (*voivode*), who acknowledged vassalage to the sultan and paid him an annual tribute. The peasantry remained in the same state of subservience to the native nobility. These regions became important sources of grain and cattle supplies for the Ottoman capital. Under Prince Vlad III, known as Vlad the Impaler and also as Dracula (*c.* 1431–1476) because of his cruelty, Wallachia offered some resistance to Ottoman rule. In Moldavia Stephan the Great (*c.* 1432–1504), successfully played the Hungarians against the Ottomans. While he did not manage to avoid Ottoman suzerainty, he did retain some autonomy. In this respect Wallachia and Moldavia as well as tiny Montenegro enjoyed some freedom of action on the periphery of the authority of Constantinople, just as Bulgaria and later Serbia had centuries before. One Wallachian prince, Michael the Brave (1558–1601), briefly united Moldavia, Transylvania and Wallachia around the turn of the seventeenth century. This incident became a basis for Romanian nationalist expectations two centuries later.

After 1453 the Ottoman Empire closely resembled its Byzantine predecessor in its location and form. It lay astride the same passages from East to West. Its capital was in the same important city. The title sultan now replaced that of emperor. As absolute ruler, the sultan controlled the empire, his power limited only by the strictures of religion. In the case of the Ottoman sultan, this was the law of Islam, the *sharia*. Adoption of

Islam by the peoples of Southeastern Europe imparted some advantages. Taxes were lower. Social status was higher. Muslims had the right to bear arms. Landowners might retain their properties. Islam found some adherents everywhere in Southeastern Europe, especially in Albania, Bosnia and Bulgaria. In these places and elsewhere both nobles and peasants converted, often under little or no duress.

The sultan regarded Christians and Jews as protected people, *zimmi*. Together with Muslims, they formed the *raya*, or flock. All of the *raya* were subject to their own religious laws through the *millet* system. There were in effect four *millets*: Islamic, Orthodox, Armenian and Jewish. This allowed the Orthodox, Gregorian Armenian (Monophysite) – who also represented Roman Catholics – and Jewish communities some lassitude under Ottoman authority. This system regarded the non-Muslim population solely on the basis of religion. The concept of nationality did not yet exist. In practice the *millet* system bestowed considerable authority on the Orthodox patriarch in Constantinople, who presided over the largest single religious group in the Balkans. Within this *millet*, the Bulgarian church retained some vestiges of identity through the continued existence of the Ohrid Autocephalous Archbishopric, as did the Serbian Church through a similar institution at Peć (Ipek) in Kosovo. This Ottoman toleration was based on the acceptance by the non-Muslims of a subordinate status in the Ottoman state.[16] Disputes were resolved within the religious communities if possible. If not, or if disputes were inter-community, the Ottoman authorities provided resolution after the payment of an appropriate fee. This tended to promote cooperation among the various communities. The system was not unwelcome to the Orthodox people. At the end of the seventeenth century the Venetians occupied the Peloponnese. The native Greek Orthodox population came to prefer the Ottomans to the Roman Catholic Venetians. This facilitated the Ottomans' return in 1718. This Orthodox preference reflected not only the Orthodox rejection of Roman Christianity but also the relative independence of the Orthodox hierarchy under the Ottoman system.

As a result of the Ottoman conquest of the Balkans, the native nobility suffered dispossession. Only conversion to Islam, as in Albania and Bosnia, preserved their landholdings. Most of the Bulgarian and Serbian nobles died or fled upon the Ottoman conquest. New Islamic landlords

The Ottoman Balkans, *c.* 1700.

arrived from Asia Minor to take possession of the land. In the Romanian lands, however, the native Christian nobility did retain their land. For the peasantry the change of masters made little difference at first. The only real immediate change was the imposition by the Ottomans of the *devşirme*, or child tax.

As the empire expanded, a regular cavalry, the *spahis*, supplemented the *ghazi* warriors. In a feudal-like arrangement, each *spahi* received a grant of land with peasants, the *timar*, from the sultan. Another military formation, the janissaries or 'new corps', also developed as the Ottomans expanded into Europe. The janissaries were composed of males of non-Muslim origin recruited through the institution of the *devşirme*, or child tax. These were taken as adolescents, converted to Islam and trained as soldiers. A minority received training as administrators. In theory they were to remain celibate. Since they were not of Muslim origin, the janissaries and the administrators were legally slaves of the sultan. This system helped the sultan to counterbalance the influence of the *spahis,* who were of Turkic origin. The child tax caused great heartbreak for many Balkan families, but also presented tremendous opportunities for advancement within the Ottoman Empire. Its use of Islamicized Bulgarian, Greek and Serbian administrators and soldiers helped to make the Ottoman Empire a Balkan institution.

One important issue differentiated the Byzantines from the Ottomans. The Byzantine commonwealth had always been fractious. Byzantine control of the Balkans was only firm in the eleventh entury. At other times the Bulgarians, Serbs and others fought against the Byzantines as well as themselves. The Ottomans imposed sufficient control over the Balkans to give this region the longest period of relative domestic tranquillity in its history. During the sixteenth and seventeenth centuries the Balkans underwent relatively few invasions or revolts. This period is sometimes known as the *Pax Ottomanica*.

During the sixteenth century the Ottomans reached the apogee of their power in Southeastern Europe. Sultan Suleiman, the Magnificent (1494–1566), defeated the young Hungarian king Louis II (1506–1526) at Mohacs in 1526 and overran most of Hungary. Louis died in the battle. The Habsburg ruler Ferdinand, Louis' heir, could not retain his inheritance, which fragmented into a Habsburg fringe in the north and west, an Ottoman core and an autonomous Transylvania. Suleiman's armies laid siege to Vienna in 1529, and Malta in 1565. After his death Ottoman power began to recede, although it maintained its grip on the Balkans until the nineteenth century. The reasons for the decline of Ottoman power are complex. One problem was the conversion of most of the old *timar* holdings into *çiftliks*. These *çiftliks* were estates owned by individuals without any obligation of military service. The introduction of new crops into the Balkans, such as corn, cotton and tobacco, made large estate-based farming attractive. The alienation of the land from the direct control of the sultan necessitated the payment of greater amounts of taxes to the central authority. This in turn imposed a greater burden of labour and production upon the peasantry, whatever its religion. The process separated both the land and the peasants from the government.

Another problem was that of the sultan himself. The holders of absolute power in the Ottoman Empire were born and raised amidst the arcane antagonisms and competitions of the harem. Some of these Ottoman scions were of Balkan origin on their mother's side. In any event, in such an environment, they did not receive the kind of education and experience necessary for the management of a world empire. Individuals fortunate enough to succeed to the Ottoman throne were often the pawns of powerful court figures who were technically the slaves of the sultan.

The janissaries gradually transformed from an elite military force to a sedentary class intent on the preservation of its privileges. After the Ottoman conquest of Hungary, the opportunities for warriors to acquire additional land and loot greatly diminished. In 1574 the previously celibate janissaries obtained the right to marry. About the same time the *devşirme* ended. The janissaries often adopted professions, and enrolled their sons in the corps. They became less interested in campaigning for loot and glory than in settling down to domestic life as a class with special rights. Thus they became a much less effective fighting force.

A particularly dangerous problem for the Ottomans was the revival of European Christian military power north of the Balkans. The *Pax Ottomanica* was over. Polish forces led by King John Sobieski (1629–1696) were critical in the defeat of a second Ottoman siege of Vienna in 1683. Poland, however, did not represent a major threat to the Ottomans. Its government would soon be in a state of disintegration. Two other dangers imperilled the Ottoman presence in the Balkans.

One of these was the revived power of the Habsburgs. After the rescue of their capital by the Poles, the Habsburgs developed a formidable military force led by Eugene of Savoy (1663–1736). This army undertook an offensive against the depleted Ottomans, conquered Hungary and brought the Habsburgs to the borders of the Balkans. The Treaty of Karlowitz (Sremski Korlovici) in 1699 confirmed these Habsburg gains and set the border between the Habsburgs and Ottomans until 1878. During the fighting against the Ottomans, Habsburg forces in 1689 advanced deep into the Balkans as far as Niš, Skopje and Prizren. They could not sustain these positions, however, in the face of stiffening Ottoman resistance. When the Habsburg troops withdrew the next year, many Serbs followed them across the Drava River. Emperor Leopold I (1640–1705) permitted these Serbs to retain their Orthodox religion and granted them other privileges, including local autonomy, in return for military service along the

Ottoman frontier. The region of historic Croatia in which these Serbs settled became known as the Military Frontier. It constituted a privileged area within the Habsburg state. As the Serbs migrated north out of Kosovo, Albanians increased their presence there. They had probably been in the region for some time, and simply took over lands the Serbs had abandoned. Border fighting between the Habsburg forces in the Military Frontier and those of the Ottomans in Bosnia continued through-out the eighteenth century.

Another strong enemy appeared to the northeast of the Ottoman holdings in the Balkans during the eighteenth century. This was Russia. In 1711 Tsar Peter I (1672–1725) invaded the Balkans and called upon the Balkan Orthodox to support him. Unfortunately for him, an Ottoman force surrounded and defeated Peter and his army at Stănilești on the Prut River in Moldavia. Somewhat surprisingly, the Ottomans permitted Peter to return home. The Russian tsar probably had to pay his way out of this predicament. He also had to concede the fortress of Azov on the Black Sea. Despite this setback, the appeal of the Russians to the Ortho-dox and Slavic peoples of the Balkans was obvious. They had the same culture and, in the case of the Bulgarians and Serbs, a similar language. While the Russians perceived in these Balkan peoples a means of facili-tating their control of the region, the Balkan peoples saw the Russians as liberators from Ottoman rule.

The first Balkan people to take advantage of the weakening of Otto-man power were the Montenegrins. In general Montenegro was too remote and unproductive for the Ottomans to pay much attention to develop-ments there. At the beginning of the eighteenth century the Montenegrin state began to coalesce around the institution of the monastery of Cetinje. The Orthodox bishop of Cetinje, loosely affiliated with the Serbian author-ity at Peć, functioned as the head of nascent state. By the beginning of the eighteenth century the office had become hereditary in the Njegoš family.[17] It was passed down from uncle to nephew.

The Ottomans reacted against the threats to their domination of the Balkans by increasing the authority of Orthodox collaborators. These were from the mainly Greek oligarchy, which was centred in the *Phanar* or lighthouse district of Constantinople. They became known as Phanariotes.[18] These families had played a prominent role in the economic and ecclesiastical affairs of the Ottoman Empire ever since its conquest of Constantinople. After Peter I's failed invasion, Ottoman authorities appointed Phanariote voivodes in Wallachia and Moldavia. Other Phanariotes moved into these principalities. This served to tie these areas more closely to Constantinople in terms of both Ottoman political rule and Greek cultural domination. It also increased the exploitation of the Romanian lands. Appointment as prince usually depended upon the proffering of large bribes to the Ottoman authorities. Prospective princes raised the funds necessary for the bribes through agricultural production.[19] Ultimately the Romanian peasants had to bear the burden of the costs of rule for their new masters.

The power of the Phanariote-controlled patriarchate in Constantinople increased during the late eighteenth century. The patriarch abolished the separate status of Peć in 1766 and Ohrid one year later. The elimination of the last vestiges of Serbian and Bulgarian administrative autonomy increased the cultural domination of the Greeks throughout the Orthodox churches of Southeastern Europe.

Russian interest in the Balkans increased under Tsarina Catherine II (1729–1796). Catherine devised a 'Greek Plan' which envisioned the projection of Russian power into the Balkans and the revival of the Byzantine Empire under the rule of her grandson Grand Duke Constantine Pavlovich (1779–1831). War between Russia and the Ottoman Empire erupted in 1768 and resulted in a Russian victory. The subsequent Treaty of Kuchuk Kainarji (Kyuchyuk-Kaynardzha) in 1774 established a permanent Russian presence on the northern littoral of the Black Sea and gave the Russians political privileges in the Romanian principalities. Furthermore, it permitted the Russians to represent the Orthodox Christians of the Balkans to the sultan's government. This became the basis of a special relationship between the Orthodox peoples of the Balkans and the Russians. The Russians increasingly supplanted the Constantinople patriarch as the advocate for the Orthodox Slavs of the Balkans in Constantinople. The subsequent Treaty of Iași in 1792 solidified Russian control of the northern shore of the Black Sea, including the Crimea.

From the fourth century until the eighteenth, a Christian and later an Islamic Empire centred in Constantinople dominated the Balkans. Both empires, Byzantine and Ottoman, imposed political domination over the region, and also world views that provided a framework for the preservation and development of the heterogeneous identities of the Balkan peoples. The Byzantines brought autocracy and Christianity to the Balkans. After the sixth century they were never able to maintain a firm political control over the region. The Ottomans adopted the autocracy and through the *millet* system reinforced Orthodox Christianity. They dominated the entire region from the fifteenth through to the eighteenth century. In the eighteenth century, however, new powers appeared on the northern periphery that would increasingly intrude into Balkan issues, and in doing so would reshape the region politically, economically and culturally.

three
The Intrusion of Modernity, 1804–78

Towards the end of the eighteenth century, Southeastern Europe began to undergo a series of significant changes. One important source of these changes lay in the transformation of the landholding system from *timars* to *chifliks*. This had begun earlier, as already noted. The economic, political and social consequences ensuing from the transformation of the landholding system became manifest by the eighteenth century. The spread of the *chiflik* system left the mainly Christian peasants at the mercy of their Muslim landlords. Landlords increased their exactions from the peasants in order to increase their income. The peasantry had little recourse for disputes from civil authorities. Great unrest developed throughout Southeastern Europe.

One result of this dissatisfaction was that some peasants fled to the more mountainous areas of the Balkan Peninsula to escape their landlords. Some of these then began to engage in brigandage. They became known as *hayduts* (Bulgarian), *klephts* (Greek) or *hajduks* (Serbian). By preying upon the wealthier elements in Ottoman society, they often became Robin Hood-like heroes among the peasantry. They were celebrated in music, song and other aspects of popular culture. Such aggrandizement of these anti-establishment forces helped to lay the foundation among the peasants for a secular sense of identification stretching beyond Orthodox Church authority.

The dissatisfaction in Southeastern Europe also brought about periodic challenges to Ottoman authority itself in the form of overall unrest and local rebellions. One of the earliest of these, although not caused directly by *chiflik* issues, was the uprising around Chiprovitsi in north-western Bulgaria in 1688.[1] The mainly Germanic Catholic population of Chiprovitsi was atypical for the region, but likely more receptive to external influence emanating from the Habsburg Empire. Nevertheless this uprising established a pattern that would increase over the next century to include many elements of the Balkan Orthodox populations. The old certainties of divinely inspired Orthodox/Ottoman authority were beginning to erode.

At the same time the increased agricultural production facilitated by the spread of the *chiflik* system brought about a growth in commerce in agricultural goods and the development of a significant Balkan merchant class. While some of these dealers in agricultural commodities arose from the traditional regional practitioners of commerce such as the Armenians, Greeks and Jews, others originated among the Orthodox Slavs who inhabited the area. Through their commercial interests these merchants developed contacts with Western Europe. In doing so they became aware of Western European ideas of reason and secularism. Merchants began to send their sons to Western European and some Westernized Russian schools. They also began to organize into secular societies which increasingly began to develop new concepts of self-awareness. As their commercial interest grew, these merchants also became more and more frustrated with the corruption, indolence and inefficiency of the Ottoman authorities. They found the rationality and secularism of the Western European Enlightenment attractive alternatives to Orthodox and Ottoman practices.

As a result, rationality and secularism intruded into the Balkans and challenged the authority of the Ottoman sultan and the Orthodox patriarch as well as existing economic and social conditions. These ideas had originated in Western Europe during the Enlightenment. Up until the eighteenth century, the Balkans had largely been isolated from Western Europe not only by geography but also by the disinclination of both Muslim political and Orthodox church authorities to accept Western Europe as a source of ideas and inspirations. The power of the Enlightenment, however, proved impossible for them to contain. It attacked the languid traditionalism that pervaded the region during Ottoman rule.

Another important idea that was intruding into the Balkans was nationalism. By the eighteenth century, Western Europeans were developing the concept that identity existed in terms of geography, language and culture, and that this shared identity naturally should have a political expression. In Southeastern Europe this meant that identity derived not just from religion but also from language and historical association. This led to greater interest in language and history in Southeastern Europe.

The concepts of rationalization and secularization intruded into the region through several vectors. After the Treaty of Karlowitz of 1699, the Habsburgs introduced policies into their new territories that facilitated the development of distinct national identities with their empire. These policies especially affected the Romanians in newly conquered Transylvania and the Serbs, who had recently migrated north into Habsburg territory. One of the most important of these polices was the establishment of a special administrative area along the border with the Ottoman Empire. Many of the Serbs who migrated north around 1690 settled in this Military Frontier. There the Habsburgs permitted them a degree of cultural and local political autonomy in return for ready military service. The Serbs established an ecclesiastical centre at Karlowitz, which established contact with the Orthodox authorities in Peć. From this contact it maintained the tradition of the medieval Serbian states among the settlers in the Habsburg Empire. This centre gained even more importance as the location of Serbian church identity and as a centre of Serbian education after the abolition of the Peć authority in 1766. The Serbian language continued to be written in an ossified form, Church Slavonic. Efforts began among the clergy and the merchants in Karlowitz to develop the Serbian language as a more viable and contemporary means of communication.

Romanian development in the Habsburg Empire was not unlike that of the Serbs. For the Romanians in Transylvania, the Uniate Church became an important factor in establishing their identity. This entity originally had formed in 1596 from the Union of Brest in eastern Poland and Lithuania as a means of proselytizing the Orthodox Ukrainians and Byelorussians living there. The Uniate Church combined Orthodox ritual and practices with Roman Catholic hierarchy. With the encouragement of the Habsburgs upon their conquest of Transylvania in 1699, the Uniate Church also sought adherents in Transylvania among the Romanian population. This institution served an overwhelmingly Romanian population and became the basis for the development of a distinct Romanian identity that soon extended south and east into Wallachia and Moldavia.

An important figure in the development of this identity was the Uniate bishop Ioan Inochentie Clain/Klein/Micu (*c.* 1700–1768).[2] Clain was an advocate for the Romanian peasants of Transylvania. He also promoted the idea that the Romanian-speaking peasants were the descendants of the Roman colonists of Dacia. The association of the Uniates with Rome brought Romanians in contact with Latin and with the Roman legacy. Some young Transylvanian Romanians studied in Jesuit institutions in Rome. Through these endeavours they realized and emphasized the Latin connection to the Romanian language. The first modern Romanian grammar appeared in Transylvania in 1780. During the eighteenth century the connection between the Romanian language and the other Romance languages became apparent to those studying Latin. Based on this correlation, the Romanian church began to substitute the Latin alphabet for the Cyrillic. Increasingly educated Romanians began to associate their language and culture with that of Italy and of the centre of the Enlightenment, France.

During the rule of Maria Theresa (1717–1780) and her son Joseph II (1741–1790), the Habsburg policy of Enlightened Rule began to affect the Romanians and Serbs living in the empire. This brought a number of changes that facilitated their development. Among the most important of these was Joseph II's Edict of Toleration of 1781. Thereafter the Orthodox church enjoyed roughly the same status in the Habsburg Empire as it did in the Ottoman Empire. This edict to some degree undercut the Uniates. Many of them in Transylvania then returned to the Orthodox fold. The growing self-awareness among the Romanians of Transylvania was a factor in the peasant uprising of 1784. Led by a Romanian Orthodox peasant named Horea (Vasile Nicola Ursu, 1731–1785), who thought he had the support of the emperor, this peasant revolt was mainly directed against German and Hungarian nobles in Transylvania.[3] By 1785 Joseph's troops had suppressed the revolt and executed its leader. Nevertheless, on the eve of the French Revolution, the Orthodox peoples of the Balkans were clearly developing a sense of national awareness similar to that in the rest of Europe.

Tiny Montenegro, a remote theocracy governed in the Adriatic Alps, was a back door for Western ideas coming into the Balkans. Since the beginning of the eighteenth century this small region had maintained sporadic contacts with western Venice and eastern Russia. While these connections were almost entirely diplomatic and the influx and dissemination of rational and secular ideas through this portal was extremely limited, Montenegro did represent an opening in Ottoman-controlled Southeastern Europe.

The French Revolution resounded throughout the region. Some educated people sought the advantages of French Enlightened Rule. By 1797 French armies appeared in Dalmatia on the periphery of Southeastern Europe, demonstrating to the peoples living there the effectiveness of revolutionary and national ideas. The Revolutionary and Napoleonic Wars also increased demand for the products of the region. This brought merchants into greater contact with Western Europeans and increased their profits. The Greeks, who dominated Ottoman maritime commerce, especially benefited from increased interactions. The continental blockade system imposed by Napoleon on Europe served to further augment these profits. Greek merchants plied their wares on both sides of the blockade and thereby derived large profits. In this way Western European ideas as well as Western European money helped to facilitate the development of national awareness in the Balkans.

By the beginning of the nineteenth century the small, educated, commercial class of Southeastern Europe had to some degree come into contact with Western European political and social ideas. The problem for them then was to act upon these ideas. The first step was to determine the cultural basis for national identity. This involved both cultural and political undertakings.

The Romanians had already begun to develop their cultural identity by the beginning of the nineteenth century. The other Southeastern European peoples endeavoured to catch up. Among the first to do so were the Greeks. The advance of secularism enabled the Greeks to more fully access their rich classical heritage, much of which lay in ruins around them. These ideas first developed among the Phanariote class, which already enjoyed a certain amount of power and influence within the Ottoman Empire through their control of commerce. The Western secular and political ideas they came into contact with through commerce eroded their loyalty to Constantinople. An important figure in the recovery of this cultural heritage was Adamantios Koraïs (1748–1833). After leaving his birthplace in Symrna (İzmir), Koraïs settled in Paris. There he absorbed many Enlightenment ideas. He particularly admired the liberal ideas of the French Revolution. Most importantly he advocated a standardization of the Greek language, eliminating foreign elements and basing the language on classical Greek. While this created difficulties because of the many changes that had occurred in written and spoken Greek since classical times, it did emphasize the connection between classical and the secular and national Greece that Koraïs envisioned. The differences between Demotic, the modern vernacular, and *Katharevousa*, the artificial form of Greek based upon classical norms and used for literary, educational and administrative purposes, were resolved only in 1976.

Among the Serbs, two figures stood out in the development of their national culture. One was Dositej Obradović (1743–1811). Obradović was born in Čakovo, a Serbian community in the Military Frontier of the Habsburg Empire. He became a monk, and travelled to Western Europe. On his journey he became influenced by Enlightenment ideas. He encouraged the development of a secular Serbian literature, and promoted a modern literary language for Serbian in place of Old Church Slavonic. In 1807 he moved to Belgrade, where he founded a school.

Among his pupils in Belgrade was Vuk Karadžić (1787–1864). He continued the work begun by Obradović for the secularization of Serbian language and literature. In 1814 he published a collection of Serbian poetry. He also promoted the use of the vernacular as the basis for the Serbian literary language. In contrast to the Greeks, who reached back over twenty centuries for their models, Karadžić advised the Serbs to 'write the way you speak'. In 1818 he published the first Serbo-Croat dictionary. Karadžić advocated the use of the western Serbian dialect (štokavian) as the basis for the literary language.[4] This tended to emphasize the similarities between Serbian and Croatian.

During the early part of the nineteenth century, Serbian secular literature also developed in Montenegro. Peter II Petrović Njegoš (1813–1851), the last prince bishop of Montenegro, became an important epic poet in the Serbian language.[5] He was best known for his poems *Ray of the Microcosm* and *The Mountain Wreath*. His literary activity helped to bring outside attention to his tiny country as a centre of Orthodox literary and political independence.

The Bulgarians also underwent a period of cultural development beginning in the eighteenth century. Their process was a little slower than that of the Romanians and Serbs because of their proximity to the centres of Ottoman and Orthodox authority and their remoteness from the Enlightenment incubator of the Habsburg Empire. A leading figure in the growth of Bulgarian cultural awareness was Father Paisii Hilandarski (1722–1773). While a monk at Hilandar Monastery on Mt Athos, Paisii became aware of his Bulgarian identity in reaction to the pervasive Greek influence there. To combat this influence he completed by hand a *Slavic-Bulgarian History* in 1762. Paisii advocated the use of the Bulgarian language and the recognition of a Bulgarian identity in opposition to the pervasive Greek culture. Handwritten copies of this work then circulated among Bulgarian monasteries and from there out into the small community of intellectuals.

Another important step for the development of Bulgarian culture was the publication by Petŭr Beron (1800–1871) of a basic primer in the Bulgarian language in Bucharest in 1824. Known as the *Fish Primer* because of the picture of a whale on the last page, this *ABC*, or really *АБВ*, included a picture for each letter. It marked the beginning of the use of contemporary Bulgarian in place of Old Church Slavonic or Greek as the literary language in the Slavic-speaking region between the Danube River and the Aegean Sea. Schools developed in a number of places in Bulgaria. Vasil Apostolov (1789–1857), an Odessa merchant, founded the first Bulgarian school in his home town of Gabrovo in 1835.

Young Bulgarians sought educational opportunities not only in Western Europe but also in Russia. Beginning around 1858 American Protestant missionaries began efforts to educate and evangelize Bulgarians.[6] They were much more successful in the first endeavour than in the second. Around the same time, the Moscow Benevolent Society offered scholarships to young Bulgarians to study in Russia. This was intended to emphasize conservative and Orthodox sensibilities among the students, but often had the opposite effect. Nevertheless many young Bulgarians came to Russia to study and to become infused with the idea of Pan Slavism. This idea was a kind of supra-Slavic nationalism, emphasizing the community of interest of all Slavic peoples, especially the Orthodox ones, and the leadership of the largest group of Slavs, the Russians.

The Bulgarians had another cultural issue to confront during their national development in the early nineteenth century. After the abolition of the Ohrid patriarchate in 1767, the Bulgarian churches came under the direct control of the church authorities in Constantinople. This meant that Greek language and culture increasingly became the norm in Bulgarian churches. The Serbian church was able to avoid this to some degree because of the existence of the independent Serbian church authority on Habsburg territory at Sremski Karlovici and because of the political unrest that developed in Serbia at the beginning of the nineteenth century. During Easter services in Plovdiv in 1854, the Bulgarian-speaking congregants ousted the Greek clergy. They demanded successfully to have Bulgarian clergy. Finally in 1870 an Ottoman decree established a Bulgarian Exarchate. While this did not restore the Ohrid patriarchate, it did acknowledge the separation between the Orthodox church in Constantinople and the Bulgarian Orthodox church, which was now free to develop as the Bulgarian national church. The Constantinople patriarch refused to recognize the Exarchate.

Despite some initial hesitations, the Orthodox churches in the Balkans adapted well to the Western European concept of nationalism. For the Bulgarians, Romanians and Serbs nationalism offered a means to escape from Phanariote domination from Constantinople. This was also a consideration for the Greek churches of Southeastern Europe. The identification of Orthodoxy with political authority then facilitated their identification of the new Serbian, Greek, Romanian and Bulgarian states. The Orthodox bishop of Cetinje had ruled Montenegro since the beginning of the eighteenth century.

Together with the development of national culture in the Balkans came increased political activity. The logic of nationalism demanded a national state to promote national culture. The evident success of national states in Western Europe, at first France and later Italy and Germany, contrasted sharply with the decadence and inefficiency of the Ottoman Empire. This disparity inspired the Balkan peoples to achieve their own national states. Political independence was necessary to obtain the economic and political success evident in Western Europe. For the first time in their development the Balkan peoples sought inspiration from the West, not the East.

The upheavals in Western Europe caused by the French Revolution and the Napoleonic Wars had a profound effect in the Balkans. They offered the Balkan nationalists an opportunity to seek support among the combatants. After the conclusion of the Napoleonic Wars and the institutionalization of the Great Power system, the Balkan nationalists recognized that to achieve their aims, they would have to work through the Great Powers. As had already become clear, Austria and Russia remained the two most relevant Great Powers to events in the region. Both continued to pursue their own aims in the Balkan Peninsula throughout the nineteenth century at the expense of the decaying Ottoman Empire. The Austrians and Russian perceived in the Balkan nationalist useful adjuncts to their own ambitions, while the Balkan nationalists sought Austrian and Russian aid to achieve national independence. Ultimately the imperialist Great Power goals were not compatible with those of the Balkan nationalists.

The failure of the Ottoman Empire to adapt facilitated the realization of these agendas. Various attempts to reform occurred during the nineteenth century. In particular the period from 1839–76 is known as the *Tanzimat* (Reorganization) in Ottoman history.[7] The Ottoman attempts to centralize and secularize society did not meet with great success. This effort to a certain degree paralleled the same efforts among the Orthodox peoples of Southeastern Europe. They were not intended to accommodate these peoples to the Ottoman regime, nor did they. If anything, the prospect of a strengthened Ottoman government only increased the determination of the Orthodox peoples of Southeastern Europe to separate from Ottoman rule. By the middle of the nineteenth century the *Pax Ottomanica* had expired. The multilingual and multicultural urban communities throughout the Balkans were coming apart along nationalist lines.

Somewhat surprisingly, the first of the Balkan peoples to achieve political success were not the Romanians, who had been the earliest to develop a national identity because of their numbers in the Habsburg Empire, or the Greeks, whose commercial contacts with Western Europe had brought them great economic resources, but the Serbs. The Serbian revolt had its origins in Serbian loyalty to the pasha of Belgrade, Hadji Mustapha (?–1801). Hadji Mustapha maintained a benevolent attitude towards the Serbs, allowing them to collect their own taxes and to form a militia under the leadership of their *knezes*. The *knez* was the head or patriarch of an extended family or clan. Hadji Mustapha's support of the Orthodox Serbs gained him the somewhat awkward title 'Mother of the Serbs'. His mild rule and friendliness towards the Serbs antagonized many Muslims. The conservative janissaries of the region particularly resented his polices. By the eighteenth century the janissaries, once among the elite of the Ottoman army, had evolved into a privileged semi military caste determined to maintain their special status. In 1801 the janissaries executed Hadji Mustapha and attempted to disarm the Serbs.

In response the Serbs began to organize resistance. The Serbian revolt originated not as a gesture of nationalism aimed at the sultan in Constantinople, but as a peasant revolt directed against the misrule of the janissaries in Belgrade. At the beginning of 1804, the janissaries and other Muslim authorities in the Pashalik of Belgrade attempted to quash the discontent by murdering the leading *kneze*s. This sparked the Serbian revolt. One *knez* who escaped the massacre, George Petrović (1768–1817), known as Karadjordje (Black George) because of his swarthy appearance, emerged as the leader of the revolt. He was a swine merchant from Topola. After some initial success in overrunning the Pashalik of Belgrade, Karadjordje assumed the position of hereditary ruler in 1808. His rule was never secure. Loyalties in liberated Serbia remained local. He sought external support from neighbouring Austria and made contact with the French. The Napoleonic Wars, however, had the full attention of the Western Europeans. Russia offered some support, men and material during the Russo-Turkish war of 1806–12. Even before Napoleon led his *Grande Armée* to Moscow in 1812, however, Russian attention to the Balkans had faltered. By 1813 the Serbian revolt had fizzled and Karadjordje fled to Austria. Ottoman troops took Belgrade that same year.

Serbia did not remain quiet for long. Initially a *knez* who was a rival of Karadjordje, Miloš Obrenović (1789–1860), collaborated with the restored Ottoman regime. Having gained a political profile, he successfully manoeuvred between the Ottoman authorities and the dissident Serbs. By 1815 he achieved recognition as the chief *knez* of the pashalik of Belgrade. Under his regime, Serbs were permitted to retain their arms and to have their own assembly (*skupština*). The somewhat murky murder of the recently returned Karadjordje in 1817 confirmed Obrenović as the Serbian leader.

Over the next twenty years Obrenović gradually expanded his authority. In 1830 in the aftermath of the Russo-Turkish War of 1828–9, the
Ottoman government accepted Serbia as fully autonomous. By 1833 the
Ottomans recognized Obrenović as the hereditary prince of Serbia, and
fixed the frontiers of the Serbian entity. Nevertheless, Obrenović's authoritarian rule alienated many of his subjects, and localism still prevented
many Serbs from understanding politics in a national context. Domestic
instability marked Serbian politics until the beginning of the next century. In 1839 Prince Miloš Obrenović abdicated in favour of his son, Prince
Milan Obrenović (1839), who died shortly thereafter, probably without
knowing of his elevation to the Serbian throne. The throne then passed
to Michael Obrenović (r. 1839–42 and 1860–68), who only lasted three
years. After he abdicated in 1842, Alexander Karadjordjević (1842–58),
Black George's son, replaced him. Prince Alexander Karadjordjević's failure to govern effectively led to his own ousting in 1858. This brought
about the return of Prince Miloš Obrenović and after his death in 1860,
the return of Prince Michael Obrenović. This time Michael managed to
secure the withdrawal of the Ottoman garrison from Belgrade in 1867. He
built up the Serbian army. With the aid of his sometime minister Ilija
Garašanin (1812–1874), Prince Michael also contemplated the formation
of a pan-Slavic Balkan league to drive the Ottomans out of the Balkans,
but in 1868 he was assassinated under mysterious circumstances.

The success of the Serbian revolt provided additional encouragement
for the Greeks to seek their own political independence from the Ottomans. The Greeks faced a formidable task. The Greek lands and islands
constituted a much more important economic and strategic part of the
Ottoman Empire than the poor and remote Pashalik of Belgrade. Even
before the Serbian revolt, some Westernized Greeks had contemplated
action against the Ottoman authorities. Notable among these was Rhigas
Pheraios (1759–1798). Born into a wealthy family in Thessaly, he had fled
Greece after he killed an Ottoman official. Eventually he made his way to
Vienna, where he came under the influence of revolutionary ideas emanating from France. He translated a number of French works into Greek
and advocated a revolution in Greece based upon these ideas. Before he
could undertake any direct action, the Austrian authorities arrested him
and turned him over to the Ottomans, who executed him in 1798.

The revolutionary and Napoleonic fighting that convulsed Europe created conditions for economic development among the Greeks of the Ottoman Empire. The French physically arrived proximate to Greece when they established control of the Ionian Islands in 1797. This economic advance was not limited to the old Phanariote class. A new more widely disbursed largely mercantile group emerged. The hold of the Phanariotes over Greek cultural, economic and political ideas began to weaken. As additional Greeks experienced economic growth from contacts with Western Europe, they sought to emulate Western European ideas. The excitement generated by the revolutionary events in Western Europe led Greeks living in Odessa to form a Friendly Society (*Philike hetairia*) in 1814. This society increasingly sought to foment revolution in Greece. Soon other such organizations developed among the Greek merchants of the Mediterranean region. They increasingly saw Orthodox Russia, a major victor over Napoleon, as a source of help against the Ottomans.

The time for direct action for the Greeks arrived in 1821. That year a former major general in the Russian army and leader of the Friendly Society, Alexander Ypsilantis (1792–1828), raised the standard of revolt. Ypsilantis came from a Phanariote family that had established itself in Wallachia. Anticipating Russian support, he led a body of soldiers known as the 'Sacred Band' from Russian territory across the Prut River into Moldavia. Unfortunately for the Sacred Band, the Russian tsar Alexander I (1777–1825) disavowed their efforts. Ypsilanitis' efforts found little favour among the Romanian peasants who constituted the majority of the population in Wallachia. Ottoman forces inflicted a decisive defeat at Drăgășanihe in Wallachia in the summer of 1821. Afterwards he fled to Austrian territory, where he eventually died.

Meanwhile other revolts against Ottoman authority erupted throughout Greece. Most of these revolts were local. One of the most important occurred in the Peloponnese at Patras, led by the local Orthodox bishop Germanos (1777–1826). The same mountainous Greek topography and the physical isolation of islands that had prevented the establishment of unified politics among the Greek city states in ancient times precluded the formation of a united military effort against the Ottomans. Often atrocities directed against Albanian-, Greek- and Turkish-speaking Muslims accompanied these uprisings. In 1822 an assembly in Epidauros proclaimed the Hellenic Republic. This government soon collapsed into civil war. Meanwhile fighting continued against the Ottomans.

The Ottoman Sultan Mahmud II (1785–1839) finally intervened in Greece with an Egyptian Army led by the Ottoman governor of Egypt, Muhammad Ali (1769–1849), himself of Albanian origin. Muhammad Ali's son Ibrahim (1789–1848) took Navarino, Missolonghi and finally Athens in 1827.[8] His success prompted Great Power intervention. Outrage at Ottoman atrocities plus a sentimental attachment to the concept of ancient Greece brought first numbers of foreign volunteers from Western Europe for the Greek cause. Among the best known of these was the British poet George Gordon, Lord Byron (1788–1824), who died at Missolonghi from a fever in 1824. A more substantive intervention came in the form of a British-French-Russian fleet, which defeated the Egyptian-Ottoman fleet at Navarino in 1827. This was the turning point in the Greek War of Independence.[9] The next year the Russians declared war on the Ottomans and a Russian army crossed the Danube. After some setbacks, it took Adrianople in 1829. The subsequent Treaty of Adrianople established the principle of Greek independence as well as Russian control of Wallachia and Moldavia. The international status of the newly independent Greek state remained unclear for the next several years.

The same local rivalries and divisions that had hampered the revolt against the Ottomans prevented the establishment of a stable national government. Assassinations and local conflicts ensued. Only in 1833 did Greece achieve a stable political situation with the arrival of the seventeen-year-old Bavarian prince Otto at the behest of the Great Powers, who detested the civil disorder in the country. He ruled as King Otho (1815–1867), aided by a Bavarian entourage in Athens. Otho never succeeded in ingratiating himself to his subjects nor in mastering the complexities of Greek politics. Disaffected Greeks called his rule *Bavarokratia*. These problems, in addition to his inability to advance the Greek national cause, led to his deposition in 1862.

With the approval of the Great Powers, a Danish prince, William George, then assumed the title of George I (1845–1913), King of the Hellenes in 1863. The British gift of the Ionian Islands in 1864, which they had controlled since seizing them from the French in 1809 and 1810, helped to bolster the position of the new king. Nevertheless as a foreigner on the throne of an ambitious but impoverished country, King George's position remained precarious.

The Romanian struggle for independence started concurrently with that of the Greeks. When Alexander Ypsilantis crossed the Prut River in 1821, a simultaneous revolt broke out among the peasantry of western Wallachia (Oltenia), led by Tudor Vladimirescu (1780–1821), who had served as a lieutenant in the Russian army. Because this effort was directed against both the immediate problem of Phanariote exploitation, as well as the more remote problem of Ottoman misrule, the Romanians were unable to sustain a common cause with Ypsilantis' Greeks. The Greeks eventually captured and executed Vladimirescu in Târgoviște in Wallachia in 1821. This incident is instructive about the difficulties of correlating rival national ideas in Southeastern Europe. After Ypsilantis' defeat, the Ottomans ceased their practice of appointing Phanariote rulers for Wallachia and Moldavia and returned to rulers drawn from the native Romanian nobility.

Intervention in the Greek War of Independence brought Russian troops into the Romanian principalities. The Russians had already occupied the Moldavian province of Bessarabia in 1812 after their war with the Ottoman Empire. This had put the Russians on the Danube. The Treaty of Adrianople of 1829 sanctioned their presence in Wallachia and the remainder of Moldavia. The rule of a single Russian governor, Pavel Kiselev (1788–1872), united Wallachia and Moldavia more closely than they had ever been before, except during the brief rule of Michael the Brave. While acting as the viceroy of the two Romanian states, General Kiselev favoured the Romanian nobles over the enserfed peasantry. He was responsible for the drafting and implementation of the Organic Statutes, the first constitutions for Wallachia and Moldavia. The Organic Statutes tended to reinforce the power of the nobles and the Russian occupation, and therefore perpetuated the semi-manorial system that afflicted the peasantry. Because the Statutes were virtually identical for Wallachia and Moldavia, they helped promote the concept of the unification of the two principalities.

The Romanian principalities were the only part of the Balkan Peninsula directly affected by the national liberal revolutions of 1848 that swept through most of the rest of Europe. While there were revolutionary stirrings in Moldavia at the beginning of that year, a well-planned revolution erupted in Wallachia in June. It seized power and announced a liberal programme, including the opposition to the Organic Statutes, abolition of serfdom and noble privileges, the establishment of a constitutional assembly and freedom of the press. A combined Russian and Ottoman invasion in September ended the brief rule of a liberal regime in Bucharest.

The situation in the two Romanian principalities remained fluid after 1848. War between the Ottomans and Russians again broke out in 1853. British, French and Piedmontese forces intervened on the Ottoman side in what became known as the Crimean War of 1853–6 after its principal theatre of action. Russian troops withdrew from Wallachia and Moldavia to be replaced by troops from Austria. The Treaty of Paris of 1856 freed the two principalities from foreign occupation and restored a small part of southern Bessarabia to Moldavia. They achieved an autonomous status under the Ottoman Empire.

By this time the unionist movement came to dominate politics in both states. In 1859 Wallachia and Moldavia both elected the same individual, the Moldavian noble Alexander Cuza (1820–1873), as prince. The two principalities were de facto united. Napoleon III (1808–1883), eager to extend the influence of France to its Latin cousins in Eastern Europe, served as a godfather to the new Balkan political entity. Through his good graces the objections of the other Great Powers to this alteration of the status quo in the east faded. The Ottoman sultan acquiesced in the arrangement of a single prince for both principalities. In 1861 the unification of the two principalities as Romania obtained international recognition.

Prince Alexander did not enjoy an easy reign. He attempted a programme of liberal reform, including most importantly universal male suffrage, an amelioration of the manorial responsibilities of the peasantry and redistribution of land to the peasants. In a reform similar to that enacted three years earlier in Russia, the peasants obtained legal freedom, but the nobles retained half the land. They were compensated for the loss of their lands by state bonds paid off by the peasants. This placed a heavy tax burden on the peasantry. This reform in particular aggravated the nobles without satisfying the peasants. Unlike in Bulgaria, Greece and Serbia, a native Orthodox nobility existed in the Romanian lands throughout the Ottoman era. Caught between the nobles and peasants, Alexander was stranded politically. Consequently a conspiracy overthrew him in 1866. His successor came from the Catholic branch of the House of Hohenzollern. Karl Hohenzollern (1839–1914) Latinized his name to Carol. His connection to his distant Lutheran relatives on the Prussian throne, later the German throne, proved an asset. Carol backed off the reforms of his unfortunate predecessor and developed Romanian connections with Austria-Hungary and Germany.

The Bulgarians lagged behind the Greeks, Serbs and Romanians in their quest for political development. The loss of the Romanian lands after the Treaty of Adrianople in 1829 increased the importance of the Bulgarians for the Ottoman Empire. The Bulgarian regions became the primary area of agricultural production for the Ottoman capital, and the Danube the first line of Ottoman defence. Bulgarian goods found ready markets in the Ottoman Empire, and a period of prosperity ensued. The relative affluence of those Bulgarians benefiting from this commerce tended to work against any agitation for political separation from the Ottomans. This even led some Bulgarians to consider the idea of a dual Bulgarian–Ottoman monarchy after the division of the Habsburg Empire into Austria-Hungary in 1867. The Ottoman sultan, however, was not interested; also, the national idea, especially as it grew in established national states in neighbouring areas, proved to be stronger than any ties to the Ottomans. Young Bulgarian revolutionaries found inspiration and shelter in Belgrade and Bucharest. In the late 1860s Bulgarian émigrés founded several organizations in Bucharest with the purpose of fomenting a mass uprising in Ottoman Bulgaria. Some returned to Bulgaria to prepare for revolt. Among these was Vasil Levski (Kunchev) (1837–1873), whom the Ottoman authorities captured and executed.

In 1875 a major insurrection broke out in Bosnia among the mainly Orthodox peasantry. Initially the peasants directed this mainly against their Islamic landlords. While the initial causes were manorial, it provided an opportunity for neighbouring Montenegro and Serbia to realize their national goals. In 1876 both declared war on the Ottoman Empire in an effort to free Bosnia from Ottoman rule.

Meanwhile in the spring of 1876, a Bulgarian rebellion broke out in the mountains of central Bulgaria at Koprivshtitsa. It soon spread to southern Bulgaria. Both the Bulgarians and the Ottomans committed atrocities, but those committed by Ottoman irregulars, the so-called

'Bulgarian Massacres', received international attention. The American journalist Januarius A. MacGahan (1844–1878) and the American diplomat Eugene Schuyler (1840–1890) did much to disseminate information about the situation in Bulgaria. This information prompted outrage throughout Europe and especially in Russia. Nevertheless the Ottomans succeeded in crushing the Bulgarian revolt, and in defeating the Montenegrin and Serbian invasions.

The Bosnian–Bulgarian crisis defied attempts at resolution by the Great Powers. On 24 April 1877 the Russians, motivated by Pan-Slavic emotions as well as by a pragmatic desire to extend their influence into the Balkans, declared war on the Ottoman Empire. The Russian army marched through Romania to cross the Danube to attack the Ottomans. Bulgarian volunteers flocked to join the Russians. Even so a spirited Ottoman defence held up the Russians at Pleven. At the request of the tsar, the Romanian prince Carol led his army to help at Pleven while Montenegro and Serbia re-entered the war. Although the Greeks were willing to intervene against the Ottomans, a British blockade of their coast prevented them from joining in the fighting. Pleven fell on 10 December 1877. The Russians crossed the Balkan Mountains and forced the Ottomans to accept an armistice. The Treaty of San Stefano of 3 March 1877, negotiated in a suburb of Constantinople, greatly diminished Ottoman holdings on the Balkan Peninsula. It established a Greater Bulgaria south of the Danube, stretching from the Black Sea through Macedonia. With the Treaty of San Stefano, the Bulgarians became the first of the Balkan peoples to realize their nationalist objectives. Because the Russians expected to dominate the Orthodox Slavic Bulgarian state, the treaty of San Stefano sanctioned Russia as the dominant power in the Balkans. In addition, the Russians took Bessarabia from Romania in order to be more proximate to the new Bulgaria and to the Balkans in general. As compensation Romania obtained northern Dobrudja, the territory between the northern curve of the Danube and the Black Sea. Montenegro and Serbia received some territorial increase; Montenegro more than doubled its territory. Montenegro, Romania and Serbia were all granted complete independence from the Ottoman Empire.

The Bulgarian provisions aroused opposition among the Great Powers and among the Balkan nations. Both Austria-Hungary and Great Britain were alarmed at the propect of Russian control of the Balkans. Austria-Hungary objected to the Treaty of San Stefano because it ignored Austrian interests in the Balkans. Great Britain objected to it because it placed Russia in a good position to dominate Constantinople and thus to establish a presence in the eastern Mediterranean. The Greeks, Montenegrins, Romanians and Serbs all denounced the treaty because it ignored their own claims to Ottoman territory in order to create the new large Bulgarian state. The Serbs had re-entered the war after the fall of Pleven and had occupied part of Macedonia, which now was assigned to Bulgaria. For the first time, the disposition of Macedonia became an issue among the Balkan nations. Before the Great Power objections led to war, the German chancellor, Otto von Bismarck (1851–1898), offered his services as an 'honest broker'. A Great Power congress then met at Berlin in the summer of 1878 to revise the San Stefano Treaty. Its decisions, announced on 13 July, completely redrew the map of the Balkans. To the great dismay of the Bulgarians, their state was trisected. A Bulgarian principality under the suzerainty of the Ottoman sultan was established between the Danube River and the Balkan Mountains. An autonomus Ottoman province under an Orthodox Christian governor was created south of the Balkans, with its capital at Plovdiv. This was called Eastern Rumelia. Rumelia was the Ottoman name for their European possessions. The treaty returned Macedonia to full Ottoman rule. Austria-Hungary received the right to occupy the Ottoman Provinces of Bosnia-Hercegovina and to garrison the Sandjak of Novi Pazar, a strip of land separating Montenegro from Serbia. This was a source of great consternation to the Montenegrins and Serbs. Both claimed these regions for themselves. The independence of Montenegro, Romania and Serbia remained intact. Each of these states also received small territorial gains. Montenegro received territories along all its Hercegovinian and Albanian frontiers as well as the Adriatic port of Bar. The Berlin settlement also confirmed the Romanian loss of Bessarabia and the acquisition of northern Dobrudja. Serbia obtained the lower Morava River region, including the important city of Niš. In addition, the Russians obtained the Transcaucasian regions of Ardahan, Batum and Kars, while Britain received the right to occupy Cyprus. At Berlin, the Great Powers totally ignored Greek territorial claims on the Ottoman Empire. The Ottomans had no input on the disposition of their territories. As one historian has written, 'The Ottomans were reduced to spectators at their own funeral, ignored and insulted by all.'[10] None of the Balkan states was satisfied. The most disappointed, however, were the Bulgarians. They had gone from the maximum realization of their nationalist objectives to the trisection of their state in only three months.

By the time of the Congress of Berlin, some ethnic changes became apparent in Balkan populations. As mainly Orthodox Christian autonomous and independent entities emerged from the Ottoman Empire, Islamic peoples often emigrated to the remaining Ottoman lands. Muslims of Slavic and Turkish origin left Serbia after 1833 and most of those of Hellenic and Turkish origin left Greece after 1829. After Berlin, some Slavic and Turkish Muslims departed from Bosnia and Bulgaria, but many stayed on under Austrian and Bulgarian rule. The Romanian lands never had a large Muslim population anywhere except for the Dobrudja. Many of these remained after Romanian independence.

The intrusion of Western European ideas into the Balkans had mixed results. The idea of nationalism and secularism had the consequence of motivating many members of Balkan society to institute economical, educational and social development. On the other hand, these ideas also led to divisiveness and violence. These conflicts generally derived from the efforts of the Orthodox peoples of Southeastern Europe to throw off Ottoman rule. In these conflicts, the Orthodox religious authorities, while not necessarily accepting Western European ideas, did support separation from the Ottoman Empire. The success of national unification in Italy and Germany spurred the Balkan peoples to liberate their co-nationals from the Ottomans. Only then could real national development ensue. As Balkan demands on the Ottomans grew, the Ottoman Empire, dubbed the 'Sick Man of Europe' by Tsar Nicholas I (1796–1855), faltered. The resolution of the fate of the 'Sick Man' became known as the 'Eastern Question', a question in which the Great Powers increasingly involved themselves. The Congress of Berlin represented their effort to control the conflicts and to ensure that their own interests in Southeastern Europe were upheld. It did not, however, succeed in quieting the increasing demands among the Balkan peoples for comprehensive national states that included all of the co-nationals.

four

The National Wars, 1878–1918

W hile the settlement imposed upon Southeastern Europe by the Congress of Berlin satisfied the immediate purposes of the Great Powers, it failed to resolve the nationalist desires of the peoples living there. Several issues were clear. These nationalist strivings would continue. Any nationalist advance, however, would have to obtain the sanction of the Great Powers. This compelled the Balkan states to establish subordinate but fragile relationships with individual Great Powers, especially Austria-Hungary and Russia. These relationships were based upon the realization that the Ottomans would make no concessions without force, and that the Balkan peoples themselves lacked the power to force the Ottomans to do so. As a consequence of the inability of the Balkan states to realize their nationalist objectives by themselves, foreign policy issues dominated domestic politics in all of the Southeastern European countries. One additional significant problem arose. The nationalist claims of the Bulgarians, Greeks, Montenegrins, Serbs and to a lesser degree the Romanians overlapped in several specific locations. There would be no easy resolution of these rivalries.

Immediately after the conclusion of the Berlin Congress, the settlement came under attack in Southeastern Europe. Among the most disappointed were the Albanians. Shortly before the Berlin Congress met, a group of Albanian notables convened in Prizren, Kosovo. Their purpose was to organize political and military opposition to any dismemberment of Albanian territory and to urge the formation of an Albanian unit within the Ottoman Empire from the *vilayets* (provinces) of Kosovo, Janina, Shkodër and Monastir (Bitola).[1] The Great Powers ignored Albanian pretentions at Berlin. Bismarck himself denied that the Albanians constituted a nation.[2] Nevertheless the thin layer of educated Albanians within and outside the Ottoman Empire increased their efforts to develop the concept of Albanian nationalism. Among their greatest successes was their use of language rather than religion as the basis for Albanian national identity. The adoption of a modified Latin script for the written Albanian language at the Congress of Monastir in 1908 facilitated this inclusiveness. Muslims, Orthodox Christians and Catholic Christians who used the Albanian language were all Albanians. This effort to establish a single literary language also helped to breach the divide between the southern Gheg dialect and the northern Tosk dialect in the Albanian language. The neighbouring Slavic peoples never quite managed this feat.

The first country to demand a formal revision of the Berlin settlement was Greece. The Berlin Congress had only suggested that the Ottomans consider Greek claims. Only in 1881, with British assistance, did the Greeks obtain some Ottoman territories. These included most of Thessaly and the district of Arta in Epirus. These acquisitions by no means satisfied the Greeks. Their irredentist programme, called the *Megali Idea*, or 'Great Idea', essentially aspired to recreate the Byzantine Empire, including Constantinople and much of Asia Minor. This concept was at the basis of Greek nationalist hopes for the next forty years.

The next to act were the Bulgarians. The truncated principality established by the Berlin Congress greatly disappointed the aspirations of Bulgarian nationalists. They established their capital at Sofia in the western part of the principality to emphasize their claims to Macedonia. To add to their frustrations, the new prince of Bulgaria remained under Ottoman suzerainty. The new prince was Alexander Battenberg (1857–1893), who obtained his throne through election by a Grand National Assembly (*subranie*) in Veliko Tŭrnovo in 1879. Battenberg was the nephew of Tsarina Marina Alexandrovna (1824–1880), the wife of Tsar Alexander II (1818–1881). He spent a difficult time on the Bulgarian throne due to his autocratic tendencies and his refusal to act as a Russian puppet. These tendencies gained him disappointment in Sofia and disapproval in St Petersburg. He attempted to consolidate his position when Bulgarian nationalists in Eastern Rumelia proclaimed union with the principality on 6 September 1885 in direct defiance of the Berlin Congress settlement.

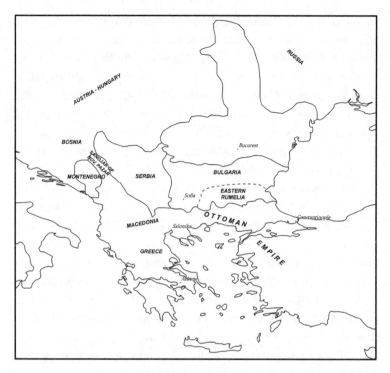

The Balkan Peninsula, 1878.

Nevertheless, after some dithering, the Great Powers and the Ottomans appeared to accept this coup. The neighbouring Serbs did not.

King Milan Obrenović of Serbia (1854–1901), who had assumed that title in 1882, sought compensation for the Bulgarian unification. He had bolstered his position in the Balkans by concluding an alliance with Austria in 1881. On 13 November 1885 he declared war on Bulgaria. The Serbs expected an easy triumph. As a sign of dissatisfaction over his cousin Battenberg's conduct and the unification, Tsar Alexander III (1845–1894) had broken off relations with the Sofia government and ordered home all Russian advisors and officers in the Bulgarian army.[3] Only young Bulgarian officers, none with rank higher than that of captain, remained to lead their army. Nevertheless, after making an agreement with the Ottomans to secure their eastern frontier, the Bulgarians sent all their forces to the west. They stopped the Serbian invasion at Slivnitsa and invaded Serbia in turn. Austrian intervention on behalf of its Serbian ally prevented the Bulgarians from taking Niš. The war ended with the Treaty of Bucharest, signed on 3 March 1886. Serbia lost no territory, but in the aftermath of the war a legacy of distrust between Bulgaria and Serbia developed. The Serbo-Bulgarian war was the first intra-Balkan conflict involving nationalist claims. Their successes in maintaining the union and defeating the Serbs lent hope to many Bulgarians that they might yet achieve their nationalist aims along the lines of the San Stefano Treaty. The Treaty of Bucharest of 1886 ended the Serbo-Bulgarian war but exacerbated the rivalry between Bulgaria and Serbia.

Another consequence of the unification and the war was Prince Alexander's loss of his throne. His success in the unification of Eastern Rumelia and in the defeat of the Serbs had ironically gained him the lasting enmity of his cousin Tsar Alexander III, who thought the Bulgarians ungrateful. After a kidnapping escapade perpetrated by pro-Russian Bulgarians, Alexander Battenberg decided he could not remain in Bulgaria in defiance of Russian wishes. He left the country for ever in 1886. Tsar Alexander III's pique with his cousin and with Bulgaria undermined Russia's strategic position in the Balkans. Russian influence waned in the Orthodox state closest to Constantinople. Not for the last time, Russians had failed to preserve their best interests in the Balkans.

The next year Bulgaria obtained a new prince. This was Ferdinand of Saxe-Coburg-Gotha (1861–1948). Ferdinand was an Austro-German prince and the grandson of Louis Philippe (1773–1850), the king of France. An individual of refined tastes, Ferdinand first promoted his own candidacy to a Bulgarian delegation at the Vienna Opera House.[4] The election of an Austro-German Roman Catholic prince for Bulgaria did little to conciliate the Russians. Ferdinand, however, achieved a settlement of sorts after the baptism into the Orthodox faith of his son, Crown Prince Boris (1894–1943), in 1896. The restoration of relations with Russia reflected the general attitude of the Bulgarian population, who still revered the largest Orthodox Slavic state for its role in the liberation of Bulgaria from the Ottoman Turks. Bulgaria assumed the anomalous status of a Russian orientation with an Austrian prince. Ferdinand consolidated his domestic position through corruption and favourites, which amounted to a policy of 'divide and conquer'. He engineered the removal from office of the powerful Prime Minister Stefan Stambolov (1854–1895) and did nothing to prevent Stambolov's assassination.[5] Ferdinand's style became known as his 'personal regime'. Political parties fragmented under this pressure. The parties were all to a greater or lesser extent pro-Russian. At the beginning of the twentieth century a strong peasant party, the Bulgarian Agrarian Union, began to emerge under the leadership of Aleksandŭr Stamboliski (1879–1923). From its inception the Agrarian Union challenged Ferdinand's 'personal regime' and those individuals and political parties that abetted it.

During the first years of Ferdinand's rule Bulgaria began to develop economically. After the liberation of 1878, most of the large Muslim landowners emigrated to the Ottoman Empire. The land was divided up among the peasants. As a result Bulgaria became an agricultural state with the land relatively evenly distributed among small peasant farms. There was no native nobility and no extremes of wealth. The government undertook efforts to diversify agriculture. Poultry products, vegetables, fruit and tobacco, as well as such exotics as lavender and rose attar, became Bulgarian staples. To facilitate development the government built railways ahead of projected traffic. This and the heavy military spending imposed a heavy tax burden on the population.

Other aspects of development were more favourable. Due in part to the efforts of American Protestant missionaries, both males and females attained the highest rates of literacy in the region. Birth rates were low, which helped prevent the division of the agricultural holdings in to untenable plots. The rapidity of Bulgarian growth after 1878 gained the Bulgarians admiration and envy, and earned them comparisons with the Japanese, among others.

As in the other Balkan states, domestic politics in Greece centred on the irredentist issue, in Greek the *Megali Idea*. Greek claims extended to the north in Epirus and Macedonia and to the islands to the east and south. Crete especially was the focus of Greek *irredenta*. Unlike the Orthodox Slavic states with Russia and Romania with Austria-Hungary, the Greeks had no obvious Great Power patron to support their nationalist aspirations. The British probably maintained the closest relations with the Athens government, but while correct, these rarely attained warmth.

In 1896 the problem of Crete confronted Greece. Crete, still a part of the Ottoman Empire, had an Orthodox majority and a Muslim minority.

Both were mainly Greek-speaking. The Ottomans had conceded some autonomy in 1868, and a little more in 1878. Nevertheless the Orthodox Cretans rebelled in 1896. The next year on 14 April Greek troops invaded the Ottoman Empire in Thessaly in support of the Cretans. An Ottoman counterattack routed the invaders and drove them back into their own territory. Another Greek thrust into Epirus also suffered defeat. Before the Ottomans could advance far into Greece the Great Powers imposed an armistice. The Greeks were forced to concede some border zones in Thessaly and to pay a small indemnity. Otherwise Crete, despite the total Greek defeat, had its autonomy expanded. Prince George of Greece (1869–1957), a son of King George, became the high commissioner of Crete; although it was under the supervision of the Great Powers it remained under Ottoman suzerainty. Greek diplomats succeeded where Greek soldiers had failed.

Greek economic development faltered at the end of the nineteenth century. Its agricultural basis was not strong. Commercial activity such as shipping was subject to varying economic conditions. Many Greeks sought opportunities abroad.[6] Remittances sent home from Greeks living in the United States and elsewhere were an important source of income for the country.

Despite its disappointment with the Berlin settlement, Montenegro had gained considerable population and territory. Through the efforts of its relentless monarch, Prince Nikola Petrović (1841–1921), who had succeeded his uncle Danilo (1826–1860) in 1860, it also managed to thrust itself into the European community. By 1880 he had secured the Great Powers' agreement to the expansion of Montenegro's tiny coastline from Bar to Ulcinj. Through the marriages of his daughters to King Victor Emmanuel III of Italy (1869–1947), two Russian Grand Dukes and the Serbian Peter Karadjordjević (1844–1921), grandson of Karadjordje and the current head of that family, he ingratiated himself with some of the most important families in Europe. Nikola maintained a strong interest in Hercegovina and northern Albania and increasingly raised pretentions to the leadership of all Serbs. He ruled absolutely until 1905, when he permitted the adoption of a constitution. This document established an assembly, some of whose members were elected; the remainer were appointed by Nikola.

Montenegro had little economic development. Its mountainous topography and stony soil greatly limited agricultural production. The ancient clans provided most of the social structure. It had little to trade. Many men were reluctant to forgo their warrior proclivities for productive labour. Much income came from abroad in the form of Russian subsidies and Austrian loans.[7]

The Berlin settlement had been a disappointment to King Carol and most Romanians. They had expected more than the loss of southern Bessarabia and the gain of northern Dobrudja in return for their intervention on the side of Russia in the Russo-Turkish War. This resentment, as well as family inclinations, led Carol to conclude a secret alliance with Austria-Hungary in 1883. This directly linked Romania to the Triple Alliance. Nevertheless many Romanians looked across the Carpathians to Transylvania and its large Romanian population as an irredentist goal. The policies of Magyarization adopted by the Hungarian government in Transylvania increased the appeal of the idea of Romanian unification on both sides of the Carpathians. The ghost of Michael the Brave beckoned to nationalists in the Romanian kingdom to take Transylvania.

Two political parties dominated Romania in the last quarter of the nineteenth century, the Conservatives and the National-Liberals. Both were committed to policies of nationalist expansion and limited domestic actions. They alternated in power. This preserved the power of the monarch, who ruled his country in a style similar to that of his Bulgarian neighbour.

Romanian economic development remained slow. Despite the land reforms of 1864, the hereditary nobility, of Romanian and Phanariote origin, continued to dominate agriculture. Wheat was grown for export, and the much less nutritious corn for domestic consumption. The introduction of foreign capital, mainly British and Dutch, to develop the oil fields around Ploeşti did little to alleviate the plight of the peasantry. Most of the product and profits from the oil industry went outside the country.

In their helplessness to improve their situation, the peasants often vented their frustrations on the growing Jewish population in the kingdom. Since the beginning of the nineteenth century, a large number of Jews had migrated first into Moldavia and later Wallachia from Austrian

Galicia and from the Jewish Pale in Russia. They often served as land agents for absentee nobles, and as tavern keepers and money lenders for the peasants. The Berlin settlement had mandated that Jews receive equal rights in Romania. This did occur in 1879; nevertheless anti-Semitism remained widespread. Among the Orthodox peoples of the Balkans only the Romanians succumbed to anti-Semitism to any degree.

In 1907 the Romanian peasantry exploded in the last major European peasant uprising before the Russian Revolution ten years later. Grievances over high taxes and absentee landlords were the immediate causes. The uprising began in Moldavia and quickly spread to Wallachia. Eventually regular army units using artillery quelled the revolt at a cost of as many as ten thousand peasant lives. The revolt had a nasty anti-Semitic dimension. The peasants often targeted Jews, whom they viewed as the agents of their misfortunes. This anti-Semitism surfaced again in post-First World War Romanian politics.

Meanwhile in Serbia, the position of King Milan Obrenović became increasingly untenable. The Austro-Hungarian occupation of Bosnia-Hercegovina outraged the Serbs. Most Serbs considered these two Ottoman provinces to be Serbian in language and culture, even though a large Slavic-speaking Muslim population also lived there. Milan further lost credibility after the Serbian defeat in the war against Bulgaria in 1885. A public quarrel with his popular wife Queen Natalia (1859–1941) also undermined his popularity. In 1889 he abdicated in favour of his thirteen-year-old son Alexander (1876–1903), although for the time being he retained his commission as commanding general of the Serbian army. King Alexander Obrenović made himself very unpopular by his marriage in 1900 to Draga Mašin (1866/1867–1903), a widow at least ten years older than himself. The Serbian population thought her to be not only of poor moral character but also infertile. Alexander was somewhat less pro-Austrian than his father. Nevertheless his personal behaviour aroused the wrath of a cabal of nationalist officers and some civilians, who hated the queen and her retinue. Among these was a junior officer named Dragutin Dimitrijević (Apis) (1876–1917). The conspirators began planning to murder the royal couple in 1901. Finally on the night of 10–11 June 1903 they broke into the palace and accomplished their purpose. Peter Karadjordjević, the grandson of Karadjordje, replaced the murdered great-grandson of Miloš

Obrenović. Under King Peter, Nikola Pašić's Serbian Radical Party increasingly dominated politics. Pašić (1845–1926) pursued a pro-Russian and anti-Austrian policy. He was determined to expand Serbia with Habsburg and Ottoman territories.

In its economic and social characteristics Serbia was similar to Bulgaria. There were few large agricultural holdings. Peasants worked their own land, producing fruit and meat products. In neither country was there a native aristocracy. Unlike Bulgaria, Serbia had access to a wider world of economic and political ideas. The Serbian community in Austria-Hungary provided an alternative source of education and economic endeavour for those Serbs living in the kingdom. The cultural, economic and political interactions of the Serbian populations living in Austria, Hungary, Bosnia-Hercegovina and the kingdom grew closer. This helped to further the idea of Serbian unification, either within the Dual Monarchy, or more likely within the kingdom.

After the Berlin settlement, the Ottoman Empire entered a period of repression and stagnation under the 'Red Sultan', Abdulhamid II (1842–1918). Although the Ottomans had adopted a constitution and established a parliament in 1876, the same year he came to the throne, Sultan Abdulhamid II preferred to rule with unimpeded authority. Of course the Ottoman Empire's international situation was difficult. It lacked the patronage of a Great Power. The territorial losses at Berlin only increased the authoritarian tendencies. These in turn prevented the implementation of real reform. A policy of Ottomanization only further alienated moderate nationalist elements, including some Muslims, in the remaining Balkan provinces.

The evident Ottoman weakness increased the Balkan peoples' appetites for the realization of their nationalist agendas. These agendas overlapped in several locations. Both the Montenegrins and Serbs coveted Dalmatia and Bosnia-Hercegovina, which was under Austro-Hungarian rule after 1878 but was still formally a part of the Ottoman Empire. The Greeks, Montenegrins and Serbs also maintained pretensions to the Albanian provinces of the Ottoman Empire.

The Balkan national rivalries converged in Macedonia. The Bulgarians, Greeks and Serbs all claimed this region on the basis of cultural, ethnographic and historical grounds. In fact the population was quite mixed. In the three Ottoman *vilayets* that comprised Macedonia, there were Orthodox Slavs, Orthodox Greeks and Orthodox Albanians. There were Muslim Turks, Muslim Slavs and Muslim Albanians. There were also Armenians, Jews, Vlachs and others. No one nationality predominated. As one historian has written recently, 'In fact Macedonia was a microcosm of the Balkans, a mosaic of Muslim, Greek, Bulgarian, Serb, Albanian, Vlach, Jewish and Gypsy communities.'[8] The Orthodox Macedonians at this point had local rather than nationalist identities. Bulgarians, Greeks and Serbs all attempted to press their claims through educational and religious endeavours. They sought to convince the Orthodox Macedonians that in fact they were Bulgarians, Greeks or Serbs.

By the 1890s the rival Balkan states also formed terrorist societies to take more direct action. The largest of these was the Internal Macedonian Revolutionary Organization (IMRO), founded in 1893. It officially advocated an autonomous Macedonia, but maintained strong Bulgarian connections. Even so, its slogan was 'Macedonia for the Macedonians'. The Bulgarian government and military sponsored another group, the so-called Supremists. The Supremists supported the direct annexation of Macedonia by Bulgaria. Through these two organizations the Bulgarians dominated the Orthodox peoples in Macedonia. Greek and Serbian armed bands also roamed through the back country of Macedonia.

Ottoman authorities attempted to play the Balkan nationalists off against each other in order to maintain control. To some extent they were successful. Bulgarian, Greek and Serbian priests and schoolteachers vied for the hearts and minds of the Macedonian population while Bulgarian, Greek and Serbian bands fought against the Ottoman authorities and each other. Even the Romanians became involved by sponsoring schools for the Latin-speaking Vlachs. The Austrians and Russians recognized the dangers looming in Macedonia and attempted to contain them. In the Goluchowski-Muraviev agreement of 8 May 1897, they agreed to maintain the status quo in the Balkans. If this were not possible they would cooperate to protect each other's interests in the Balkans against the intervention of any other Great Power.[9]

By the turn of the century the situation in Macedonia had become explosive. After a premature revolt in Gorna Dzhumaya (Blagoevgrad) in northeastern Macedonia in 1902, IMRO rose throughout much of central

Macedonia in August 1903. This became known as the *Ilinden* (St Elias Day) revolt. The Ottomans quickly suppressed this revolt at a high cost in lives and property. The Sofia government found itself impotent to help. In the short term Bulgarian influence in Macedonia waned because of this failure to intervene. In October 1903 the Austrians and Russians proposed a policy of reform in Macedonia, the so-called Mürzteg programme. This reform envisioned the reorganization of the police and the judiciary of Macedonia under some Austrian and Russian oversight. In reality it accomplished little.

The bloody end of the Obrenović dynasty and the restoration of the Karadjordjević dynasty in Belgrade isolated Serbia internationally. In particular, it earned Serbia the enmity of its Austro-Hungarian neighbour. In this circumstance, the Serbs sought to reach an arrangement with Bulgaria. In April 1904 Belgrade concluded a treaty of friendship and a military alliance with Sofia.[10] The next year the two Balkan allies signed a trade agreement. This understanding did not withstand Austro-Hungarian hostility and Bulgarian inconsistency. In 1906 the Austrians undertook a trade war against Serbia, closing their frontiers to Serbian production. This became known as the 'Pig War' after a major Serbian export. The Bulgarians reverted to their rivalry with the Serbs by 1907. The Bulgarian–Serbian agreements of 1904 became moot.

The pace of events quickened throughout Southeastern Europe in 1908 when on 23 July the Committee for Union and Progress seized power in Constantinople. This organization, known as the Young Turks, had formed from an amalgamation of several reform-minded groups in the Ottoman Empire the previous year and was based in Salonika. Many of its members were junior officers in the Ottoman army. After their coup, the Young Turks announced a programme of reform. These reforms included restoration of the 1876 constitution, promotion of an Ottoman identity and military modernization. After an attempted countercoup the next year, Abdulhamid II lost his throne. His replacement, Mehmed V (1844–1918), was a non-entity.

The possibility of a reformed and strengthened Ottoman Empire alarmed the Great Powers, especially Austria-Hungary and Russia. In an effort to protect their interests, Russian foreign minister Alexander Izvolsky (1856–1919) met with the Austro-Hungarian foreign minister Alois von Aehrenthal (1854–1912) at Buchlau, Moravia on 16 September 1908. There the two ministers agreed that Russia would not oppose an Austrian annexation of Bosnia-Hercegovina. In return the Austrians would not object to an increased Russian presence in the Straits. Before the Russians could gain the agreement of the other Great Powers, the Austro-Hungarians announced the annexation of the Ottoman Provinces on 6 October. The day before, by prior arrangement with the Austrians, Prince Ferdinand declared Bulgaria's complete independence from the Ottoman Empire and assumed the title *tsar* in emulation of his medieval predecessors. These actions provoked the so-called Bosnian Crisis. These actions enraged the Russians. They thought the Austrians had betrayed the agreement made at Buchlau. The Montenegrins and Serbs also were furious. The Montenegrins had long coveted Hercegovina, while the Serbs wanted Bosnia. Austria-Hungary's evacuation of its garrisons in the Sandjak of Novi Pazar did little to assuage either Montenegro or Serbia. Yet they were unable to act against Austria-Hungary without Great Power support, which was not forthcoming.

The implications of the Young Turk Revolt and the breach of the Berlin settlement resulting from the Bosnian Crisis had a profound impact on the Balkan states. Clearly they too had to act to obtain their national agendas before the Young Turk reforms reinvigorated the Ottoman Empire. As early as October 1908, mainly in response to the annexation crisis, the Montenegrins and the Serbs began to explore the possibility of an alliance. By the next year this effort had waned. However in August 1909 a coup in Athens by a cabal of military officers resulted in the assumption of prime minister by Eleutherios Venizelos (1864–1936) the next year. A native of Crete, he was determined to realize the *Megali Idea*. In 1910 he made an overture to Sofia for an alliance.

That same year the Ottoman position began to deteriorate in Albania. Up until the turn of the century the Albanians had been among the most loyal Ottoman subjects in Europe. Concerns about the Ottomanization policies of the Young Turks, however, led to the outbreak of a revolt in the northern Albanian regions. Montenegro's King Nikola, who had adopted the regal title in 1910, abetted and encouraged this revolt.

Before action began on the Greek initiative, Bulgarian–Serbian negotiations resumed. With the strong support of the Russian minister in

Belgrade, Nicholas Hartwig (1855–1914) and the Russian minister in Sofia, Anatoli Neklyudov (1856–1934), the Bulgarian and Serbian governments reached an arrangement. On 13 March 1912 the Bulgarians and Serbs signed a treaty of alliance which provided for joint action against any aggressor. The real purpose of this agreement was a war against the Ottoman Empire. A secret annex assigned specific Ottoman territories to Bulgaria and Serbia, and nodded to the concept of Macedonian autonomy. By this agreement, Serbia was to obtain the Sandjak of Novi Pazar, Kosovo, while Bulgaria would receive southern Macedonia. Macedonian territory southeast of the Šar Mountains and northwest of Veles, including Skopje and Kumanovo, was regarded as a 'contested zone', the disposal of which Russian tsar Nicholas would arbitrate if the Bulgarians and Serbs could not agree between themselves.

Other bilateral arrangements among the Bulgarians, Greeks, Montenegrins and Serbs soon followed the Bulgarian–Serb alliance. The most important of these was the Bulgarian–Greek alliance signed on 29 May 1912. Significantly it contained no territorial provisions. After the poor performance of the Greek army in 1897, the Bulgarians thought that they would have little difficulty in realizing their territorial ambitions to the south. By the summer of 1912 a loose Balkan League had formed. The Balkan allies were anxious to act before the Ottomans concluded their war in North Africa against Italy.

The Montenegrins began the war on 8 October. The other Balkan allies followed on 18 October. Each Balkan ally fought a separate campaign against the Ottomans. Geography dictated that Thrace, located between the Bulgarian border and the Ottoman capital Constantinople, became the main theatre of war. Three Bulgarian armies invaded eastern Thrace. One Bulgarian army screened the important Ottoman fortress town of Adrianople (Odrin, Edirne), while on 29–31 October the other two smashed the Ottoman forces in the battle of Lyule Burgas–Buni Hisar (Lüle Burgaz–Pinarhisar). The victorious Bulgarians pursued the Ottomans to their defensive positions at Chataldzha (Çatalca), about 20 miles outside of Constantinople. There, on 16–17 November, the Bulgarians attempted to force the lines and seize the ancient imperial city. Cholera and exhaustion plus determined Ottoman resistance prevented the Bulgarians from attaining their objective.

Meanwhile the Serbian army crushed the Ottoman forces in western Macedonia at Kumanovo on 24 October. While Ottoman army remnants retreated into central Albania, the Serbs occupied Kosovo and much of northern Albania. To the south, the Greek navy played an important role in bottling up the Ottoman fleet in the Dardanelles. This meant that the Ottomans could not transfer troops from Anatolia to the Balkans by sea. Their control of the sea also enabled the Greeks to occupy the Aegean islands of Chios, Limnos and Mitylene. The Greek army advanced into Ottoman territory along two axes. One element hurried north to Salonikia (Thessaloniki), which it entered on 8 November, one day ahead of a Bulgarian force which had the same objective. The other Greek army moved in the northwest to bring the town of Ioannina (Janina) under siege. A small Montenegrin force entered the Sandjak of Novi Pazar. Most Montenegrin troops, however, brought the northern Albanian town of Scutari (Shkodër) under siege. All their attempts to take the town by direct assault failed.

Having suffered defeat on every front, the Ottomans requested an armistice. This was finalized at Chataldzha on 3 December 1912. At this point, the Ottoman Empire consisted of only the territory between the Chataldzha lines and Constantinople, the Gallipoli peninsula and the three besieged cities of Adrianople, Janina and Scutari. After the conclusion of the armistice, negotiations between the Balkan allies and the Ottomans shifted to London. The Greeks remained apart from the armistice negotiations. Two parallel conferences held there during December attempted to resolve the conflict. The first was a meeting of the representatives of the belligerent sides. Delegations from Bulgaria, Greece, Montenegro, Serbia and the Ottoman Empire attended the London Peace Conference. At the same time the ambassadors of the Great Powers to Great Britain also met at the London Ambassadors Conference, presided over by the British foreign secretary Edward Grey (1862–1933), to ensure that their own interests in the Balkans were preserved by the settlement.

When the extent of the Ottoman defeat became clear, a group of Albanian notables in Vlorë proclaimed an independent Albanian state on 28 November 1912. Urged on by the representatives of Austria-Hungary and Italy, the Ambassadors Conference soon recognized the new state. This new Albania claimed much territory that had been overrun by the

Serbs. The Austrian and Italian protectors of the new state insisted that the Serbs evacuate northern Albania. Meanwhile the London belligerents' conference foundered mainly on the issue of Adrianople, which the Ottomans insisted on retaining. When the Young Turks again seized power in Constantinople at the end of January 1913, they denounced the armistice.

The war resumed on 3 February 1913. The three besieged Ottoman cities soon fell. Janina surrendered to the Greeks on 6 March. The Bulgarians, with some Serbian help, took Adrianople on 26 March. Austro-Hungarian pressure forced Serbian troops aiding the Montenegrins at Scutari to withdraw in April. Even though the Great Powers decided at London to assign Scutari to the new Albanian state, Montenegrin forces continued their siege. The weary defenders of Scutari finally negotiated its surrender on 22 April. This provoked an international crisis. On Austro-Hungarian insistence, the Great Powers backed their demand that the Montenegrins withdraw with threats of armed intervention. Under these circumstances, the Montenegrins agreed to leave Scutari on 5 May 1913. After these further losses, the Ottomans agreed to terms. The Balkan War belligerents signed a preliminary peace treaty in London on 30 May 1913. This agreement limited the Ottoman presence in Europe to territory east of a straight line drawn from Enez (Enos) on the Aegean Sea to Midye (Midia) on the Black Sea.

Meanwhile tensions were rising among the Balkan allies. The failure of the Serbs to retain northern Albania increased their determination to hold Macedonia in the face of growing Bulgarian opposition. The Bulgarians and Greeks never reached any agreement for the disposition of conquered Ottoman territories and soon fell to skirmishing over northern Macedonia. By 5 May 1913 the Greeks and Serbs had concluded an alliance directed against Bulgaria. To complicate the situation, the Romanians, who wanted compensation for any Bulgarian gains in the war, began to make demands on Bulgarian (southern) Dobrudja. A Great Powers ambassadors' conference in St Petersburg in April 1913 failed to resolve the issue to the satisfaction of either the Bulgarians or Romanians. The conclusion of the London Treaty enabled the Bulgarians to transfer the bulk of their army from the Chataldzha lines to the southwestern part of their country in order to enforce their claims to Macedonia. Before the Russians could act upon their promise to mediate the dispute, an explosion occurred.

On the night of 29 June 1913 Bulgarian troops attacked Serbian positions in southeastern Macedonia. This began the Second Balkan War. Greek and Serbian counterattacks drove the Bulgarians back. By early July, however, the Bulgarian army had largely contained the Greek and Serbian advance along the line of the old Bulgarian frontier. At this point, the Ottomans and the Romanians intervened against Bulgaria. The Romanians wanted all of Bulgarian Dobrudja. The Ottomans sought to regain Adrianople, which they had lost earlier that year. The Romanians invaded Bulgaria on 10 July, the Ottomans two days later. The Bulgarian army, committed along the southwestern Bulgarian border against the Greeks and Serbs, could not oppose either action. With no help forthcoming from any quarter, the Bulgarians had to seek terms. Negotiations with the Greeks, Romanians and Serbs resulted in the Treaty of Bucharest, signed on 10 August 1913. Here Bulgaria acknowledged the loss of most of Macedonia as well as southern Dobrudja. A separate treaty signed in Constantinople on 30 September 1913 confirmed the loss of Adrianople and eastern Thrace to the Ottomans. Bulgaria, the main victor of the First Balkan War, became the victim of the Second Balkan War.

The two Balkan Wars resulted in significant changes to the map of Southeastern Europe. A fragile Albania emerged, challenged by Greek and Serbian territorial claims and protected by Austria-Hungary and Italy. Bulgaria, despite its defeat in the Second Balkan War, gained territory all along its southern frontier, including an outlet to the Aegean with the port of Dedeagach (Alexandroúpolis). Greatly disappointed by Russia's failure to save them from defeat, the Bulgarians turned away from Russia and increasingly to the Triple Alliance. Greece obtained a clear title to Crete, Epirus, much of southern Macedonia – including the important city of Salonika – and the islands of Chios, Limnos and Mitylene. The Greeks remained without an overt Great Power sponsor. Montenegro received half of the Sandjak of Novi Pazar but was denied Scutari. Romania took southern Dobrudja. The Romanians began to waver between the Triple Alliance and the Triple Entente. Serbia got Kosovo, the largest portion of Macedonia and half of the Sandjak of Novi Pazar. The great victor of the Balkan Wars, Serbia was now Russia's only reliable Balkan connection. The Serbs were determined to take advantage of this situation. Even though they were exhausted by their efforts during the Balkan Wars, the

Serbs understood that they had Russian protection. They had realized their objectives against the Ottoman Empire and against Bulgaria. They then turned to their Austro-Hungarian antagonist in order to unite with the Serbs of Bosnia.

The Great Powers made some effort to establish the new Albanian state on a firm footing through an International Control Commission. The Commission set up a police force directed by Dutch officers and invited a Prussian officer, William of Wied (1876–1945), to be the new country's first prince. Albania at this point still lacked an infrastructure and clearly defined borders.

The end of the Balkan Wars did not mean an end to the fighting in the Balkans. Albanians in Kosovo resisted the Serbian occupation. Serbian troops remained in northern Albania. On 18 October the Austro-Hungarians delivered an ultimatum in Belgrade demanding that the Serbs withdraw from Albania. Although the Serbs agreed to remove their forces from Albania, some stayed there to enforce Serbian claims to the region and to assist in the suppression of the Kosovo insurgency. For the third time in a year, the Serbs antagonized Austria-Hungary.

The actual event to ignite the Austro-Serb conflict was not a dispute over Albanian frontiers, as it had been the three previous times. On the Serbian national holiday, St Vitus Day (*Vidovdan*), 28 June 1914, the 525th anniversary of the Battle of Kosovo, a Bosnian Serb teenager, Gavrilo Princip (1894–1918), assassinated the Austrian heir Franz Ferdinand (1863–1914) and his wife Sophia Chotek (1868–1914) on the streets of Sarajevo. A cabal of officers in the Serbian army, many of whom, like their leader, Colonel Dimitrijević (Apis), had been active in the plot against King Alexander Obrenović, abetted the actions of Princip and his cohorts. The Austrians quickly determined this connection and decided to utilize it to put an end to their ongoing problems with their southern neighbour. The Austrians declared war on 28 July, one month after the assassination. The European alliance systems engaged, with France, Great Britain and Russia joining the Serbs and Germany supporting Austria-Hungary. Montenegro joined the Serbs. Bulgaria, Greece and Romania affirmed their neutrality.

The Serbs, led by the indomitable Vojvode Radomir Putnik (1847–1917), turned back the first Austrian invasion at the battle of Cer Mountain on 16–25 August. A second Austrian attempt later that autumn also failed. The Austrians did succeed in occupying Belgrade on 2 December 1914. A determined counterattack ejected them from Serbian territory for the third time by 15 December.[11] The Serbian victories were among the few Entente successes of 1914.

The situation in Serbia, however, remained perilous. The Serbian army lacked sufficient ammunition and other military supplies. Cholera and typhus ravaged the civilian and military populations. The country teetered on the edge of exhaustion. Serbia's British and French allies decided to send support. The only viable access to Serbia was through the Greek port of Salonika. Greek Prime Minister Venizelos favoured the Entente and invited the Entente forces to use the port on 3 October 1915. However, he resigned on 5 October and a neutralist government then assumed power. The British and French troops began landing in Salonika that same day, either as invited guests or as violators of Greek neutrality.

At this point the role of Bulgaria became critical. After the outbreak of the war, both sides recognized the importance of Bulgaria and sought its adherence to their efforts. For the Central Powers, Bulgaria would ensure communication with the Ottoman Empire and the destruction of Serbia. For the Entente, the adherence of Bulgaria would greatly facilitate an attack on Constantinople and would support Serbia. Bulgaria was prepared to intervene on whichever side could guarantee the attainment of Bulgaria's nationalist objectives, especially in Macedonia. The Gallipoli campaign made Bulgaria particularly attractive to the Entente. Bulgarian pressure on Constantinople would likely insure an Entente success. The price for Bulgarian intervention on the side of the Entente was Macedonia. Because the Serbs were unwilling to concede Macedonia, their prize from the Balkan Wars, the Entente could not meet the Bulgarian demand. Serbia, for the Entente, was the ally whose distress had been a cause for the outbreak of the war. At best, the Entente could offer Bulgaria a part of Macedonia after the war when Serbia had presumably taken Bosnia. The Central Powers, however, had no such inhibitions. Bulgaria could have Macedonia immediately. Given the apparent Entente failure at Gallipoli and the German victories in Poland at Gorlice-Tarnow, the choice appeared obvious. Bulgaria could have a part of Macedonia at the end of the war, or all of it immediately. On 6 September 1915, Bulgaria joined the Central Powers.

A Central Powers attack on Serbia from two sides began the next month. One Austro-Hungarian and one German army crossed the Danube in the north on 6 October. Two Bulgarian armies attacked Serbia from the east one week later. The Serbs were soon overwhelmed. Cut off by the Bulgarians from a retreat to the south, the remnants of the Serbian forces retreated in winter conditions during November and December 1915 to the southwest across the Albanian Mountains to the Adriatic Sea. Eventually they found refuge on the Greek island of Corfu. Austro-Hungarian and Bulgarian troops occupied Serbia. Both occupying powers imposed a harsh regime on the Serbian civilian population. In 1917 Bulgarian troops brutally suppressed a Serbian revolt in Toplica.

Entente troops began landing on 7 October in neutral Greece at the port of Salonika. Their plan was to move north up the Vardar River valley to aid the beleaguered Serbs. The Bulgarians halted the British and French in a series of sharp engagements and forced them back across the Greek frontier in December 1915.

At German insistence, the Bulgarians stopped their pursuit of the British and French at the Greek frontier. The Bulgarian halt allowed the Entente to augment its forces with additional British and French troops as well as contingents from Italy and Russia. After some rest and refurbishment on the island of Corfu, the survivors of the Serbian retreat joined the Salonika army. The Macedonian Front then developed in the pattern established on the Western Front. Both sides fortified their positions along the Greek frontier, and sought advantage in air raids and small ground attacks.

The Montenegrin army helped to cover the Serbian retreat. Without the Serbs, however, the Montenegrins were vulnerable. Early in 1916 the Austrians launched an invasion of the smallest Balkan country. Cetinje fell on 11 January 1916 and Montenegro formally surrendered on 17 January, the first country to leave the war. King Nikola went into exile in Italy. Austro-Hungarian troops occupied the country.

The fragile young Albanian state collapsed soon after the beginning of the war. Lacking support anywhere in the country, Prince William returned to Germany in September 1914. Serbian troops had never entirely left the northern part of the country. Meanwhile in the south, Greek irregulars seeking unification with Greece fought against local Albanians.

In the spring of 1915 Italian troops occupied the south. After the defeat of Serbia, Austrian soldiers confronted Italian troops along a line from Lake Prespa to the Adriatic Sea south of Vlorë.

Romania, which like Bulgaria had wavered between both sides since the beginning of the war, appeared ready to join the Entente. Like the Bulgarians, the Romanians wanted to realize nationalist goals. Unlike Bulgaria, these goals were divided between the belligerents. Austria-Hungary had Transylvania and Bukovina, long coveted by Romanian nationalists. Russia, however, had Bessarabia, taken from Romania in 1878. Romania had also had a formal arrangement with Austria-Hungary from 1882 until 1914. In the summer of 1916 the apparent success of the Brusilov offensive tilted Bucharest in favour of the Entente. As the Romanians made final preparations to enter the war, the Entente readied an offensive along the Macedonian Front to divert and distract the Central Powers from Romania, which lay exposed between Austria-Hungary and Bulgaria. The Bulgarians attempted to precipitate the Entente offensive on the Macedonian Front by launching one of their own. The pending threat from Romania persuaded the Germans to lift their ban on a Bulgarian attack into Greece. This effort involved attacks on the eastern and western wings of the Front. In the east Bulgarian troops advanced into Greek-held eastern Macedonia. Against little Greek resistance they occupied Drama, Seres and the Aegean port of Kavala. In the west they seized Florina (Lerin). The Entente countered this effort and through the autumn of 1916 drove the Bulgarians out of Florina north into Macedonia as far as Monastir.

Romania finally entered the war on the side of the Entente on 27 August and invaded Transylvania, the main Romanian objective in the war. The Romanians soon found themselves in a two-front war. The Bulgarian 3rd Army, augmented by German and Ottoman troops, crossed the Romanian frontier in Dobrudja in conjunction with an Austro-Hungarian and German counterattack against Romania. The Bulgarians advanced quickly against determined Romanian opposition. By December, they had defeated a Romanian attempt to cross the Danube to invade Bulgaria and overrun the entire Dobrudja. On 6 December the Austro-German force occupied Bucharest. The Romanians held on in Moldavia through 1917. They won important – mainly defensive – victories at Mărăaşti and

Mărăşesti in July and August respectively of that year, but at a heavy cost in Romanian lives. The collapse of Russia and the subsequent Treaty of Brest-Litovsk left the Romanians isolated and forced them to come to terms with the Central Powers. Romania signed the Treaty of Bucharest on 7 May 1918, conceding Dobrudja, territories all along the Carpathian border with Austria-Hungary and important economic concessions to the Central Powers.

By 1917 Greece was a divided country. Supporters of Venizelos advocated entering the war on the side of the Entente, whose forces were by then ensconced in the north of the country. Supporters of King Constantine (1868–1923), who was himself of Danish origin and married to Sophie (1870–1932), the sister of the German Kaiser William II (1859–1941), inclined towards the Central Powers. Given the presence of a significant Entente force on his territory, he was in no position to join the Central Powers. He therefore favoured neutrality for Greece, as did important elements in the army. This dichotomy in the Greek reaction to the war resulted in the so-called 'National Schism'. On 30 August 1916 a group of pro-Venizelos army officers seized power in Salonika and established a pro-Entente government there in opposition to the neutralist government in Athens. Meanwhile the Entente imposed a blockade on the Athens government. After almost a year, Entente pressure finally forced King Constantine to abdicate in favour of his son Alexander (1893–1920) on 12 June 1917. Alexander appointed Venizelos prime minister, and Greece declared war on the Central Powers on 27 June 1917. Greek army units then joined the Entente forces at the Macedonian Front.

Meanwhile morale and material conditions within Bulgaria deteriorated. As the Germans prepared for their Western Front offensive, they began to shift their forces away from Macedonia in 1917. By April 1918 few Germans troops remained there. Another issue was the lack of a material basis on which to continue the war. Food was a major problem. Hunger appeared in Bulgarian villages and towns and on the front line. There was also a great lack of adequate clothing. Some soldiers went into battle barefoot and in rags.

On 14 September French and Serbian forces launched a massive assault on Bulgarian defences at Dobro Pole in the centre of the Macedonian Front in northern Greece.[12] After the second day of heavy fighting, the Bulgarian soldiers began to fall back in disarray. Troops retreated towards Bulgaria, forming angry mobs, seeking redress for the suffering they had endured at the Front. French and Serbian troops surged north into Macedonia. Even so at this late date, other Bulgarian units were still able to defeat a British-Greek attack at Lake Doiran.

Despite the defensive success at Doiran, Bulgarian forces at the Front to the east and west of Dobro Pole had to withdraw to avoid being cut off. Discipline continued to deteriorate. Almost six years of fighting, lack of food and clothing and concerns about their families at home caused many Bulgarian soldiers to reject frantic attempts by Bulgarian officers to impose discipline. Disorganized mobs of Bulgarian soldiers moved north, determined to punish those in the capital they regarded as responsible for all the suffering. This effort became known as the Radomir Rebellion, after the city in western Bulgaria at the centre of the disorders. Many of the soldiers came under the influence of peasant revolutionary leaders from the Agrarian Party, such as Alexandŭr Stamboliski. The Austro-Hungarians and Germans could promise only that six divisions were on the way.

Threatened by revolution and lacking meaningful help from the Central Powers, on 25 September the Bulgarian government decided to seek an armistice. The Bulgarian delegation signed an armistice agreement with the Entente on 29 September in Salonika. Bulgaria became the first of the Central Powers to leave the war. Montenegro and Romania as well as Russia had preceded Bulgaria in leaving the war. While Entente military strength was superior to that of the Bulgarians, the years of bad food, shoddy materiel and uncertain relations with their allies proved to be as effective weapons as Serbian infantry and French artillery in the defeat of September 1918.

When the Austro-Hungarian and German troops arrived in Bulgaria, they participated in the suppression of the army mutineers. At a battle near Pernik outside Sofia, on the same day the armistice was signed in Salonika, Bulgarian military cadets, German troops and some IMRO forces turned the mutineers back. Afterwards they scattered, their goal of ending the war achieved. Shortly afterwards, on 3 October, Tsar Ferdinand abdicated. His 24-year-old son assumed the Bulgarian throne as Boris III.

As Austro-Hungarian and German units retreated to the north, victorious Serbian soldiers moved through Macedonia and on into Serbia. They reached Niš on 10 October and Belgrade on 1 November. Austrian and Bulgarian occupation had lasted three years. The Serbs continued on over the Danube and had moved into southern Hungary to enforce Serbian claims to the Vojvodina by the time the war ended. The Austro-Hungarians only evacuated Albania and Montenegro at the end of October. They finally left Cetinje on 6 November. By this time Habsburg authority had collapsed everywhere. Serbian troops filled the power vacuum in Croatia and Slovenia, drawn by a need to expel the Hungarians and thwart Italian expansionism.

Even though defeated by the Central Powers, Romania made some territorial gains. As early as January 1918 Romanian troops intervened in the chaotic situation that existed across the Prut River in Bessarabia as a result of the Russian revolutions. On 9 April 1918 the *Sfatul Ţării*, the Bessarabian National Council, voted to unify with Romania.[13] With the defeat of the Central Powers obvious, the Romanians re-entered the war on 10 November. This ensured that they would be among the victors of the war.

By any reckoning the wars from 1912 to 1918 were disastrous for the Balkan states in men and materiel. The fighting had spared no place in the Balkans. Romania and Serbia in particular had experienced heavy combat on their own territories. Soldiers died in large numbers: in the Balkan Wars, Bulgaria lost as many as 66,000, Greece around 8,000, Montenegro 3,000 and Serbia about 37,000.[14] In the fighting from 1914 to 1918 101,224 Bulgarian soldiers were killed, 28,000 Greeks, 3,000 Montenegrins, 335,706 Romanians and 127,535 Serbians.[15] In the fighting after 1914 alone Serbia lost more than one-third of its army, Romania one-quarter and Bulgaria one-fifth.[16] This means that as many as 710,000 Balkan soldiers died in the fighting from 1912 to 1918. The wounded were even more numerous. The fighting displaced civilians everywhere. Civilians died throughout the Balkans from the privations in food, fuel and other materials caused by the fighting as well as from disease. The fighting displaced hundreds of thousands throughout the region.

Yet for the most part, the foreign soldiers left the Balkans. The victors maintained only small numbers of troops in defeated Bulgaria. Some

Greek, Italian and Yugoslav units remained in Albania until 1920. Amid the debris of war, some hopes existed that within the pending peace based on American and Wilsonian idealism, the potential of the Balkans could achieve full realization.

five

The Interbellum, 1919–39

The waning of conflict in the Balkan Peninsula at the end of 1918 brought important changes to the configuration of the Balkan national states. As a result of the six years of fighting, Bulgaria, Greece, Romania and Serbia had all gained territory, and a new Albanian state had come into existence. Despite the destruction and the exhaustion brought about as a result of six years of war, the Balkan peoples anticipated that the aftermath of the conflict would bring some realization of their desires for national development.

The most important of these changes was the establishment of the new state of the Kingdom of Serbs, Croats and Slovenes, popularly known as Yugoslavia or Land of the South Slavs. This state had its cultural origins in the realization by some in the nineteenth century that the Slavic languages spoken in the southern and western parts of the Balkan Peninsula, including Slovene, Croatian, Serbian and Bulgarian, were quite similar. This idea initially became known as Illyrianism. An initial advocate of this idea was Ljudevit Gaj (1809–1872), who noted that a walker from 'Villach (Slovenia) to Varna (Bulgaria)' would encounter only slight changes in the local Slavic dialect from village to village.[1] Illyrianism envisioned that the Slavic peoples of the Balkan Peninsula had a single cultural identity. Gaj himself promoted Vuk Karadžić's use of the Serbo-Croatian štokavian dialect. He also modified the Latin alphabet so that Slavic sounds could be more easily represented. This enabled the modern forms of Croatian, Slovene and Serbian to be written with the Latin alphabet. Serbian also retained Cyrillic, as did Bulgarian and Macedonian. Gaj thus helped bridge the divide between Western Catholic Slavs and Eastern Orthodox Slavs in Southeastern

Europe. This greatly facilitated the flow of Western European ideas into the Balkans.

The idea of Yugoslavism assumed a political dimension in the Austro-Hungarian Empire after the *Ausgleich* of 1867, which transformed the Habsburg Empire into Austria-Hungary. It served as a means to further South Slavic interests in Austrian Dalmatia as well as to balance Magyarization policies in the Hungarian part of the state. Croat and Serb politicians sought mutual advantage through cooperation in the Austrian and Hungarian parliaments.

Austro-Hungarian South Slavs formed the Yugoslav Committee in order to maintain their interests at the beginning of the First World War. It favoured a federated South Slav state. This conflicted with the Serbian aim of a Greater Serbia, which would include Bosnia-Hercegovina, Vojvodina and part of Dalmatia. When Italy entered the war on the side of the Entente in May 1915, the Treaty of Rome promised the Italians extensive Austro-Hungarian territories on the eastern side of the Adriatic Sea. These areas included mainly Slovenes, Croats and some Serbs. This Italian threat to their national interests motivated the Slovenes, Croats and Serbs within Austria-Hungary to strengthen contacts among themselves. As the Austro-Hungarian war effort weakened, these South Slavic peoples sought protection against Italy.

Meanwhile in 1915 the Central Powers occupied Serbia. The February 1917 revolution in Russia demonstrated to the Serbs that little help could come from Petrograd. The result of the mutual weakness of the Serbs and the Austro-Hungarian South Slavs was the Pact of Corfu, signed on 20 July 1917 between Nikola Pašić of the Serbia government in exile and Ante Trumbić (1864–1938), a Dalmatian Croat from the Yugoslav Committee. The Pact of Corfu called for the establishment of a democratic South Slav state, or Yugoslavia, at the end of the war, with equality of religions and alphabets, under the Serbian Karadjordjević dynasty. A token Yugoslav unit, mainly consisting of Serbian prisoners of war from the Austro-Hungarian army, went to Salonika to participate in the fighting on the Macedonian Front.

The Serbian breakthough of the Bulgarian lines at Dobro Pole in September 1918 established the conditions to realize a South Slavic State. Events after Dobro Pole developed rapidly. The Serbian army advanced

The Balkans, 1921–1939.

from Macedonia and Serbia into Croatia and southern Hungary. There it established order as Austro-Hungarian authority collapsed.[2] On 28 October, on the verge of Austria-Hungary's disintegration, Habsburg authorities ceded authority to the Yugoslav National Council. In Geneva on 11 November this body, the Yugoslav Committee and the Serbian government signed an agreement which provided for autonomy for the former Habsburg provinces within a Yugoslav state. On 26 November an assembly in Podgorica, Montenegro deposed the exiled King Nikola and proclaimed the unification of Montenegro with Serbia. Then on 1 December 1918 at a meeting in Belgrade, the National Council accepted unification with the Kingdom of Serbia. That same day, Prince Regent Alexander (1888–1934) announced the establishment of the Kingdom of Serbs, Croats and Slovenes. Left unresolved were the power dynamics of the new state. The presence of the victorious Serbian army throughout the territory of the new entity, and the participation of many Croats and

Slovenes in the defeated Habsburg forces, however, indicated the strong likelihood of Serbian predominance. Also left unresolved were the precise frontiers of the new state, especially in regard to Albania and Italy.

This South Slavic state came into being not as an expression of the popular will of the Serbian, Croatian and Slovene people, but as a means of mutual self-interest and protection against outside predation. While it may well have represented the best political option for the South Slavs at the time, its benefits for the non-Slavic peoples in the region were dubious. The state distrusted the Germans and Hungarian inhabitants of the former Habsburg territories. The Kosovo Albanians had never accepted the Serbian conquest of 1912. They had harassed retreating Serbian soldiers in 1915. They resisted the return of the Serbs in 1918. Those Albanians who fought against the reinstatement of Serbian control of Kosovo after 1918 were known as the Kachaks.[3] Fighting in Kosovo between the Kachaks and the Yugoslav army continued until the late 1920s.

The Paris Peace Conference, which convened in January 1919, held some promise for the Balkan states. If the Wilsonian ideal of national self-determination prevailed at the conference, perhaps the disputes that had plagued the region with the waning of Ottoman power could achieve resolution. Even Bulgaria had a chance of retaining some of its wartime gains. After all, Bulgaria and the United States had not gone to war against each other. The Bulgarians hoped that the Americans might support their claims to Macedonia at the conference.

The country to benefit most from the peace process, however, was Romania. In April 1918, the Romanians had signed the Treaty of Bucharest with the Central Powers and exited the war. A year later they were contemplating the realization of their maximum nationalist aspirations. As a result of the Treaty of St Germain with Austria, signed on 10 September 1919, Romania obtained the old Habsburg province of Bukovina, which had a mixed population but a Romanian plurality. As a consequence of the Treaty of Trianon, signed with Hungary on 4 June 1920, Romania obtained not only Transylvania, but also significant parts of northeastern Hungary and the Banat. The participation of the Romanian army in the summer 1919 campaign to oust the Bela Kun's (1886–1938?) Communist regime in Budapest undoubtedly helped to advance Romanian claims against Hungary. The resulting 'Greater Romania' also included Bessarabia, which had been annexed the previous year from the crumbling Russian Empire, and southern Dobrudja, which had been first taken from Bulgaria during the Second Balkan War. Greater Romania contained large numbers of minorities, including Bulgarians, Germans, Hungarians and Ukrainians. It also had the largest Jewish population in Southeastern Europe.

The Bulgarians were bitterly disappointed by the outcome of the peace process. The anticipated American support proved to be only 'platonic'.[4] National self-determination did not apply to them in Paris. By the Treaty of Neuilly, signed on 27 November 1919, Bulgaria lost three western enclaves to the new Serb-Croat-Slovene state, western Thrace, including its Aegean coastline to Greece and southern Dobrudja to Romania. Macedonia, the main object of Bulgarian national aspirations since the Treaty of San Stefano, once again was denied to the Bulgarians. Additional stipulations demilitarized Bulgaria, limited its army to 33,000 men and imposed reparations payments of us$445 million. The Bulgarians were greatly frustrated that the victors permitted no plebiscites in the lost territories.

For Albania and Greece, however, the conclusion of peace in Paris did not bring an end to conflict. Italian troops remained in central Albania, while Greek irregulars operated in the south and Yugoslav (Serbian) bands remained in the north. The Treaty of Rome of 26 April 1915 had promised Italy control of Vlorë and the island of Sazan (Saseno), which controlled the harbour of Vlorë. At Paris, the Greeks pressed claims to southern Albania. Nevertheless the victors gave Italy an effective mandate over Albania, but the Italians lacked the resources to enforce their control over the country and increasingly faced scattered resistance throughout the country. The Italians evacuated their forces in August 1920, but retained Sazan. Even before the Italians left, a national congress convened in Lushnja in January 1920. Little enthusiasm existed in Albania for the return of Prince Wied and the resumption of the monarchy. The congress held a general election. Those elected then met on 27 March in Tirana as the Albanian National Assembly. They established a rather inchoate republic.

After the resolution of the 'National Schism' the Greeks, under Venizelos' leadership, sought to expand their position in Anatolia at the expense of the defeated Ottoman government. This represented the implementation of the *Megali Idea,* the 'Great Idea' of Greek nationalism that sought the re-establishment of the Byzantine Empire. In May 1919 a Greek army occupied Symrna (Izmir) on the west coast of Anatolia in anticipation of its assignment to Greece in the peace settlement. The Greeks subsequently extended their control over the hinterland. The Treaty of Sèvres signed with the Ottoman Empire assigned most of this region to Greece. A resurgent Turkish army under the leadership of the former Young Turk and hero of the defence of Gallipoli, Mustapha Kemal (1881–1938), the future Atatürk, however, contested these Greek attempts to extend their control of Anatolia. At the battle of the Sakarya (Sangarios) in central Anatolia in August and September 1921, Kemal's Turkish forces routed the overextended Greeks. The Greek army then slowly retreated to the Aegean. The army evacuated Symrna in September 1922, accompanied by hundreds of thousands of Greek civilians. The dream of the *Megali Idea* had turned into a nightmare. In the aftermath of this disaster, the Greek and Turkish governments negotiated a population exchange in the Treaty of Lausanne in January 1923.[5] Muslim Greeks, whatever their language, went to Turkey. Christians from Anatolia, both Greek- and Turkish-speaking, went to Greece. With this disorganized exodus, over three thousand years of Greek presence in western Anatolia ended. The Greeks also had to evacuate Adrianople and eastern Thrace, which they had occupied in 1920. In 1924 Greek forces evacuated southern Albania, where they had supported a Greek state called Northern Epirus, although the Athens government continued to maintain claims to the region.

The wars left all the Balkan states in poor material and physical condition. War-damaged infrastructure and hordes of refugees formed a significant obstacle to economic development, and undermined chances for political stability. Regional agreements remained difficult because of lingering hostilities. All the Balkan countries experienced problems of integration. The Bulgarians and Greeks had to incorporate Macedonian and Anatolian refugees. This burden quickly overtaxed state resources. The Romanians had to integrate infrastructures – including railways, telegraphs, school systems and commercial patterns – from four main sources, Austrian, Hungarian, Romanian and Russian, as well as from the slice of Bulgaria that they had acquired in 1913. The Yugoslav kingdom had to integrate infrastructures from five sources: Austrian, Hungarian, Montenegrin, Ottoman and Serbian. The bureaucracies established throughout the Balkans were overgrown, inefficient and corrupt. Integration often proved beyond the capabilities of limited state resources.

The agricultural economy was in poor condition throughout the region. Land reform first occurred in Romania during the war as a belated means to quell the discontent that had erupted in 1907 and to motivate the peasant soldiers to fight in the World War. This reform later dispossessed Austrian landowners in Bukovina, Hungarian landowners in the Banat and Transylvania and Russian landowners in Bessarabia. A similar process gave land to the peasantry in the former Austrian and Hungarian parts of the new South Slav kingdom. Nevertheless demographic pressures resulting from higher birth rates, lower death rates and the influx of refugees caused rural overpopulation throughout the region. Peasant land became divided into increasingly smaller plots. These plots were frequently widely disbursed strips. Peasants exhausted themselves just in travelling to their plots. Obviously this adversely affected production. The small peasant producers lacked the capital to purchase agricultural machinery, fertilizers, seed and livestock. All of the Balkan states lacked the transportation and processing infrastructure to utilize their agricultural production. As a consequence many of their crops rotted in the fields or in storage facilities. Because of the inadequate processing, Balkan-produced grain frequently cost more in European markets than that from Argentina, Canada and the United States.

Industrialization failed to take hold in the Balkans during the interwar period. The few large industrial enterprises, notably the Ploeşti oil-refining complex in Romania, remained in the hands of foreigners. Consequently most of the profits left the country, and few locals developed upper-level management skills. As in the case of agriculture, there was little domestic capital available for investment. Some of the limited capital went to the production of arms.

A 'scissors crisis' resounded throughout the region in the late 1920s. The price of agricultural production fell as the cost of industrial goods rose. The Balkan countries lacked the buying power for imported goods. This left them vulnerable to the economic machinations of foreigners.[6] Nazi Germany in particular derived advantage from this situation.

Another problem that afflicted the Balkan states was that of national minorities. Only Greece had largely avoided this issue, through the population exchanges with Bulgaria and Turkey in 1923. Large numbers of Anatolian and Thracian refugees, some of whom did not even speak Greek, resulted from these exchanges. They often existed in conditions similar to those of national minorities in the other Balkan states. A small but self-aware Greek minority who still hoped for unification with Greece remained in southern Albania. A large Turkish-speaking minority lived in Bulgaria, which together with the Slavic-speaking Islamic group known as *Pomacks*, constituted almost 10 per cent of the population. In Romania roughly a quarter of the population was made up of ethnic minorities, including 8 per cent Hungarians, 5 per cent Jews, 5 per cent Germans and 5 per cent Ukrainians. Yugoslavia was nationally complex. No one group constituted a majority. There were Serbs, who were the largest single national group, Croats and Slovenes. The national status of Bosnian Muslims and Macedonians remained unresolved. Also there were large numbers of non-Slavs, including Albanians, Germans and Hungarians. All of the Balkan states contained significant though largely uncounted populations of Roma (Gypsies), who remained beyond the parameters and often the interests of state authorities. None of the nationalist Balkan governments wanted to expend their limited resources on minority groups which were sometimes potential enemies.

The mutual suspicion and dislike between town and country, already in evidence especially in Bulgaria and Romania, became more pronounced elsewhere in the Balkans during the interwar period. Peasant political movements gained importance. Briefly in the early 1920s a Green (Peasant) International movement arose among the peasant parties of Bulgaria, Yugoslavia and Czechoslovakia. Ironically greater educational opportunities helped to widen the town and country divide. The peasants' sons who obtained an education in cities often demonstrated little inclination to return home so that the countryside could benefit from their achievements. Frequently they failed to find meaningful employment in the cities. Out of a sense of frustration they often became susceptible to authoritarian political movements.

These problems all undermined Balkan state governments. Although occasionally a government based upon real democracy emerged, such as the Stamboliski government in Bulgaria, democratic governments in general were few and unsuccessful. By the 1930s all of the Balkan states had succumbed to royalist authoritarian governments.

In 1921, nine years after its declaration of independence, Albania finally achieved international recognition of its frontiers. Greek and Yugoslav forces withdrew, at least for the time being. Only then did Albania begin to achieve some long-desired political stability. The country nevertheless underwent frequent changes of government. A leading figure was Fan Noli (1882–1965) who served as Albanian delegate to the League of Nations, foreign minister and in 1924 prime minister. Born in Ottoman Thrace, Noli had moved to the United States, where he graduated from Harvard University and then served as a bishop of the Albanian Orthodox Church.[7] His programme of land and political reform aroused the opposition of traditional Muslim landowners. A force led by a northern Albanian landowner and former prime minister, Ahmed Zogu (1895–1961),[8] overthrew Noli with the help of some White Russian veterans of General Peter Wrangel's (1878–1928) army and the assistance of the Yugoslav government. Zogu then proceeded to eliminate opposition and establish a regime based upon his personal power. He quickly turned his back on his Yugoslav allies and sought help from Mussolini's Italy. In 1928 he proclaimed himself 'King of the Albanians' under the name Zog I. The pretensions of the title did little to improve relations with his Greek and Yugoslav neighbours. This did not matter to Zog, whose army had Italian advisors, whose finances had Italian oversight and who permitted Italian settlement in Albania. The influx of aid from across the Straits of Otranto nevertheless did little to improve the material condition of Albania, which remained the least developed country in the least developed region of Europe.

Bulgaria's second defeat in six years left the country broke, demoralized, exhausted and overrun with refugees. Agrarian party leader Aleksandŭr Stamboliski came to power through a reasonably clean election in 1919. He made some effort to govern the country in the interests of the peasant majority. He initiated some land reform measures and introduced legal reform that made justice more accessible and cheaper for the average Bulgarian.[9] To supplement the treaty-limited army, he instituted compulsory labour service to help build up the county's infrastructure.

This also helped to dilute the power of the officer corps. Stamboliski made efforts to curb the power that IMRO exercised in southwestern Bulgaria. He also attempted to establish links with other Eastern European agrarian movements in Croatia, Czechoslovakia and Poland, seeking to form a 'Green International'. Stamboliski's peasant demeanour alienated some more refined urban dwellers. Even more, his acceptance of the Treaty of Neuilly and its limitations for Bulgaria and his signing of a friendship treaty at Niš in 1923 with the new South Slav state outraged many irreconcilable Bulgarian military officers and members of IMRO. In June 1923 they, with the complicity of Tsar Boris, staged a coup to overthrow the Agrarian government. Before murdering Stamboliski, the rebels cut off the right hand that had signed the despised Treaty of Niš earlier that year.

After the destruction of the Stamboliski government, Bulgaria entered a period of parliamentary ineffectiveness and instability. Some Communists belatedly and unsuccessfully attempted a revolt later in 1923. The government easily quashed it. On 16 April 1925 other Communists blew up St Nedelya cathedral in downtown Sofia in an attempt to kill the tsar and his ministers. Due to his late arrival, Boris escaped harm. More than 169 other Bulgarians died, however, and over five hundred were injured.[10] Meanwhile IMRO ruled Pirin Macedonia (southwestern Bulgaria) virtually without interference from the government in Sofia. A part of IMRO's income came from the cultivation and processing of poppies in the region.

In 1934 a group from within the Bulgarian military which called itself *Zveno* (link) ousted the government and established a military dictatorship. They curbed IMRO and re-established the authority of the central government in Pirin Macedonia. The next year Tsar Boris, who did not want to lose his personal authority to a military clique, ejected *Zveno* from power with the help of rival elements in the military, and established a relatively mild royal dictatorship. Parliament continued to function, and censorship was light. Unlike his fellow Balkan rulers in Albania, Romania and Yugoslavia, Tsar Boris' direct rule managed to evoke a sense of relief and even satisfaction from his subjects.

Greece emerged from the wars in bad shape. New lands in western Thrace were acquired from Bulgaria. The dream of the *Megali Idea*, however, was shattered beyond any recovery. Hordes of Anatolian refugees taxed the limited resources of the government, and traces of the national schism remained to obstruct and destabilize politics. Basically this conflict devolved to a struggle between liberals and republicans against conservatives, monarchists and militarists for control of Greek politics. In 1922 in the aftermath of the defeat by Turkey, King Constantine abdicated once again. His son and successor, King George II (1890–1947), did not remain on the throne for long. Elections held in 1923 established a republic the next year. This second Greek republic lasted for twelve turbulent years until 1935.[11] From 1928–33 the old nationalist Eletherios Venizelos, who had lived outside the country following the Anatolian debacle, returned to become the leading figure in the government. In 1935, however, elements in the military associated with the former king seized power and restored the monarchy. Although King George returned to the country, General Ioannis Metaxas (1871–1941), a Balkan War hero and leading supporter of King Constantine during the national schism, effectively governed the country as a military dictatorship.

In the aftermath of the First World War, Romania was perhaps the most fortunate of the Balkan states. Romania recovered from defeat by the Central Powers to emerge on the winning side at the end of the war and to realize its maximum nationalist expectations. Greater Romania had many advantages, including rich agricultural land, a large population and an oil industry around Ploeşti. Yet almost immediately the political situation deteriorated. Old patterns re-emerged. Parliamentary practices that had prevailed in Austrian Bukovina and Hungarian Transylvania did not mesh easily with the choreographed corruption of the old kingdom. The Liberals maintained their grip on politics.

A new problem arose upon the death of King Ferdinand (b. 1865) in 1927. His son Carol (1893–1953) had forfeited his right to the throne through a series of scandalous escapades. On King Ferdinand's death, Carol's six-year-old son Michael (1921–) succeeded his grandfather as king of Romania, while his father lived in exile. In 1930, however, the Peasant Party leader Iuliu Maniu (1873–1953), sensing a political advantage, agreed to the return of Carol as king of Romania so long as he renounced his mistress Elena (Magda) Lupescu (1895–1977). Carol agreed to do so, but within three weeks of his return he had openly resumed his relationship with Madam Lupsecu. The outraged Maniu resigned. On this issue the British historian Hugh Seton-Watson (1916–1984) observed, 'Bourgeois sexual morality is probably less esteemed in Romania than anywhere else on the continent of Europe. It was not the right issue to base the whole conflict between Democracy and Dictatorship.'[12] The parliamentary system struggled to manage the country until 1938, when Carol imposed a royal dictatorship. Romania became the last country in the Balkans to install an authoritarian regime.

The lack of job opportunities, the persistence of corruption and the slow pace of development in interwar Romania all contributed to a sense of frustration and disappointment that Greater Romania had not lived up to its promise and potential. The government seemingly had no solutions for Romania's problems. These issues contributed to the rise of the main Romanian fascist party, known in its final form as the Iron Guard. Although fascist movements also developed in Bulgaria, in Greece and among the Yugoslav peoples, the Iron Guard was by far the largest and most popular such movement to arise in the interwar period in the Balkans. The charismatic leader of the Iron Guard was Corneliu Zelea Codreanu (1899–1938), who was of mixed German–Ukrainian or possibly Polish descent. He first gained notoriety when he killed the police chief of Iași in 1924. His movement combined nationalist and Orthodox elements as well as pronounced anti-Semitism. This was the only major Orthodox-tinged fascist movement to develop in Europe. Other fascist movements did rise in Bulgaria and Serbia, but for the most part they remained on the political fringe. Codreanu and the Iron Guard developed a large following among both the peasants and the urban population of Romania. Although he had earlier subsidized the Iron Guard, King Carol later perceived it as a threat. In 1938 he had Codreanu and some of his followers arrested. On 29 November 1938 they were shot 'while trying to escape'. The elimination of the leadership of the Iron Guard did little to improve Carol's political position. By this time his royal dictatorship retained very little support in Romania.

After its establishment in 1918, the Kingdom of the Serbs, Croats and Slovenes had a difficult existence. It set a standard for complexity, even in the Balkans. Basically the Serbs envisioned this south Slav state as a unitary state that reflected their status as the single largest nationality. The non-Serb nationalities, however, wanted the south Slav state to become a federal state that protected them from Serbian domination. From the start Serbian generals and Serbian bureaucrats managed the country. The first constitution was enacted on 28 June 1921, the seventh anniversary of the assassination of Franz Ferdinand and the 532nd anniversary of the battle of Kosovo Pole. This *Vidovdan* (St Vitus Day) constitution, based on the pre-war Serbian constitution, provided for a single legislative body, the *skupština*. It imposed a Serbian-based centralism on the country.[13] The Serbs asserted the right to control the new state because they constituted the largest single nationality and because they, unlike the Austro-Hungarian south Slavs, had emerged on the winning side in the war. The others nationalities, especially the Croats who were the second largest group in the country, increasingly felt alienated from the Serbian-dominated south Slav state. Initially the Muslims, mainly in Bosnia, and the Slovenes acted as swing elements between the Croats and the Serbs. Nevertheless political deadlock soon ensued. On 20 June 1928 a Montenegrin advocate of Serbian centralism named Puniša Račić (1886–1944) shot five Croatian deputies in Parliament. Two of those subsequently died, including the leader of the Croatian Peasant Party, Stephan Radić (1871–1928).

After this catastrophe, King Alexander imposed a new regime on the country. He officially changed the name to Yugoslavia and attempted to forge a Yugoslav identity for the country. He abolished the old national regions and formed new provinces which theoretically cut across national lines. In 1931 he enacted a new constitution that superseded the Vidovdan constitution. It provided a legal basis for the royal dictatorship. He even named his second son Tomislav after a medieval Croatian ruler. The new arrangements failed to ameliorate the growing national crisis. Not even all Serbs supported Alexander's regime. The economic collapse of the 1930s only intensified nationalist divisions in Yugoslavia. On 9 October 1934 IMRO operative Vlado Chernozemski (1897–1934), abetted by Hungarian, Italian and Croatian (Ustaša) sources, murdered King Alexander together with his host, French foreign minister Louis Barthou (1862–1934), in Marseilles, France.

Because Alexander's son and heir, Crown Prince Peter (1923–1970), was a minor, a regency assumed power. Alexander's first cousin, Prince Paul Karadjordjević (1893–1976), was its main figure. A Serbian banker, Milan Stojadinović (1888–1961), headed the government and the foreign office after 1935. He attempted to develop a personal following and formed a political movement that adopted some fascist trappings, including uniformed followers and the use of the term *vojda* (leader).

Meanwhile in Italy, a Croatian fascist party, the Ustaša, awaited an opportunity to impose itself on its homeland. Its leader, Ante Pavelić (1889–1959), had fled to Italy with some of his followers after the establishment of the royal dictatorship in Yugoslavia. There he founded the Ustaša. Benito Mussolini maintained the Ustaša as a potential weapon against Yugoslavia. Periodically the Ustaša committed acts of terrorism within Yugoslavia. Nevertheless it commanded little support within Croatia.

The Stojadinović government's attempt in 1937 to reach a settlement with the Roman Catholic Church provoked a strong response from Serbian Orthodox authorities and congregants. Their reaction in turn further alienated the Catholic Croats and Slovenes and alarmed the Muslims. Up until then the Slovenes, together with the Muslims, had largely attempted to stay out of the growing Serb-Croat controversy.

Tiring of Stojadinović's authoritarian and grandiose tendencies, Prince Paul fired him in 1939 and opened negotiations with the leader of the Croat Peasant Party, Vladko Maček (1879–1964). Growing concerns about the unsettled international situation added to the urgency of obtaining an accord. These efforts resulted in the *Sporazum* (agreement) of 26 August 1939. The *Sporazum* provided for an autonomous Croatia with its own assembly. Maček then joined the Yugoslav government. This agreement did not meet with universal support in the country. Not surprisingly, the Slovenes and Slavic Muslims demanded similar arrangements, and some Serbs resented Croat 'privileges'. Before the *Sporazum* had a chance to succeed, international events overwhelmed Yugoslavia.

The manner in which the war ended, with pronounced winners and losers, provided little basis for the establishment of regional cooperation in the Balkans. This greatly hampered economic progress. It also precluded the establishment of any kind of viable security arrangement for the region.

All of the Balkan states faced some kind of external security threat. Albania had barely managed to gain international sanction for independence after the war. Greece coveted Albanian territory in the south while Yugoslavia wanted northern Albania. In addition the issue of Yugoslav-ruled Kosovo and its large Albanian population remained unresolved. From across the Adriatic Italy exercised a huge influence over Albanian affairs.

Bulgaria, thwarted in its attempts to obtain Macedonia three times in the past fifty years, was frustrated and hostile to most of its neighbours. Territorial disputes remained with Greece, Romania and Yugoslavia. In 1923, after Bulgarian border guards shot a Greek officer, the Greek army undertook an incursion in force into Bulgarian territory. The mediation of the League of Nations finally resolved this problem. Bulgarian pretensions to Macedonia remained. IMRO conducted raids from Bulgarian territory into Yugoslavia.[14] After the overthrow of the Stamboliski government, Bulgaria sought the amelioration or end of the Neuilly sanctions.

Greece also had hostile frontiers. Problems remained with Turkey in delineating boundaries in the Aegean waters off its coast. Greece still retained hopes of obtaining 'Northern Epirus', but this made normal relations with Albania impossible. Bulgaria resented the loss of its Aegean coastline to Greece. The two states were unable to work out an arrangement for the Bulgarian use of a Greek Aegean port. Yugoslavia also had pretensions to obtaining a corridor down the Vardar valley to the Aegean, but was unable to negotiate an agreement with the Greek government. Italian aspirations to control the Adriatic and eastern Mediterranean from its bases in the Dodecanese Islands also presented a serious threat to Greece.

Romania was in an especially difficult international situation. To the west was Hungary, which had not accepted the loss of Transylvania. To the east was Soviet Russia, which did not recognize Romania's annexation of Bessarabia. To the south was Bulgaria, which continued to resent the loss of Dobrudja in the Second Balkan War. Romania enjoyed relatively small but friendly frontiers with only Czechoslovakia, Poland and Yugoslavia.

Yugoslavia had the most complicated international circumstances. Tensions remained over the existence of a Slovene population in the Austrian region of southern Carinthia. After the *Anchluss* of 1938 Nazi Germany would take up this issue. Hungary retained hopes of regaining lost regions along the Danube, including Vojvodina. Albania had the hope but not the ability to acquire Kosovo. Bulgaria continued to maintain aspirations to Macedonia. The greatest interwar threat to Yugoslavia came from Italy. The Paris Peace Conference had thwarted the 1915 Treaty of Rome's promise that Italy could obtain much of Dalmatia. As early as 31 October 1918 Italy had demonstrated this hostility by sinking the Austro-Hungarian battleship *Viribus Unitis*, which was designated for the new Kingdom of Serbs, Croats and Slovenes. Italy did obtain the Dalmatian city of Zara (Zadar) and some Adriatic Islands after the war. In 1922 Italy added the former Hungarian/Croatian port of Fiume (Rijeka) to its Adriatic possessions after a group of Italian freebooters seized the city in 1919. After 1929 Italy harboured the Ustaša and maintained strong connections with Bulgaria. In 1937 the Stojadinović government did sign a friendship treaty with Italy, but this did not bring an end to Italian aspirations against Yugoslavia.

Several alliance arrangements bolstered region security. One was the so-called Little Entente, which tied France to Czechoslovakia, Romania and Yugoslavia. This arrangement was in place by 1927, but it lacked internal cohesion. Czechoslovakia's main threat came from Germany, Romania's from Soviet Russia and Yugoslavia's from Italy. The only real value of the arrangement was its guarantee against the revisionist aspirations of relatively weak Hungary. Romania also enjoyed an alliance with Poland. Both feared the power of Soviet Russia.

Probably the most important international regional arrangement was the Balkan Entente, established in 1934 after a series of four conferences beginning in 1930. The dismal economic situation and a general distrust of the larger powers provided the impetus for these Balkan conferences. Greece, Romania, Turkey and Yugoslavia participated in these Balkan Conferences. This marked the return of Turkey to Balkan affairs for the first time since the Balkan Wars. The conferences established intra-Balkan commissions for communications, economic affairs, social and health problems and intellectual cooperation. The Balkan Entente itself provided for mutual security of frontiers, consultation among the members if any were attacked and preservation of the status quo in the Balkans. The agreement was left open so that Bulgaria and even Albania could join in the future. In 1938, as the international situation in Europe became more threatening, the Balkan Entente did sign a treaty of friendship with Bulgaria. In any event, the Balkan Entente never had the opportunity to implement any of its mutual security provisions.

Three large external powers represented serious security threats to the Balkan Peninsula during the interwar period: Italy, Germany and Soviet Russia.

During this time the menace of Soviet Russia was confined to Romania. The two states did not maintain diplomatic relations until 1934, and regarded each other as hostile. Italy was the first of the large states to seek influence in the region. Benito Mussolini promoted the concept of Italian predominance in the Mediterranean region. The Italians made Albania a virtual colony and supported Bulgarian and Hungarian revisionist claims in the region. In 1926 the Italians, emphasizing their mutual Latin heritage, signed a friendship treaty with Romania. In 1930 the daughter of Italian King Victor Emmanuel III, Giovanna (1907–2000), married Tsar Boris of Bulgaria. Nevertheless the Italians lacked the resources to maintain a sustained presence in the Balkan lands.

German influence grew substantially in the region after Adolf Hitler (1889–1945) came to power in 1933. Some antagonism had developed during Bulgaria's wartime alliance with Germany. Nevertheless, German revisionism appealed to Bulgaria. Nazi ideology attracted General Metaxas' authoritarian regime. The German economic revival under the Nazis provided opportunities for all the Balkan countries to improve their own poor economic conditions. The Germans traded arms and manufactured goods for agricultural production and raw materials. This brought the Bulgarian, Romanian and Yugoslav economies to some degree of prosperity. By 1939 these states were all in economic thrall to Nazi Germany. Political defiance to the Nazis by any of the Balkan states would have meant economic disaster. British and French behaviour at Munich not only meant the effective end of the Little Entente, but also the diminished expectations of any help from those powers. Rightly or wrongly, the Greeks and Yugoslavs saw in the Nazis some measure of protection against the Italians. The Bulgarians perceived them as supporters of their revisionist claims. The Romanians expected protection from them against their mutual enemy, Soviet Russia.

The interwar period began with high expectations. Albanian independence was re-established. The Stamboliski government offered an opportunity for real democratic development in Bulgaria. Greater Romania achieved wide nationalist expectations. The Kingdom of Serbs, Croats and Slovenes presented an opportunity for multiethnic development. Only Greece began the period in defeat and despair. None of the expectations was achieved anywhere in the Balkans. Economic development remained elusive. The dubious trade relationship with Nazi Germany provided relief from a dismal economic situation. Democracy failed everywhere. By the 1930s every Balkan state had an authoritarian government, with the monarch exercising personal power. In Greece monarchal authority faded before the power of a military dictator in the manner of Miguel Primo de Rivera's (1870–1930) Spain or Mussolini's Italy. During this time, the national minorities that lived in every state received little attention. Militaries gained inordinate portions of national treasure. Civil rights remained a hope rather than an expectation. Corruption prevailed everywhere. The overall situation portended ill as Hitler directed Germany towards conflict in Europe.

six

Renewed War, 1939–45

Unlike the war of 1914, the European war of 1939 did not originate in the Balkans. Nevertheless, the machinations of the Italians and the Germans throughout Europe were not lost on the Balkan states, nor were overt German preparations for war. By 1939 the economies of the Balkan states were subordinate to that of Nazi Germany. The Balkan Entente was fragile. There existed little prospect of any united Balkan effort to resist Germany. For some in Greece and Yugoslavia, the Germans were preferable to the Italians, simply because the Germans were more remote geographically and did not press claims on national territories. The economic ties to Germany were strong, the fears of Soviet Russia were fierce and the Western powers were remote.

Nevertheless the first fighting of the Second World War in Europe did start in the Balkans. This occurred during the Italian invasion of Albania in April 1939. To a considerable degree this invasion was unnecessary. Albania was already under Italian control. King Zog acknowledged this in a message he sent to Italy in 1938: 'Albania is now in Italy's hands, for Italy controls every sector of the national activity. The King is devoted. The people are grateful. Why do you want anything more?'[1] Zog's marriage that year to Géraldine Apponyi (1915–2002), a half-American Hungarian countess, apparently had disquieted Rome. The Albanian king could now perpetuate a dynasty. Also, Mussolini was eager to replicate the success Germany had had the previous month in dismembering rump Czechoslovakia: disregarding the Munich Agreement of the previous year, Hitler had annexed Bohemia and Moravia and turned Slovakia into a German satellite state.

On 25 March 1939, the Italians demanded the establishment of a formal protectorate over Albania. King Zog stalled for time, but no help was forthcoming from any quarter. The British and French were far more concerned about the fate of Czechoslovakia. In the absence of a response, the Italians launched an invasion on 7 April. In spite of their pervasive influence in the country, they did encounter some resistance, especially at Durrës. They overcame this quickly, and soon occupied most of the country. Zog, Geraldine and their two-day-old son Prince Leka (1939–) fled the country, going first to Greece and after some travails finally settling in Great Britain. After the Italians occupied the country, an Albanian legislature continued to function with Italian advisors. King Victor Emanuel III added the title of King of the Albanians to those of King of Italy and Emperor of Ethiopia. The Italians also presented themselves as the champions of Albanian unity. Some Albanians collaborated with the Italian regime and a small Albanian Fascist Party emerged. Economic development increased. Even so, the Italian presence was largely limited to coastal and lowland regions.

The increased Italian presence on the Balkan mainland alarmed the governments in Athens and Belgrade. Concern about the possibly Italian attack from new bases in Albania led General Metaxas to accept the British offer of a guarantee against aggression in April. At the same time, King Carol's Romania also accepted a British offer of support. Yugoslavia drew closer to Nazi Germany.

As fighting swirled around the rest of Europe during the next year, the Balkans remained uncharacteristically quiet. Tensions rose, however. Particularly problematic was Romania. The Nazi–Soviet Pact of August 1939 allied Romania's possible Nazi saviour with its potential Soviet enemy. A secret part of this agreement sanctioned the Soviet acquisition of Bessarabia, which had been ruled by Russia until 1918. The Soviets hesitated to implement this part of the agreement until the defeat of France in June 1940. After that, Romania was left without any possible source of help.

On 26 June 1940 the Soviets demanded not only Bessarabia, but also northern Bukovina. Bukovina had been an Austrian province before 1918. The Romanians had 24 hours to respond. Without allies, King Carol's government accepted the Soviet demands. The Soviets advanced into these territories so quickly that the Romanian army lost significant amounts of materiel and 150,000 men, presumably to Soviet captivity.[2] Considerable disorders resulted from the rapid Soviet advance and the hasty Romanian retreat. The obvious Romanian weakness opened the way for other neighbouring states to make demands on Romanian territory.

To obtain support against its enemies, Carol's government attempted to ingratiate itself with Nazi Germany. It renounced the 1939 British guarantee, adopted stringent anti-Semitic laws and invited a German military mission into the country to train the Romanian army and to protect the Ploeşti oil complex. Hitler agreed to protect Romania on the condition that the Romanians reach a settlement with Hungary and Bulgaria. The Germans especially wanted to avoid a war between Hungary and Romania which might invite Soviet intervention and which could threaten the vital oil complex. After direct negotiations between the Hungarians and Romanians failed to reach any resolution, German and Italian arbitrators took up the problem. With the Second Vienna Award, announced on 30 August 1940, these German and Italian 'arbitrators' gave northern Transylvania to Hungary.[3] This amounted to around two-fifths of Transylvania. Significant numbers of Romanians were included in the territories awarded to Hungary, while large numbers of Hungarians remained in Romania. From the German perspective, the Second Vienna Award was most satisfactory, because it disappointed both the Hungarians and Romanians and left both of them open to further German manipulation in the hopes of amending the verdict. From the Romanian perspective, the Second Vienna Award was a disaster. A further humiliation occurred with the Treaty of Craiova on 7 September when the Romanians returned southern Dobrudja to Bulgaria. The Romanian army had seized this territory in 1913 during the Second Balkan War. It had never had a large Romanian population. The return of the territory was far more significant to the Bulgarians than its loss was to the Romanians.

The rape of Romania was now complete. Greater Romania, shorn of most of the gains of the First World War, was lost. The truncated Romanian state was totally in thrall to Nazi Germany. Carol's government did not survive the disasters of the summer of 1940. The king himself abdicated on 5 September in favour of his son Michael, who returned to the throne as an adult. Carol fled the country with Madame Lupescu and his famous stamp collection.

King Michael, in his second time on the Romanian throne, did not get the opportunity to exercise any real authority. In place of the failed royal dictatorship, an odd coalition between the army and the Iron Guard assumed power. The head of this 'National Legionary' government was an army general, Ion Antonescu (1882–1946). Lacking any alternatives, he kept Romania firmly in the German camp. He also tried to contain the unruly Iron Guard, now led by Horia Sima (1907–1993), who held the title of deputy prime minister. This increasingly proved to be problematic as the Guard engaged in anti-Semitic outrages during the fall of 1940. They blamed the Jews for Romania's national humiliation. Iron Guardsmen also murdered a number of prominent political opponents, including the renowned historian Nicolae Iorga (1871–1940). This unstable coalition did not last.

On 21 January the Iron Guard attempted to seize power in Bucharest. When the Germans indicated they would not intervene, the Romanian army suppressed the revolt. With the invasion of Soviet Russia planned for later that year, the Germans wanted stability in Romania. They could not entirely trust Antonescu, however. Guardist leader Sima and some confederates fled to safety in Germany. There the Nazis maintained them as a threat to ensure Antonescu's good behaviour. Romania became a full military dictatorship under General Antonescu.

Meanwhile, during the autumn of 1940, open fighting returned to Southeastern Europe. Once again the fighting began in Albania. Throughout the summer of 1940 the Italians had attempted to provoke the Greeks by attacks, even sinking the light cruiser *Hellas* on 15 August. On 28 October 1940 the Italian ambassador in Athens presented an ultimatum to the Greek government, announcing an imminent Italian attack unless certain strategic points were surrendered to Italian forces. General Metaxas responded in the negative, and requested British aid. Italian units crossed the Greek frontier into Epirus the same day. The Italian action was ill-prepared from the start. The Bulgarians rejected Italian overtures to participate in the attack on Greece. This meant the Greeks could concentrate most of their forces in the west. The mountain roads along the Greek–Albanian frontier could not handle heavy Italian equipment. Italian supplies stacked up in Albanian ports. British aid, in the form at first of vehicles, Royal Air Force men and anti-aircraft weapons, proved to be important in stopping the Italians.[4] General Metaxas limited the British presence, because he feared that a large British force might provoke the Germans. By mid-November the Italian advance into Greece had stalled. Greek forces pushed the Italians back into Albania, occupying Korista on 22 November. With the turn of the year, the Greek advance had stopped due to logistical difficulties, and the war stalemated with the Greeks in possession of about one-quarter of Albania. The Albanians, who had initially hoped the Italian attack on Greece would be a means of unification with the Albanians living in Greek Epirus, now perceived the weakness of their Italian occupiers. Fighting continued in southern Albania into the next year.

After the death of Metaxas on 29 January 1941 the Greek government agreed to accept British land forces in an effort to break the stalemate in Albania. This portended ill for Southeastern Europe. Although he had not been informed in advance of his Italian ally's attack on Greece, Hitler soon afterwards decided to intervene in the war. By the fall of 1940 he was planning the attack on Soviet Russia. He wanted to eliminate the British presence on his right flank before undertaking Operation Barbarossa, especially the threat of the RAF to the vitally important oil complex around Ploești, Romania.

In order to attack Greece, the Germans sought arrangements with the other Balkan states. This was easy in the case of Bulgaria and Romania. Romania had already joined the German alliance system and hosted German troops. Bulgaria joined the German–Italian alliance on 1 March 1941. By then German soldiers were already in the country preparing for the attack on Greece. The Germans also sought the assistance of Yugoslavia. They dangled before the Yugoslav government the prospect of the acquisition of Salonika. For a while Belgrade dithered, but in the end recognized that German power in the region was much stronger and more immediate than that of the British. On 25 March 1941 Yugoslav representatives signed the alliance with Germany in Vienna. The terms were rather mild. The Yugoslavs agreed to the passage of German forces through their country on the way to attack Greece. No direct Yugoslav participation in the upcoming campaign was required.

Nevertheless, when news of the signing reached Belgrade the Serbian part of the Yugoslav population exploded in outrage. Crowds in the

Yugoslav capital denounced the arrangement with the slogan 'Better war than the pact'. The next day, 26 March, a cabal of Serbian officers in the Yugoslav air force seized power in the name of the seventeen-year-old king, Peter II. The plotters hustled the regent Prince Paul out of the country, and at the same time informed the Germans that they intended to adhere to the pact. This assurance was to no avail. Hitler immediately decided to attack Yugoslavia along with the attack on Greece. This action was code named Operation Maritsa.

On 6 April the German air force opened the campaign with the bombing of Belgrade. German, Hungarian and Italian troops then crossed all of Yugoslavia's land borders except for that with Greece. They replicated the Austro-Hungarian, Bulgarian and German invasion of Serbia of October 1915, with the addition of a supplemental attack from Albania. The Yugoslav armed forces, which attempted to defend the entire country, quickly collapsed. Some Croat units refused orders. Croat officers abandoned their posts and sought instructions from Zagreb. The Yugoslav navy, whose ships were manned mainly by Croat seamen, remained paralysed. The invaders took large numbers of prisoners and sustained light casualties. German forces entered Zagreb on 10 April and Belgrade two days later. The Yugoslav government surrendered on 17 April. By that time, King Peter and most of his ministers had fled the country. Ultimately they established a government in exile in London.

Meanwhile the attack on Greece proceeded concurrently with that on Yugoslavia. Crossing the frontier from Bulgaria, the Germans breached the Greek defences north of Salonika known as the Metaxas Line by 9 April. The breakthrough in Macedonia forced the Greeks to withdraw from Albania. The British units could do little to help. After failing to stop the Germans on the ancient battlefield of Thermopylae on 24 April, the British began to withdraw their forces from Greece. Although scattered resistance continued in the Peloponnese, German entry into Athens the next day effectively ended the campaign. German airborne forces then seized Crete 20 May–1 June.

At relatively low cost to themselves in the spring of 1941, the Germans had established control over the entire Balkan Peninsula.[5] The entire region had not experienced such overall power since Ottoman rule at the beginning of the nineteenth century. Only Albania escaped direct

German influence. There the Italian occupation diluted German power, at least for the time being. The poor showing of the Italians in the war against Greece undermined their position in Albania.

The Italians posed as champions of Albanian unity. After the conquests of Greece and Yugoslavia, the Italians annexed portions of northwestern Greece and almost all of Kosovo to Albania. For the first time a Greater Albania existed, albeit under Italian control. The Italians also invested heavily in developing the infrastructure in their Albanian possession. These actions did little to secure the popularity of their rule. By the end of 1941 several anti-Italian guerrilla bands began to operate in Albania. By 1942 a Communist Partisan force became active. This was led by the French-educated Enver Hoxha (1908–1985), who had considerable support from the Yugoslav Partisans. Another force coalesced about the same time to oppose both the Communists and the Italians. This was the *Balli Kombëtar* (National Front). British efforts to unify these two organizations in order to direct them against the Germans had little success. Civil war soon broke out between the two factions.

The collapse of the Italians in September 1943 led to the immediate German occupation of lowland Albania. The Germans formed a theoretically independent collaborationist government, which attracted some *Balli Kombëtar* elements. The Germans were even able to form an ss 'Skanderbeg' unit, mainly made up of Kosovars (Kosovo Albanians). It enjoyed mixed success and committed some atrocities against Serbian populations. Towards the end of 1944 the Germans disbanded it. The German retreat in 1944 left the *Balli Kombëtar* at the mercy of the Partisans. Hoxha and his forces entered Tirana on 18 November 1944. By the beginning of 1945 all German troops had left Albania.

Albania had only a small Jewish population. Albanian Jews suffered no restrictions during the period of Italian rule. Some Jews from Greece and Yugoslavia even sought refuge there.[6] After the Germans occupied Albania, however, they deported the Jews of Kosovo.

Bulgaria enjoyed probably the most favourable situation of all the countries in the Balkans during the Second World War. Tsar Boris maintained a clever policy of cooperation without commitment with the Germans. Although Bulgarian troops did not participate in the military campaigns against Yugoslavia and Greece, Bulgaria gained significant advantage from these campaigns. Following the German invasion of the Balkans, the Bulgarians annexed their main nationalist goal, Macedonia. In contrast to the First World War, they did not have to fire a shot to annex Macedonia in 1941. They also obtained the region of eastern Serbia around Pirot, Greek Macedonia and a part of Greek (western) Thrace. The Sofia government acted quickly to spread its influence in these regions. Initially Bulgarian rule was popular in Macedonia, after over twenty years of Yugoslav policy that treated the region as 'South Serbia'. The Bulgarians established as many as eight hundred schools throughout Macedonia, founded Tsar Boris III University in Skopje and opened a national theatre there. Bulgarian occupation forces brutally suppressed an uprising in Greek Macedonia around the city of Drama in 1941–2. The Bulgarians also defended their interests in Macedonia in 1942 by clashing with Italian troops over a disputed portion of the Albanian-Macedonian border.[7] An incompetent and corrupt administration, which contained few local people and was mainly run from distant Sofia, eventually led to the alienation of much of the Macedonian population.

Tsar Boris avoided involvement in Operation Barbarossa, the German attack on Soviet Russia. The majority of the Bulgarian population was Russophile, and Bulgaria stood to gain little and lose much from any fight against Russia. Bulgaria and Soviet Russia maintained relations throughout the war. To placate the Germans, the Bulgarians did declare war on Britain and the United States. The Bulgarians and Americans had not gone to war against each other during the First World War. In July 1943 the Bulgarians agreed to extend their presence in Serbia, much as they had done during the First World War. This time they occupied all of rump Serbia, except for the northwestern corner around Valjevo. Other than conducting anti-Partisan actions in Greece and Yugoslavia, the Bulgarian army avoided fighting during the first part of the war. German presence in the country was minimal. Bulgarian peasants profited from the sale of their agricultural produce to the Germans.

In 1943 the good war began to go bad for Bulgaria. American bombers on their way back from hitting targets around Ploești dropped excess ordinance on Sofia and other Bulgarian cities.[8] The British undertook punitive raids directed at Bulgaria itself.

Even worse, the popular Tsar Boris died on 28 August 1943 at the relatively young age of 49, soon after his return from a confrontational meeting with Hitler at the Führer's headquarters in East Prussia. Rumours circulated that the Germans had caused his death. He seems, however, to have died from heart disease.[9] His funeral was the occasion for a public demonstration of grief and concern over the fate of the country. A triune regency headed by Boris's brother Prince Kyril (1895–1945) assumed the authority to rule for six-year-old Tsar Simeon II (1937–). The regency immediately began to seek a way out of the war.

Also by 1943 a small Partisan movement had begun to emerge. The Bulgarian Communist Party had organized the Partisans two years earlier as a means of supporting Soviet Russia. Initially they remained small in number and were confined to remote parts of the country. Because there were few Germans in the country and because most of the Bulgarian army was in Macedonia and Serbia, the Partisans mainly fought the local police. This and the fact that the war induced prosperity in the country did not help their cause. By 1943 growing awareness of Soviet victories and the approach of the Red Army to the Balkans increased Partisan numbers. Despite the Partisans' clear Communist orientation, the British made some effort to air-drop them supplies. A small British liaison unit did make contact with the Partisans in late 1943. By the summer of 1944 Partisan numbers had increased. They counted as many as ten thousand often very idealistic men and women in their ranks. They became more brazen in their activities and attacked some of the small German units in the country as well as elements of the Bulgarian police.

Also in 1943 the Germans began to assert some pressure on Bulgaria to resolve the 'Jewish Question'. Around fifty thousand Jews lived in Bulgaria, of both Ashkenazi and Sephardic origin. They were well integrated into Bulgarian society. There existed little inclination towards anti-Semitism in the country. Nevertheless Tsar Boris' government had adopted some anti-Jewish measures in 1941, including a tax on Jewish-owned property and limitations on residence and employment. When news of the German plans to deport the Jews spread through Bulgaria in March 1943, opposition arose from all segments of society, including high officials of the Bulgarian Orthodox Church, among them Exarch Stefan (1878–1957). Tsar Boris dithered but did not capitulate to the German demands. Although some Jews had to leave their homes for rural camps, by 1944 almost all had returned. While Jews within the pre-war borders of Bulgaria survived the war, many of those in the annexed territories of Macedonia and western Thrace did not. In these areas Bulgarian authorities cooperated with the Germans to deport the mainly Sephardic populations. This action somewhat undercut the heroism of the Bulgarians in protecting their domestic Jewish population.

In August 1944, after Romania changed sides in the war, the Red Army appeared on the north bank of the Danube. The Bulgarian government sent a delegation to surrender but was told that no surrender could take place at that time because no state of war existed between Bulgaria and the USSR. This was duly arranged. On 5 September the Fatherland Front, a Communist organization, seized power in Sofia. Bulgaria then declared war on Nazi Germany on 7 September. Bulgarian troops participated in the so-called 'Fatherland War' in Yugoslavia, Austria and Czechoslovakia. Fighting alongside the Red Army, they suffered heavy losses with at least thirty thousand killed. The new Fatherland Front government undertook this effort in part in the hope that Bulgaria could retain Macedonia and western Thrace.

During the Second World War Greece underwent not only the burden of foreign occupation but also the horrors of civil war. After the success of the German invasion became obvious, King George II and his government fled to form a government in exile. In the aftermath of the invasion Albania, Bulgaria, Germany and Italy partitioned Greece. Italian-controlled Albania took northwestern Greece, including Janina. The Bulgarians annexed Greek Macedonia, except for the region of Salonika. The Germans ran the part of western Thrace on the Turkish frontier for strategic regions. They also administered Athens, the Salonika region of Greek Macedonia, including that city, Limnos, Lesbos, Chios, several smaller islands and Crete. The Italians administered everything else. After the Italian surrender in September 1943, the Bulgarians expanded their holdings in Greek Macedonia and the Germans took over everything else. General Georgios Tsolkoglou (1886–1948) formed a Quisling government based in Athens. Some elements within the Greek military had always admired the Germans going back to the time of the Balkan Wars. Also the collaborationist government attracted some royalist elements, in effect continuing the National Schism of the First World War years. After the resignation of General Tsolkoglou, Constantine Logothetopoulos (1878–1961) and then Ioannis Rhallis (1878–1946) replaced him. Cooperation with the Germans, however, yielded few tangible results. By the end of 1941 famine had gripped the country due to German expropriation of food resources. As many as 250,000 Greeks died of starvation during the most intense part of the famine from 1941 to 1943.[10]

Resistance movements soon developed in occupied Greece. The National Liberation Front (EAM) formed in September 1941. It was a political umbrella organization that drew together various individuals and groups opposed to the foreign occupation of the country. At the end of 1942 EAM formed a military wing to coordinate ongoing fighting in several parts of the country against the occupation. This was the National People's Liberation Army (ELAS). This movement was somewhat analogous to the Partisan movement to the north in Yugoslavia. It was generally republican and socialist in political orientation. Both of these affiliated organizations came under the influence of the Greek Communist Party (KKE). The other main resistance movement was the National Republican Greek League (EDES). The leader of this nationalist and royalist organization was Colonel Napoleon Zervas (1891–1957). It was much smaller than EAM/ELAS and was mainly limited to Epirus. EDES was somewhat analogous to the Četnik movement of General Mihailović in Yugoslavia. It did receive some British aid. When the Italians left the war in September 1943 ELAS managed to seize most of their equipment and supplies. Initially EDES acted against the Germans and the Italian-supported Albanians in northwestern Greece. By the end of 1943 ELAS and EDES had come into conflict against each other. ELAS easily dominated EDES. As a result EAM established political control of much of Greece. The Germans and the collaborationist government only maintained a presence in the major cities. After the defection of Bulgaria and Romania from the German side in the autumn of 1944 the position of the Germans in Greece became impossible to sustain. In October 1944 they began a systematic retreat out of the country. As they left, EAM spread its control.

A new force arrived, however, to contest EAM power: the British Army, which landed in Athens on 18 October 1944 with a number of anti-Communist Greek politicians in tow. Initially EAM/ELAS cooperated with the British, but by December 1944 this had ended. Athens became the arena of heavy fighting between EAM/ELAS forces and the British. A number of collaborationists eager to redeem themselves supported the British. A ceasefire on 11 January 1945 ended the fighting but not the hostility. Outright civil war began anew the next year.

During the initial phase of the occupation the Jewish population of Greece suffered restrictions only in the German-occupied regions, notably Salonika, which had a large Sephardic Ladino-speaking Jewish community. Jews from Salonika had to wear the Star of David and work in labour battalions, among other things. In March 1943 the Germans deported the Jews from Salonika, mainly to Auschwitz. The vast majority died there. After the withdrawal of Italy from the war, the Germans imposed strictures on the Jews elsewhere in Greece. Deportations began in January 1944 from Athens and some of the islands, including Crete, Corfu and Rhodes. Most of these unfortunates also perished in Auschwitz.

During its comparatively brief intervention in the First World War the Romanian Army had sustained heavy casualties. In the Second World War their losses were even higher. Romanian oil and foodstuffs were vital to the German war effort. Operation Barbarossa made the Romanian army the most important German allied formation on the Eastern Front. On relatively short notice from their German allies the Romanians agreed to participate in the campaign. Their immediate objectives were the recovery of Bessarabia and Bukovina. Marshal Antonescu also wanted to remain in Hitler's good graces in regard to his Hungarian rivals. The recovery of the lost eastern territories went fairly smoothly, but the Romanians suffered very heavy casualties in the conquest of Odessa in October 1941. The latter Soviet designation of Odessa as a 'Hero City' can be understood as a backhanded recognition of the effort of the Romanian army.[11] After this effort the Romanians occupied but did not annex the region around Odessa, which they named Transnistria. They feared that outright annexation of this area might suffice for compensation for their loss of northern Transylvania. The region had a mixed Romanian, German and Ukrainian population, and served as a dumping-ground for Jews from Bessarabia.

The next summer the Romanians participated in the bloody conquest of Sevastopol. They also increased their presence in the Russian campaign by fielding Third and Fourth armies in the land bridge between the Black Sea and Caspian Sea. Their other two armies remained at home to guard against Hungarian aggression. The Third and Fourth armies held the flanks on either side of Stalingrad, and were almost entirely destroyed during the Soviet Russian offensive in November 1942. The Romanians shared in the German catastrophe at Stalingrad.

After the Stalingrad disaster, Marshal Antonescu realized that any opportunity for victory was gone and sought to limit Romanian participation in the east. He began to search for a way out as the Soviet Russians relentlessly pushed the Germans and Romanians out of Ukraine and Crimea in 1943 and 1944. In 1943 the Romanians made contact with British representatives in Ankara, Turkey, but received only the advice to reach some accommodation with the Russians. By this time the Romanian homeland was coming under attack. As early as June 1942 the Americans began to undertake bombing raids on the Ploeşti oil facilities. These raids continued until the arrival of the Red Army in 1944.

Comparatively little opposition developed against the Antonescu regime during the initial years of the war. The partial restoration of Greater Romania, the national hostility to Hungary and Russia and the relative prosperity that came with supplying the German army with oil, wheat and cattle all tended to preclude active resistance. The extent of Romania's military defeat, however, emboldened some to resist. The very top of the political system roused itself to proceed. On 23 August, with the Red Army on the Prut River poised to invade Romania, King Michael and some senior military officers arrested Marshal Antonescu, surrendered to the Allies and declared war on Germany. For this action the king received Soviet Russia's Order of Victory from Joseph Stalin (1879–1953). The Romanian army then helped the Russians drive the Germans out of the country. The Romanians continued the fight on the Russian side on into Hungary and Austria until the end of the war, and suffered heavy casualties. The hope that Romania might regain Transylvania provided some incentive for the fight against the erstwhile German allies and the Hungarians.

The 757,000 Jews in Greater Romania constituted the largest Jewish population in the Balkans. They experienced much travail during the war. Romania was singular among the Balkan states because of its anti-Semitism. The Iron Guard had made anti-Semitism a part of its ideology and had undertaken murderous pogroms directed against Jews. King Carol's government had enacted anti-Semitic legislation expelling Jews from government service and imposing limitations on their economic and professional activities. Such strictures increased under the Antonescu regime.

During the invasion of Soviet Russia the Romanian army, regarding the Jewish populations of Bessarabia and northern Bukovina as pro-Soviet, undertook a number of massacres of Jews. The Romanian army expelled Jews to Transnistria, the Romanian administered territory east of the Dniester River, where they had to live in wretched conditions. The Romanian army also participated in *Einsatzgruppen* massacres of Jews in Ukraine. After the Stalingrad disaster Antonescu realized the war was lost, and changed Romania's policies towards the Jews. He rebuffed German efforts to deport the Romanian Jews. He also decided to allow Romanian Jews to buy their way out of the country. He established contact with foreign Jewish organizations to alleviate the conditions of Romanian Jews and to facilitate their departure from the country. While 250,000 Jews from Bessarabia and Northern Bukovina died in massacres and in the horrible conditions in Transnistria, most of the remainder of Romanian Jews survived the war.

The wartime situation that developed in Yugoslavia was hideously complex. The rapid collapse of the Yugoslav state in the face of the German, Italian and Hungarian invasion emphasized its failure to develop a feeling of loyalty among many of its citizens. The invaders dissolved the state and partitioned its lands among themselves and their allies. They found collaborators wherever they appeared. The Germans annexed two-thirds of the Slovene-speaking lands, and maintained a direct military administration in the nationally mixed area of Vojvodina, which had a sizeable German minority. After the Italians exited the war the Germans annexed their part of Slovenia. The Hungarians took two regions south of the Danube, Bačka and Baranja and two areas west of the Drava River along the Mura River, Prekurje and Medjimurje, with significant Magyar populations. The Italians annexed one-third of Slovenia, including the city of Ljubljana, and Dalmatia, which consisted of the three coastal regions Zara, Split (Spaleto) and Kotor (Catero) as well as some Adriatic islands, including Korčula, Mljet and Vis. They also annexed Kosovo, a strip of western

Macedonia and a strip of southeastern Montenegro to their Albanian lands. Bulgaria, for the second time in 25 years, annexed Macedonia.

Three political entities emerged from the wreckage of Yugoslavia. The Italians restored the nominal independence of Montenegro. Italian King Victor Emmanuel III, married to the Montenegrin princess Elena (1873–1952), however, did not revive the Montenegrin crown of his late father-in-law, King Nikola. Italian troops occupied the country. At least initially, they gained some support from Montenegrin separatists, known as Greens.

Croatia, known as the NDH (*Nezavisna Država Hrvatska*: Independent State of Croatia), became an independent state for the first time since 1102. It included the *sporazum* borders of Croatia plus Bosnia-Hercegovina. Only about half of the population was Croatian. Large numbers of Serbs and Bosniaks resided within its frontiers. The Ustaša regime made some effort to attract the Bosniaks, whom it regarded as Islamic Croats. Several Bosniaks participated in government. The NDH was nominally a kingdom under Victor Emmanuel's cousin Aimone, Duke of Spoleto (1900–1948). He assumed the title Tomislav II, but due to the problematic relations that developed between the Italians and the Ustaša regime, never visited 'his' kingdom. When the Germans failed to persuade Vladko Maček to assume the leadership of the country, they turned to the Ustaša and Ante Pavelić. The Germans and Italians divided the NDH into zones of influence, with the Italians taking the remaining coastal areas and the Germans controlling the railway lines between the Reich and the Balkans passing through Zagreb. The NDH overtly favoured the Germans over the Italians, mainly because of the Italian annexation of Dalmatia and the absence of any direct German designs on Croatian territory.

The Germans dominated the NDH.[12] When the Italians left the war in September 1943 the NDH took control of all the Italian possessions in Dalmatia. The Germans trained and equipped the regular Croatian army, the *Domobrani*. Most of the senior officers of this organization had served in the old Austro-Hungarian army. Some Croatian troops participated in the Russian campaign. One Croatian brigade was destroyed at Stalingrad. The Ustaša themselves maintained their own armed forces, similar to the Nazi SS. These troops became infamous for their brutality. At no time did the Ustaša government control its entire claimed territory.

The third political entity emerging from the debris of Yugoslavia was the 'Serbian Residual State', whose borders corresponded roughly to those of the pre-1912 Serbian kingdom with the addition of half of the old Sandjak of Novi Pazar.[13] The Germans established a harsh military occupation in Serbia. To strengthen their position they established a puppet government. They were aided by cooperation from several sources. Most important among their helpers was General Milan Nedić (1877–1946), who headed the Serbian government of National Salvation. He played a role in Serbia similar to that of Marshal Philippe Pétain (1856–1951) in France. He frequently threatened to resign over issues such as the Bulgarian occupation of Valjevo, but remained at his post throughout the war. Another collaborator was Dimitrije Ljotić (1891–1945), leader of the small Serbian fascist movement *Zbor* (Rally). The Nedić regime organized its own Serbian State Guard. Other collaborationist forces in rump Serbia were Ljotić's Serbian Volunteer Corps and a unit of anti-Communist (White) Russians designated as the Russian Defence Corps.

None of the occupation regimes established in Yugoslavia proved popular. The occupation authorities initially varied in their relations to the local populations. The Italians were relatively lenient, the Bulgarians, Germans and Hungarians were more brutal. Especially horrific, however, was the Ustaša regime in the NDH. From its inception it regarded its Jewish and Serbian populations as undesirables, and worked to expel or murder them. Even as the Yugoslav government collapsed, notices appeared in Croatia: 'No Serbs, Gypsies, Jews and dogs'.[14] The actions of the Ustaša death squads provided a powerful incentive for the Serbs to organize resistance.

By the summer of 1941 opposition to the occupation regimes developed throughout the territory of the former Yugoslav state. This opposition centred around two main sources of inspiration. One was Serbian nationalism. So rapid was their pace in April 1941 that the invaders failed to round up all the Yugoslav military formations. Some mainly Serbian units coalesced under the leadership of a Yugoslav Army colonel, Dragoljub (Draža) Mihailović (1893–1946). These Serbian units became known as *Četniks*, from the Serbo-Croatian word *četa*, or armed band. Mihailović established a base in Ravna Gora, about 60 miles southwest of Belgrade. From there he exercised a loose control over Četnik forces springing up in Montenegro, Serbia and in the Serbian-inhabited regions of the NDH, including Bosnia. There Serbian formations developed in response to Ustaša terror. The commanders of these Četnik forces often acted as local warlords, enacting taxes and dispensing justice to Serbian populations. Mihailović also maintained contact with the Nedić government in Belgrade. In November 1941 the royal government in exile recognized Mihailović as Minister of War and promoted him to general. In so far as he had a political programme at all, Mihailović sought a return of the Serbian-dominated Yugoslav state.

The other main resistance movement to arise from the ashes of the Yugoslav state was the Partisans. Organized and lead by Communists, the Partisans became active only after the German invasion of Soviet Russia on 22 June 1941. Their commander was that relative rarity, a real Yugoslav. Josip Broz Tito (1892–1980) was the son of a Croat father and a Slovene mother.[15] He was captured while serving as a non-commissioned officer in the Austro-Hungarian army on the Russian front during the First World War. He later joined the Reds during the Russian Civil War and eventually returned to Yugoslavia to become active in the Communist party there. In contrast to the Četniks, the Partisans offered a vision of Yugoslavia based upon social reform, if not outright Communism. They favoured self-determination for all nationalities, and recognized Albanians and Macedonians as distinct groups.

The first Yugoslav uprising against the foreign occupation began in Montenegro in July 1941. Initially the Četniks and Partisans cooperated. During the autumn of 1941 they even undertook joint action against the Germans. The brutal German retaliation at Kraljevo and Kragujevac in October 1941, in which they shot over 4,500 hostages, however, convinced Mihailović that the occupying forces were too strong and that his best hope was to maintain the Četniks in a state of readiness and await the eventual British and American appearance in the Balkans. In contrast the Partisans sought confrontation with the occupiers as a means of rallying the population against the occupiers and their collaborators.

By the beginning of 1942 the Četniks and Partisans had become mutually hostile. Civil war between them compounded the difficulties of the foreign occupation. In the increasingly confused situation, the lines among the various participants blurred. After 1942 much of the conflict took place in Bosnia. This region was nominally part of the NDH but in addition to Croatian *Domobrani* and Ustaša formations a large variety of military groups operated, including Italians, Germans, Bulgarians, Četniks and Partisans, as well as local militias with shifting loyalties. Contacts developed among all of them, and the Četniks in particular accepted Italian aid. When the Italians left the war in September 1943, however, the Partisans were able to secure much of their weapons and munitions. By this time, Tito had established a capital at Jajce in central Bosnia. The British and later the Americans in 1943 had supported Mihailović materially and morally. By February 1943, however, they had shifted their support to the Partisans. Their calculation was simple: the Partisans fought the Germans but the Četniks did not.

In 1944, as the Russian army neared the Balkans, the Partisans become more overtly Communist. The Germans and their NDH allies were able to garner some support by portraying themselves as anti-Communist. This enabled the Germans to raise anti-Communist formations in Slovenia. Mihailović realized by then that the Americans and British were not coming. Četnik contacts with the Germans increased. The Russian army swept into eastern Serbia in the autumn of 1944. With Soviet help the Partisans liberated Belgrade on 20 October 1944 and cleared Serbia of the Germans.[16] The Red Army then advanced into Hungary. The Partisans continued to fight the Germans, who slowly withdrew from the Yugoslav lands accompanied by formations of their collaborators. Fighting between the Partisans and Germans, NDH units, Četniks and other Serbian nationalist formations, Russians, Slovene nationalists and others continued until the very end of the war. The Partisans entered Sarajevo on 6 April, Ljubljana on 7 May and Zagreb on 9 May. The NDH remained steadfast to Germany to the end, the only one of Hitler's European allies to do so. The fighting from October 1944 to May 1945 allowed the Partisans to claim credit for the liberation of Yugoslavia and to eliminate many of their domestic opponents. With the conquest of Zagreb, they controlled all of Yugoslavia. Near Bleiburg Partisan forces then massacred around seventy thousand members of NDH units and other collaborationist formations who were trying to flee into Austria.[17] The British even turned over to the Partisans some of the collaborators who had surrendered to them.

The Jews of Yugoslavia suffered greatly during the war. At first those in the Italian-occupied regions enjoyed relative safety. Jews from other regions fled to the Italian areas. In Serbia the Germans voraciously hunted down the Jews. By the beginning of 1942 they proclaimed Serbia to be free of Jews. The Bulgarians, the Hungarians and the NDH all cooperated with the Germans to deport Jews from the regions under their control. After the exit of the Italians from the war, the Jews in their zones came under German and NDH control. This resulted in their destruction. Only around twenty thousand of the pre-war Jewish population of eighty thousand survived the war.

The end of the Second World War left Southeastern Europe devastated. Huge human and material losses affected every country. Albania had experienced six years of foreign occupation and a nasty civil war. Bulgaria had escaped combat on its territory, but had suffered from American and British bombing, and Bulgarian troops had sustained heavy casualties in fighting the 'Fatherland War' on the side of the Red Army. Greece had endured war, occupation, starvation and civil war. Romania had lost much of its army in the failed Russian campaign, and many of the survivors died in the service of the Russians. In addition the oil complex around Ploeşti had suffered heavy destruction from American bombing. Yugoslavia had endured the worst losses of all the Balkan states. Probably around 1 million Yugoslavs lost their lives in the war.[18] Much of the infrastructure of the country was in ruins. Insidiously the complex civil wars left a legacy of hate and revenge which unscrupulous politicians would revive in the 1990s for their own purposes.

After the Second World War, the old order was gone in Southeastern Europe. Its defenders were often dead and its supporters demoralized. Considerable material destruction and much loss of life resulted from the end of the old regimes. The surviving populations awaited the establishment of something new in economics, politics and society, with fear and hope.

seven

The Establishment of
Soviet Control, 1945–53

The end of the Second World War brought a new ideology and a new conflict to the Balkans: Soviet-style Communism and the Cold War. The collectivist ideology of Communism had found few adherents in Southeastern Europe before the war. The preconditions for Communism were largely absent: there was little industrialization anywhere; the mainly peasant population had no desire to trade its individual land-holdings for collective farms; and the Orthodox churches still dominated the spiritual and to some degree the intellectual life of the region. The fate of the Russian Orthodox Church under the Soviet regime increased the concerns of Orthodox establishments throughout the region. All the interwar Balkan governments had adopted strong, often brutal anti-Communist policies.

Nevertheless Soviet Russian Communism did exercise some appeal for the people of the region. There were several reasons for this appeal. Democracy had never thrived in the Balkans. The old economic, political and social order was defunct. Its defenders had died opposing the invaders or assisting them. Much of the leadership of the Orthodox churches had compromised themselves by supporting the authoritarian regimes of the interwar period. Then they had often condoned collabora-tion with the occupation forces.

The Balkan peoples recognized that the Western powers had little interest in the Balkans. If they had, they would have invaded the region in 1943 or 1944. Also they knew that the Americans and British had supported Partisan movements in Albania, Bulgaria and especially Yugo-slavia. At the Moscow Conference in October 1944, Winston Churchill (1874–1965) and Stalin had agreed on a division of Eastern Europe which assigned predominance in Romania (90 per cent/10 per cent) and Bulgaria (75 per cent/25 per cent) to Soviet Russia and split Yugoslavia (50 per cent/50 per cent) between the Soviets and the others, meaning British and Americans. Why the Soviets wanted a 15 per cent greater role in Romania than in Bulgaria remains unclear. Perhaps Stalin felt more comfortable about the imposition of Soviet control in traditionally Russophile Bulgaria than he did in habitually Russophobe Romania. Greece was to be divided in a 90 per cent/10 per cent split between others and Soviets. Albania was not considered.

Soviet Russian Communism also offered the prospect of rapid development and modernization. It had established an industrial economy in Soviet Russia. This industrialization had been instrumental in Soviet Russia's defeat of the German armed forces, the most powerful military in the world. The Soviet success in self-industrialization might possibly serve as a model for Balkan industrialization and modernization.

The presence of the Red Army in Bulgaria and Romania, and its participation in the ejection of the Germans from Yugoslavia, however, was the main reason for the implementation of Communist regimes in the region. The Red Army did not enter Albania, but Yugoslav Partisans provided important assistance to assure the success of the Partisan movement there. The Red Army did not invade Greece. There initial British support for the anti-EAM/ELAS forces proved to be vital in the defeat of the Communists. The implementation of Communist regimes proved to be relatively easy everywhere but Greece.

The Communist regimes in the Balkans all followed the same basic patterns of extending their power. They abolished or subsumed the other political parties. They adopted autarchic economic policies based on the Soviet economic model. This meant the implementation of Five Year Plans for industrial development and use of human capital, often by means of coercion, for labour in big projects. They took over control of the banks and the main economic enterprises, and ended convertible currencies. They collectivized agriculture, a policy very unpopular throughout the region. They subverted the religious establishments and curtailed religious and private education. They co-opted education and the media. The Russians served as guides and role models for all these endeavours. Russian advisors directed Balkan militaries and security

The Balkans, 1945–1991.

apparatuses. Joint stock companies which gave the Soviets partial owner-ship of Balkan economic enterprises helped send Balkan production and wealth to Soviet Russia. The influence of Soviet Russia became pervasive. The Soviet state and its leader, Josef Stalin, were glorified in the media, culture and education. Russia assumed a leading role among all the Communist nations. While the concept of Russophilia was not difficult for the Orthodox Slavic Bulgarians and Serbs to understand, it was much more problematic for the Romanians. Varna, Bulgaria and Brașov, Romania changed their names to Stalin and Orașul Stalin respectively to glorify the Soviet leader.

The process of Sovietization began in Bulgaria and Romania in 1944 with the arrival of the Red Army. Initially it proceeded slowly. The presence of Allied control commissions in these two defeated enemy countries caused the Soviet to temper their efforts for control for the time being. Only after the Allies signed peace treaties with Bulgaria and Romania in 1947 did complete Soviet control ensue. The Albanian and Yugoslav Partisans began these processes in 1945 and progressed comparatively rapidly.

Each Balkan country developed its own particular perspective on Communism. In Albania, no Communist movement existed before the Second World War. The country was too underdeveloped to support a Communist movement. Its organization and the support it received from the Yugoslav Partisans were the direct consequence of the war. The Italian surrender, the German withdrawal and the defeat of the *Balli Kombëtar* left Enver Hoxha and the Partisans in power in Albania. Initially Hoxha chose to exercise authority through the facade of a coalition, the People's Front. Trials of 'war criminals' removed the remaining opposition figures along with some genuine collaborators with the Italians and Germans. In 1946, however, he proclaimed Albania a republic. Albania shared the anti-Western position of its Yugoslav protector. In three separate incidents during 1946 the Albanians demonstrated overt hostility towards British warships in the Corfu Channel. In the most serious of these incidents, two British destroyers struck mines in the channel on 22 October 1946, causing the deaths of 44 sailors.[1]

After the end of the war, Hoxha continued to rely heavily upon the Yugoslavs for economic, military and political advice. After the brutal suppression of the Kosovo Albanians in 1945, Tito seems to have contemplated turning over Kosovo to Albania, but feared a Serbian nationalist reaction.[2] During 1948 Stalin even told Tito's emissary Milovan Djilas (1911–1995) that Yugoslavia could 'swallow' Albania.[3] The annexation of Albania by Yugoslavia would have had several advantages for Tito. It would have solved the problem of Kosovo. It would also have established the basis for a Balkan federation under his leadership, which might also have attracted Bulgaria and possibly a Communist Greece. However, it would have enormously complicated his efforts to overcome the national rivalries already existent in Yugoslavia.

In Bulgaria a viable Communist party had existed before the war, centred primarily in the large towns. Part of the appeal was the traditional Russophilia of the Bulgarians. There was also an indigenous basis for Communism in Bulgaria. The Macedonian-born Dimitŭr Blagoev (1859–1924), had promoted Marxist Leninist ideas in Bulgaria. After several Communists attempted to kill Tsar Boris by blowing up Sveta Nedelya cathedral in 1925, the party had to go underground. It still retained an urban following, however.

The Bulgarian Partisan movement remained too small to have much post-war authority. Initially the Communists participated in a coalition known as the Fatherland Front, which included some individuals associated with the old *Zveno* organization as well as some from the Agrarian Party. The presence of the Red Army proved to be of considerable importance. The new government held 'War Criminal' trials in 1945 and 1946 to eliminate the political vestiges of the old regime. There were many executions. Among the victims were the three regents, including Prince Kyril, other government officials and high-ranking military officers. The high number of victims, perhaps as many as 2,138 executed, 1,940 sentenced to twenty years in prison and 1,689 to ten to fifteen years, stands in contrast to the relative lack of war crimes in Bulgaria during the Second World War.[4] In 1946 Georgi Dimitrov (1882–1949), the former head of the Communist international organization Comintern, returned to Bulgaria from Moscow. In 1933, while on trial in Nazi Germany for complicity in the Reichstag fire, he had gained some notoriety by wining a verbal duel with Hermann Goering (1893–1946). Dimitrov presided over the imposition of a Soviet regime in Bulgaria. In September 1946, after a plebiscite abolished the monarchy, the young Tsar Simeon and his family went into exile. Bulgaria became a People's Republic. Contrary to the hopes of many Bulgarians, their country did not retain any of the parts of Macedonia and Thrace occupied in 1941. Southern Dobrudja did remain Bulgarian, however. The peace treaty required Bulgaria to pay reparations to Yugoslavia. After 1947, with the Allied control commission now gone, the Dimitrov government disposed of the remnants of the opposition. Nikola Petkov (1889–1947), an Agrarian with democratic sensibilities, bravely opposed the Communist takeover of Bulgaria. He waited in vain for American intervention. Petkov was tried and executed in September 1947, immediately after the signing of the peace treaty. The regime permitted the part of the Agrarian Party within the Fatherland Front to exist as a token opposition party. This facilitated the rapid and ruthless implementation of collectivized agriculture.

Communism developed slowly in Greece. The Greek Communist Party (KKE) was organized in 1918. Its collectivist concepts held little interest for the Greek peasants. Nor did its position on autonomy for Macedonia attract many followers. Nevertheless there was little anti-Russian sentiment in Greece. Soviet Russia was too far away to have any claims on Greek territory, and some Greeks perceived in Soviet Russia a potential ally against Turkey. During the depression, the KKE began to garner support. As a result of its role during the war in the resistance activities of EAM/ELAS, the KKE gained tremendous prestige in Greece.

Although Romania did develop an industrial infrastructure around Ploeşti, the Communist movement found few adherents there before the Second World War. A major reason for its failure to thrive was the interwar hostility between Romania and Soviet Russia over Bessarabia. Support for the Romanian Communist Party was tantamount to support for the return of Bessarabia to Russia and thus against Greater Romania. As a result much of the leadership and membership of the illegal Romanian Communist party came from the country's Hungarian, Jewish and Ukrainian minorities.

The Red Army's invasion of Romania changed this situation. In the absence of any prominent local Communists, the Soviet member of the Allied Control Commission, Deputy Commissar for Foreign Affairs Andrei Vyshinsky (1883–1954) functioned as a Russian viceroy for Romania, much as General Kiselev had a century earlier. He pressured King Michael into accepting a pro-Soviet 'National Democratic Front' government. This was a facade behind which the Communists, lead by Ana Pauker (1893–1969) and Vasile Luca (1898–1963), manipulated the political situation. Many lower-level Iron Guardists, seeking to evade punishment for their previous political orientation, sought refuge in the Communist-controlled security service, the *Securitate*. In 1946 show trials pronounced death sentences upon senior leaders of the old regime, including Marshal Antonescu. These were carried out post-haste. Other political remnants of the opposition and the old regime found themselves after show trials sentenced to long terms of hard labour. Work on the Danube–Black Sea Canal, begun in 1949, cost the lives of many of these people. The Communists also abolished the Uniate Church in Transylvania and deeded its properties to the Romanian Orthodox Church.

Such repression caused much resentment. With the issue of the disposition of Transylvania pending, however, the Communists appeared to offer some hope of its return to Romania. The Romanian nation, which had sustained enormous losses only 25 years earlier during the First World War, was again exhausted after the huge losses in manpower and materiel as a result of fighting on both sides in the Second World War. The elections of 1946, fraudulent like most of the preceding Romanian elections, gave the pro-Communist coalition 89 per cent of the vote. By the end of the next year the government had forced King Michael to abdicate and leave the country. Romania then became, like Bulgaria, a People's Republic. The peace settlement of 1947 confirmed Romania's loss of Bessarabia and northern Bukovina to the Soviet Union and the loss of southern Dobrudja to Bulgaria, but did sanction the return of all of Transylvania to Romania.

The traditional Russophilia of the Montenegrins and Serbs provided a basis for development of a Yugoslav Communist party. When some members assassinated a cabinet minister in 1921, the Belgrade government outlawed the party. It nevertheless maintained support in Orthodox Macedonia, Montenegro and Serbia. During the Second World War, this support became an important basis for the Partisan movement.

The prestige of its military success against their domestic and foreign opponents buoyed the Partisan movement even before the conclusion of the war. This made the return of the Yugoslav government in exile and King Peter problematic. Stalin urged Tito to be pragmatic on this issue, to no avail. A constitutional assembly in November 1945 declared Yugoslavia to be a federal state comprised of six republics: Serbia, Croatia, Slovenia, Bosnia-Hercegovina, Macedonia and Montenegro. In order to prevent Serbia from dominating the federation, two autonomous regions diminished its size and influence. One was Vojvodina, which contained a large Hungarian population. The new government forced most of its German inhabitants out. The other autonomous region was Kosovo Metohija. The overwhelming majority of inhabitants of Kosovo were Albanians. Some internal border changes occurred as well. Montenegro received a part of the old Dalmatian coast. This new iteration of Yugoslavia recognized the Macedonians and later the Bosniaks (Bosnian Muslims) as distinct nationalities. It also permitted the Albanian minority a role in the South Slav State. Although the state represented the major nationalities, overt displays of nationalism were punishable by severe penalties.

Pockets of resistance to the new state remained on into 1946. Pockets of Četnik resistance remained active in southwestern Serbia. A former subordinate betrayed Mihailović in March 1946. The Tito government subsequently brought him to trial and executed him on 17 July 1946.[5] At the same time a number of other former Četniks, Nedić supporters and Ustaša received prison sentences or death. Among the other prominent victims of the elimination of domestic opposition was the Primate of Croatia, Archbishop Aloijž Stepinac (1898–1960), whom Tito's court sentenced to sixteen years of hard labour.

The Tito government initially confronted its international opponents as aggressively as it had its domestic enemies. Partisan troops occupied Trieste ahead of a New Zealand force in April 1945. After a tense confrontation, Anglo-American pressure compelled the Partisans to withdraw. Nevertheless Tito continued to press claims to the city, which did have a significant Slovene minority. The Yugoslav government also renewed an interest in the southern part of Carinthia around the city of Villach. The old Kingdom of Serbs, Croats and Slovenes had never really accepted the results of a 1921 plebiscite in this region, which voted to remain in Austria. Probably the most serious hostile incident occurred in August 1946, when the Yugoslav air force shot down a US Air Force cargo plane in Yugoslav air space, killing the entire crew.

Before these issues could escalate to further hostilities between Yugoslavia and the United States a major dispute erupted between Tito's government and its Soviet patrons. Resentment over Soviet behaviour had been growing for some time in Yugoslavia. Red Army personnel had committed atrocities, including looting, rapes and murders, when they marched through northeastern Yugoslavia in 1944. After the war, the Soviets imposed joint stock companies, military advisors and secret police on the Yugoslavs, as they had elsewhere in Eastern Europe. Soviet Russia treated Yugoslavia, its victorious wartime ally, in a similar manner to that in which it had treated the former German allies Bulgaria and Romania. Because of their success in the Second World War, the Partisans thought they needed little advice from the Red Army. The Soviets' failure to support Yugoslav claims to Trieste and southern Carinthia also caused antipathy. Even more, the patronizing demeanour of the Soviets offended Partisan idealism.

The Soviet–Yugoslav dispute was not one-sided. The upstart Yugoslav Communist regime had aroused Soviet suspicions and Stalinist paranoia. Tito's pretensions to Trieste seriously undermined the Italian Communist Party, which after the war had attracted considerable popular support. This jeopardized Stalin's hopes for a Communist election victory in Italy. Tito had assumed a high profile among Eastern European Communist leaders. His apparent ambitions in the Balkans especially disturbed the Soviets. He already dominated Albania. He had undertaken talks with the Bulgarian Communist leader Georgi Dimitrov in 1947 towards the formation of a Balkan federation, in effect a real 'Yugoslavia'. Tito also gave strong support to Greek Communist insurgents operating in the northern part of that country. The Yugoslavs promoted the concept of a united Macedonia, including the Bulgarian and Greek parts of that region, in a Balkan federation. Tito was clearly the most prominent Eastern European Communist leader. As such, he appeared to trespass on Stalin's prerogatives.

At the beginning of 1948 the Soviets initiated an anti-Tito campaign. They rejected a trade treaty with Yugoslavia. Stalin ordered the Bulgarian and Yugoslav leaders to Moscow in March. Tito sent subordinates, so Dimitrov had to bear the brunt of Stalin's wrath for the idea of the Balkan Federation. This must have been somewhat galling for the Bulgarian leader. He and his fellow countrymen cannot have been eager to lose Pirin Macedonia to a Macedonian Republic, nor did they want to subsume their state as the seventh republic in Yugoslavia. The Bulgarians had in fact demanded equal status with Yugoslavia in any new Balkan arrangement. In March Soviet military advisors to the Yugoslav armed forces returned home. Then on *Vidovdan*, 28 June, the Soviets expelled Yugoslavia from Cominform, their umbrella organization for world Communist parties.

Stalin expected that the withdrawal of Soviet support would quickly undermine the Yugoslav regime. A barrage of anti-Tito propaganda arose from Soviet Russia and Eastern Europe. The Russians and their satellites refused to honour prior economic arrangements made with Yugoslavia. Incidents occurred along Yugoslavia's Bulgarian, Hungarian and Romanian frontiers.

Stalin reportedly said that he would 'shake his little finger' and Tito would fall.[6] This did not prove to be the case. Although a few Yugoslav

Communist stalwarts fled or attempted to flee the country, most supported Tito. Stalin was unable to utilize Yugoslavia's ethnic diversity to undermine Tito. Most of his domestic opposition had fled or was dead. Those who remained loyal to Stalin were incarcerated in a prison complex on the Adriatic Island of Goli Otok (Bare Island). Tito's refusal to bow to Soviet pressure undoubtedly gained him support for himself and his party within the country. The years 1948 and 1949 were difficult because of the absence of external support. By 1950, however, Yugoslavia began to receive American economic and military aid.

The consequences of the Stalin–Tito split resounded throughout the Balkans. The Belgrade government eased its relations with Austria and Italy. The Yugoslavs dropped their overt pretensions to southern Carinthia without quite abandoning them. They also eased tensions over Trieste. They accepted a proposal which divided Trieste into two zones. Zone A, mainly the city of Trieste itself, was under Anglo-American occupation; Zone B, the surrounding territory, under Yugoslav control. In 1954 the London agreement formalized this division, with Italy obtaining clear ownership of Zone A and Yugoslavia of Zone B. Most importantly, in July 1949, Tito closed Yugoslavia's borders to the Greek Communist rebels. No longer could they gain supplies and succour in Yugoslav Macedonia.

The split had important consequences elsewhere in the Balkans. In Yugoslavia's Albanian dependency the leader, Enver Hoxha, demonstrated his gratitude for Partisan help in establishing his regime by supporting Stalin in the split. The Hoxha regime arrested the main conduit for Yugoslav authority in Albania, Defence and Interior Minister Koçi Xoxe (1917–1949) in September 1948, and after a show trial executed him in June 1949. With this ploy, Hoxha freed Albania from Yugoslav domination. In its place he established a subordinate but more distant relationship with Soviet Russia. His ambitions as an Albanian nationalist became clearer, as did his suspicions about his Greek and Yugoslav neighbours. Given Albania's brief experience as an independent state, such suspicions were not without justification. The Soviets established a naval base on the island of Sazan to maintain a presence in the Adriatic Sea. This same location had been an Italian base in the interwar period.

Nevertheless the relative isolation of Albania from its Soviet patron tempted the Americans and British to intervene. They sent in a number of agents between 1946 and 1952 in an effort to foster rebellion and perhaps overthrow the Communist government there. Albanian authorities arrested the Western agents soon after their arrival in the country. The Albanians acted on information supplied by the notorious H.A.R. 'Kim' Philby (1912–1988), an important figure in British intelligence in the pay of the Soviets. This failed Western effort only increased Hoxha's paranoia about Albanian security.

In Bulgaria the Soviets utilized the split to eliminate any Communists who potentially could emulate Tito: those Communists who had spent little or no time in Moscow and who maintained local bases of power. Most prominent among such individuals in Bulgaria was Traicho Kostov (1897–1949). After the failed 1923 coup, government authorities arrested Kostov. While under interrogation, he jumped out of a window in an effort to escape his torturers. In 1949 he, along with ten other defendants, endured a show trial. At its conclusion Kostov and another defendant were executed. The others were imprisoned. Along with Kostov, as many as 100,000 Bulgarian Communist Party members were also purged.[7] The more unfortunate among them were executed or sent to the grim prison on the Danubian island of Belene. Dimitrov escaped this fate by dying in 1949, although suspicions lingered that his death was actually murder through medical procedure.

Assuming Dimitrov's place was his brother-in-law, Vŭlko Chervenkov (1900–1980). Chervenkov was a strict Stalinist. He oversaw the collectivization of Bulgarian agriculture. Not surprisingly in this peasant country, collectivization had aroused considerable opposition. This opposition caused many peasants to join the former Communists in Belene. In a demonstration of his Cold War rigour, in 1950 Chervenkov broke off relations with the United States.

Romania's experience in the aftermath of the Tito–Stalin split contrasted with that of Bulgaria. In Bulgaria native Communists were purged. In Romania native Communists ousted those who had spent time in Moscow. Among those purged were Ana Pauker and Vasile Luca, who were among the architects of the original Communist regime in Bucharest. Pauker, who was of Jewish origin, had been imprisoned during King Carol II's regime. She later went to Moscow after an exchange of prisoners between the Romanians and Soviet Russians, then returned in 1944 with the Red Army. Luca was an ethnic Hungarian whom the Russians had released from prison when they occupied northern Bukovina in 1940. He too returned to Romania in the wake of the Red Army in 1944. In the summer of 1952, rather late for action of this sort, a party faction headed by Gheorghe Gheorghiu-Dej (1901–1965) began to agitate against the Moscow group. Antonescu's police had imprisoned Gheorghiu-Dej during the war. He accused Pauker in particular of 'cosmopolitism', an anti-Semitic Stalinist euphemism. Both Pauker and Luca were expelled from the party the next year. Gheorghiu-Dej evidently was able to persuade Stalin that the Romanian Communist Party would be on firmer ground if an ethnic Romanian, such as himself, managed it, instead of drawing upon leadership from Romania's ethnic minorities. While Luca died in prison, Pauker received a sentence of house arrest, from which she was soon freed. Gheorghiu-Dej thus achieved, with Stalin's approval, his own type of national Communism.

The Soviets had seized Bessarabia, which had been under Romanian rule since 1918, in 1940 and held it until 1941. It was back firmly in Soviet hands at the end of the war. The Soviets established the Moldavian Socialist Soviet Republic from this territory and joined it with some of the former Moldavian Autonomous Soviet Socialist Republic, which they had erected earlier on territories on the east bank of the Dniester River.[8] The coastal region of Bessarabia was detached and affixed to the Ukrainian SSR. Under Soviet rule the region, the scene of wartime atrocities directed against its Jewish inhabitants and heavy fighting between German and Romanian forces against the Red Army, underwent further devastation due to the policies of collectivization and Sovietization imposed by the new authorities. The Soviets made an effort to present the Moldovians as culturally distinct from the Romanians. The Cyrillic alphabet replaced the Latin. In this way the Romanian of Moldavia became similar to Romanian written before the nineteenth century. Geographic names were Russified. Families were urged to adopt Russian-style patronymics. Deportations spread many inhabitants of the region to other parts of the Soviet Union. With most of the German inhabitants of the region flown and most of the Jews killed during the Second World War, many Russians and Ukrainians came to settle in the region, especially in the area east of the Dniester River. Leonid Brezhnev (1906–1982), who later led the entire Soviet Union, oversaw the Sovietization of the Moldavian SSR.

During the time immediately after the Second World War, Greece remained the great exception in the region. Fighting that ended elsewhere in the Balkan Peninsula continued in Greece. The Athens government established under the protection of British arms in the autumn of 1944 was led by a former Venizelist and anti-Communist, George Papandreou (1888–1968). An agreement in February 1945 between the Papandreou government and EAM/ELAS provided for a plebiscite to decide the fate of the monarchy and parliamentary elections. During the rest of 1945 and into 1946 the situation deteriorated into civil war as government forces containing rightists and former collaborators harassed EAM/ELAS around Athens. EAM/ELAS refused to participate in the 1946 plebiscite and elections, which sanctioned the return of King George II, and established a rightist government. The Greeks retained the only monarchy left in the Balkans, albeit on a dubious basis. Many in EAM/ELAS, including members of the KKE, refused to accept the outcome of the elections. Fighting began in the mountains in the northern part of the country. Guerrilla tactics gave them control of much of the rural north during 1947. The next year, however, the situation changed in favour of the government. The Americans replaced the exhausted British as the chief material support of the Athens government. The Truman Doctrine, announced in 1947, provided the royalist government with military aid and advisors for the Greek armed forces. The aid began to arrive in quantity in 1948. At the same time the guerrillas changed their tactics. Because they sought control of a major city in which to base their provisional government, they decided to fight on a more conventional basis. This forced them to confront the material superiority of the American-supplied royal army. Stalin had little interest in supporting the rebels.[9] He had conceded Greece to the British in his meeting with Churchill in Moscow in October 1944. Furthermore he did not want to confront the United States in Greece.

After the Soviet–Yugoslav split, Albania and Bulgaria denied refuge to the Greek rebels. Finally, in July 1949, Tito closed Yugoslavia's Macedonian frontiers to them. Outgunned and denied sanctuary, the Communist rebels suffered defeat. By the end of 1949 the Greek civil war was over. The fighting caused heavy human losses and material destruction.

As many as 150,000 soldiers and civilians died.[10] The fighting displaced many people, and in some locations depopulated the countryside. The large cities swelled with refugees, as they had in 1922. Many Slavic speakers from Greek Macedonia sought refuge across the border in Bulgaria and in Yugoslav Macedonia. As with the First World War, the Greeks were involved in fighting long after the formal conclusion of hostilities of the Second World War. And, as after the end of fighting in Anatolia, after the end of the Greek civil war Greek civil strife continued.

The main factor in the importation of Communism to Southeastern Europe was the success of the Red Army against Nazi Germany. Even in Yugoslavia, where an indigenous force fought for four years, the advance of the Red Army was critical. The implementation of Stalinist-style Communism found a few brave opponents. Most people, however, were too exhausted and demoralized to oppose the Communists or were enthusiastic about the opportunities they presented to bring about significant change to a region that had lagged behind the rest of Europe in every economic, political and social aspect.

The overall experience of the Balkan peoples during the imposition of Communism was similar. All had totalitarian regimes established with the help of foreign military forces, all had directed economies and collectivized agriculture, and the strict curtailment of individual liberties. State security forces brutally suppressed any surviving political opposition. Show trials emphasized the determination of the first to eliminate the remnants of the old regimes. After their subordination to Nazi Germany, the region's economies reoriented themselves eastward in subservience to Soviet Russia.

While the Soviets attempted to impose their system directly from Moscow and uniformly onto each of the Balkan countries, local conditions soon altered these efforts. In Bulgaria Stalinist directives for maintaining Soviet control resulted in closer Soviet control under Bulgarian Communists who had spent the war years in Soviet Russia. As a result many Partisans who had fought the Bulgarian police and the few Germans in the country were purged from the party. In Romania ethnic Romanians established a nationalist basis for the party when they removed from power leaders drawn from Romania's national minorities. Yugoslavia, based on the prestige the Communist movement and its leader had amassed during the Second World War, successfully broke away from Soviet control. At the same time Albania freed itself of Yugoslav domination and accepted direct subordination to Moscow. Greece avoided Communist rule only through the victory of the anti Communist forces in a civil war. Any surviving Četniks, *Balli Kombëtar* supporters and other Balkan anti-Communists must have regarded the royalist success in Greece with envy and frustration.

The imposition of Communism continued and even increased the practice of authoritarian government and political repression in the Balkans. Tens of thousands suffered torture, death and long terms of imprisonment. Collectivization of agriculture stripped away cherished family holdings from the peasantry. The Orthodox churches were subordinated to the governments. The Orthodox concept of *caesaropapism* facilitated their subservience to the new Communist rulers. The Communists, however, did provide more accessible health care and educational opportunities than had existed previously in the region. The centralized economic planning in many cases facilitated reconstruction after the devastation of the war, and extended many of the already extant transportation infrastructures. The entire region also became more urbanized. National minorities became more fully integrated into the body politic. While discrimination remained everywhere at local levels, minorities gained wider access to the social and economic benefits provided by the states.

The Soviet–Yugoslav split in 1948 did not in general alter these changes. It brought new factions to power in Bulgaria and Romania, and confirmed the power of the existing rulers of Albania and Yugoslavia. It increased Soviet influence in Albania, Bulgaria and Romania, and diminished it in Yugoslavia. Above all, it demonstrated that the application of Soviet-style Communism in the Balkans was not monolithic, but depended upon already established local and national conditions. The split also facilitated the defeat of the Communist insurgency in Greece.

In Greece, the only country in the region to escape Communism, trends similar to those to the north developed. American aid through the Marshall Plan facilitated reconstruction and further economic development. Education and health care became more widely available. The population of the major cities, Athens and Thessaloniki (Salonika), boomed. Democracy, however, remained problematic there as well.

eight

Erosion of Soviet Control, 1953–85

The death of Joseph Stalin in April 1953 brought about significant changes in Southeastern Europe. These changes depended to a considerable degree on the political processes that occurred within Soviet Russia after Stalin's death. As the direction of Soviet leadership became clear and the process of de-Stalinization appeared evident, the Balkan Communist regimes started to adjust to the new policies. Each regime developed its own particular accommodation to the new circumstances. Communism in the Balkans fragmented further. Meanwhile Greece recovered from its civil war economically, but still confronted political difficulties.

The first major indication in the Balkans of a change of direction by the Soviets was the Soviet–Yugoslav rapprochement. As early as the summer of 1953, the two countries exchanged ambassadors, ending a five-year gap in diplomatic relations. In May 1955 Stalin's successor, Nikita S. Khrushchev (1894–1971), flew to Belgrade and upon disembarking from his aircraft embraced Tito, who was at the airport to meet him. At this meeting Khrushchev conceded Yugoslavia's right to pursue its own domestic and foreign policies.[1] This indicated to the Balkan Communist governments that the Stalinist regime was over. What it would be replaced by, however, was not yet entirely clear.

Another major sign of a Soviet change of course was Khrushchev's 'secret speech' to the twentieth party conference of the Soviet Communist Party in Moscow on 25 February 1956. Here he laid out the basis for de-Stalinization; Stalin was bad, Tito was good and peaceful coexistence with the United States was desirable. This seemed to open up new opportunities for the Balkan Communist regimes. The suppression of the Hungarian Revolt later that year, however, clearly demonstrated to them that there were limits to Soviet reform and to the willingness of the Soviets to tolerate reform in Eastern Europe.

Khrushchev also curbed some of the authoritarian excesses of the Stalinist model. Terror, although still present everywhere, eased. Relations with Western countries developed. The 'cult of personality' that had glorified Stalin was muted and then extinguished. Stalin, Bulgaria resumed its former name of Varna in 1956; Orașul Stalin in Romania reverted to Brașov in 1960.

Khrushchev undertook some specific actions to emphasize his new regime. He institutionalized Soviet control over all of Eastern Europe. The Soviets had established an economic alliance with their Eastern European satellites in 1949. This was the Council for Mutual Economic Assistance, known as CMEA or COMECON. This was intended to be a response to the Marshall Plan and to tie the Eastern European economies more firmly to the Soviets. It remained formal until Stalin's death. Khrushchev utilized COMECON to further suborn the Eastern European economies to the Soviets. Under the concept of 'Socialist Division of Labour', the economies of the three Balkan COMECON countries, Albania, Bulgaria and Romania, assumed obligations to be providers of agricultural goods and raw materials. These restrictions displeased many Albanians, Bulgarians and Romanians, who had hoped to industrialize on the comprehensive Soviet model.

In 1955 the Soviets established a military alliance for Eastern Europe. Up until this time, each Eastern European state had signed bilateral military agreements with Soviet Russia. The new overall alliance, named the Warsaw Pact for the location of its establishment, was intended to be the Soviet response to NATO. NATO's admission of West Germany in 1955 was the ostensible reason for the Warsaw Pact, which enabled the Soviets to impose a more uniform control of the Eastern European militaries, all of which had issues of reliability.

On the other side of the Iron Curtain, Greece joined NATO together with Turkey in 1952. In an echo of the Balkan Entente of 1934 Greece, Turkey and Yugoslavia signed a Balkan Pact at Bled, Yugoslavia on 9 August 1954. This appealed to Tito because at that time Yugoslavia appeared vulnerable in the Balkans between Soviet-allied Albania, Bulgaria and Romania on one hand and NATO members Greece and Turkey on the other. This agreement provided for mutual military aid in the event of an attack against any one of them. The Balkan Pact proved to be ephemeral because of Greek and Turkish antagonism over Cyprus, and because of Yugoslavia's improved relations with Soviet Russia after 1955. The Balkan Pact lapsed by 1960.

The Balkan Communist leadership reacted individually to the new situation emanating from Moscow. The Albanian leadership viewed the process of de-Stalinization and especially the improvement of relations between the Soviets and the Yugoslavs with alarm. This rapprochement raised the possibility that Yugoslavia might again try to subsume Albania. Enver Hoxha remained steadfast as the other Eastern European regimes began to distance themselves from Stalinism. His stance placed the substantial Soviet aid Albania received in jeopardy. At a November 1960 meeting in Moscow attended by Communist leaders from around the world, Hoxha vigorously condemned Khrushchev's policies. Albania thereafter sided openly with China in the Chinese–Russian dispute. The Soviets abandoned their submarine base on Sazan, and discontinued their economic and military aid to Albania. On 25 November 1961 the Soviet ambassador left Tirana. The lack of a physical connection between the two countries limited the repercussions of the Albanian–Soviet split for the Hoxha regime. The split was also undoubtedly a source of satisfaction to Albania's Greek and Yugoslav neighbours because it eliminated Russian influence and presence in the western part of the Balkans. After 1961 Albanian membership in COMECON and the Warsaw Pact lapsed, although they only officially ended their membership of the Warsaw Pact in 1968 in the aftermath of its deployment in the suppression of the liberal Communist government of Czechoslovakia.

After the break with the Soviets, Hoxha turned to the Chinese to protect Albania. Albania became Communist China's only European ally. This arrangement undoubtedly brought more advantages to the Albanians than to the Chinese, although it did allow the Chinese to claim that their Maoist ideology was global and gave them a presence, however backward and remote the location, in Europe. The Albanians received massive amounts of aid from China in the form of food and technical assistance. To a degree Chinese aid replaced the lost Soviet assistance. For Hoxha, China's distance from Albania made the Chinese munificence even more attractive. There was little chance that the Chinese would attempt a physical occupation of Albania. Albanian propaganda proudly proclaimed that 'We and the Chinese are one billion strong.'

The Albanians followed the lead of their large Asian ally in ideology. In 1967 Albania endured its own form of Cultural Revolution. In conjunction with this effort that same year, Albania proclaimed itself the first real atheist state in the world. Authorities closed mosques and churches. Names of religious origin were forbidden.[2] In 1975 Albania was the only European country not to send a delegation to the Helsinki Conference.

By the beginning of the 1970s, however, Hoxha's enthusiasm for the Chinese began to wane. The Chinese had established diplomatic relations with Yugoslavia in 1970. Two years later they opened relations with the United States. To the paranoid regime in Tirana these connections with Albania's enemies appeared to be a conspiracy directed against Albania. After opening themselves up to the outside world the Chinese lost interest in maintaining an isolated European outpost. In addition, by that time Chinese technology and military hardware were becoming dated. The Chinese demonstrated little interest in providing the Albanians with more modern equipment. Chinese aid to Albania ended in 1978, and thereafter the Albanians began to emerge from their self-imposed isolation.

The response of the Bulgarian Communist Party to the new situation in Moscow contrasted considerably with that of the Albanians. After an intra-party struggle, Todor Zhivkov (1911–1998) wrested power from Chervenkov in 1954. The old Stalinist hung on as prime minister until 1956. After the devastations of the Titoist purges, there was little interest in Bulgaria in a new round of anti-Stalinist purges. Zhivkov pursued a policy of absolute loyalty towards Soviet Russia and its leadership. He asserted that Bulgaria and Soviet Russia 'act as a single body, breathing with the same lungs and nourished by the same bloodstream'.[3] He also expressed an interest in having Bulgaria join the Soviet Union as the sixteenth republic. Bulgaria did not deviate from Soviet foreign policy positions. At home Zhivkov maintained a strictly conservative domestic regime that permitted no dissent.

This obsequious attitude gained real benefits for Bulgaria. Soviet raw materials and manufactured goods became readily available. The Bulgarians then frequently sold Soviet oil and gas to Western customers to obtain valuable Western credits. In a large part due to this lucrative trade, consumer goods greatly improved throughout the country during the 1960s. Within the cities especially the standard of living improved. Large blocks of drab but serviceable apartments appeared on the peripheries of Sofia, Plovdiv, Burgas and other urban locations. Jobs and apartments drew the population from the countryside to the cities. Vacations to state resorts in preserved mountain villages or on the Black Sea coast became possible for many Bulgarians. Through the 1970s the Bulgarian population could credit Zhivkov with real material improvement in their lives.

Loyalty to the Soviets also provided Bulgaria with security. During the first half of the twentieth century Bulgaria had had problematic relations with all of its neighbours. By the 1960s Greece and Turkey were in NATO, Yugoslavia had an independent policy and Romania, although formally a Warsaw Pact member, had increasingly pursued its own independent policy. The Red Army had gone home in 1947. In these circumstances Bulgaria maintained a direct military connection with Soviet Russia by means of Black Sea barges that operated between the large Soviet naval base at Nikoleav and Varna.

Perhaps the most important security service the Soviets provided to the Zhivkov regime was a 1965 tip that elements within the Bulgarian Communist Party and Bulgarian military were planning a coup to oust Zhivkov.[4] Officially the plotters wanted to establish a pro-Chinese regime in Sofia. A more likely reason was that they opposed Zhivkov personally as well as his cronies from his home town of Vratsa. Acting on the information obtained from the KGB, Zhivkov foiled the plot and imprisoned the principals.

In Romania Gheorghiu-Dej adopted a separate distinctly Romanian strategy for dealing with Communism and Soviet Russia. As in Bulgaria, the regime maintained a strict, even Stalinist domestic policy. After elimination of the 'cosmopolitans' Gheorghiu-Dej turned on the ethnic Romanians in the party. He had his chief ethnic Romanian rival, Lucreţiu Pătrăşcanu (1900–1954) executed in 1954. Pătrăşcanu was both the last victim of the Titoist purges and the first victim of the de-Stalinization process.

Initially Gheorghiu-Dej also supported the Soviets loyally in foreign relations. In 1956 Romania served as a conduit for Soviet forces moving into Hungary to suppress the revolution. The Soviet crushing of the

Hungarians was undoubtedly a source of satisfaction for many Romanians. The Hungarian leader Imre Nagy (1896–1958) was imprisoned for a
while in Romania, where he could encounter little likelihood of sympathy.
Gheorghiu-Dej's assistance during the Hungarian Revolt apparently convinced the Soviets of his loyalty. In 1958 Soviet armed forces left Romania.

With the Russian armed forces out of Romania, Gheorghiu-Dej
pursued a more distinctly Romanian approach to Communism. He began
a policy of economic deviance. Refusing to conform to Khrushchev's
consignment of Romania to agriculture, Gheorghiu-Dej sought to develop
an industrial economy. He began with that icon of the Five Year Plans,
the steel mill. Even though Romania lacked the necessary raw materials
to produce steel, Gheorghiu-Dej built a steel mill in Galați on the
Danube River.

After Gheorghiu-Dej's death in 1965 his successor, Nicolae Ceaușescu
(1918–1989), accelerated the development of an independent Romanian
Communism. His version of national Communism initially engendered
some domestic support for him. Russia was historically unpopular in
Romania, and memories of the war, occupation and loss of territory
remained. Ceaușescu deviated sharply from Soviet foreign policy. After
1965 Romania's relations with the Warsaw Pact cooled. The Romanians
refused to allow Warsaw Pact exercises on their territory, and discontinued their participation in exercises elsewhere. Romania continued to
maintain relations with Beijing, the only country in Eastern Europe to do
so apart from Albania. Romania was also the only country in Eastern
Europe not to break off relations with Israel during the Six Day War in
1967. Ceaușescu denounced the Warsaw Pact invasion of Czechoslovakia
in 1968. This gained him great credibility in the West. Romania also
maintained a military relationship with Yugoslavia. Both had mobilized
in August 1968 when the Warsaw Pact had invaded Czechoslovakia in
August 1968. They even discussed the joint production of a fighter jet, the
Orel (eagle).

Most importantly, under Ceaușescu, Romania sought ties with the
West. Romania opened up to Willy Brand's (1913–1991) *Ostpolitik*, and
established relations with West Germany in 1967. In 1969 Richard M.
Nixon (1913–1994), who also went to Yugoslavia at this time, became the
first American president to visit the Balkans. This opening to the West

provided Romania with access to Western credits and technology. West-ern firms built 'turn key' factories in Romania, so complete that all the Romanians had to do was turn the key to make the factory work. The Romanians also attempted to develop a tourist industry. For this they drew heavily on the Dracula legends.

The divergence from Soviet policies came at the cost of severe inter-nal repression. While abroad, Ceaușescu appeared to be a new Tito; at home he was strictly a Stalin. Because of this any benefits the Romanian people gained from the Western exposure were limited by the *Securitate*. Undoubtedly Ceaușescu's repressive domestic policies allayed Soviet concerns that Romania would become a Western outpost behind the Iron Curtain.

After the limits of Stalinist retribution became clear, Tito confidently began to develop distinct and unique policies for Yugoslavia. The first of these was federalism. The parameters of federalism had already been established in the 1945 constitution. The six republics and two auto-nomous areas reflected the national composition of the state and defused its power, if not the power of its dictator. The federal state strengthened the national identities of some of its components. Macedonia in particu-lar developed a national identity separate from those of Bulgaria, Greece and Serbia. A major factor in this was the establishment in the early 1950s of a distinct Macedonian literary language.[5] This was based upon the dialect from the western part of the country in order to emphasize its differences from Bulgarian. It employed a modified form of the Cyrillic alphabet. In 1968 the Macedonian Orthodox Church broke away from the authority of the Serbian Orthodox Church in Belgrade and became autonomous, with its administrative seat in Skopje.

Another group who benefited were the Bosnian Muslims, or Bosniaks. Long regarded by the Croats as apostate Catholics and the Serbs as rene-gade Orthodox, and called 'Turks' by both, the Bosniaks gained sanction of their distinct identity through Yugoslav federalism. In 1968 the Yugoslav Communists recognized the Muslims of Bosnia as a secular nation rather than a religious community.[6] This became the legal basis for their national identity.

While nationalities achieved recognition and development in federal Yugoslavia, overt expressions of nationalism were strictly forbidden. This ban helped to obscure the national bases for the intra-Yugoslav conflicts of the Second World War. As in the first Yugoslavia, the military remained the preserve of the Serbs. More than 70 per cent of the members of the Yugoslav National Army (JNA) officer corps were Serbian or Montenegrin.

The attempt to quash overt expressions of nationalism encountered some difficulties. In 1966 the Serbian head of the Ministry of the Interior, Aleksander Ranković (1909–1983) lost his position when Tito's offices were discovered to have secret police listening devices. Ranković's centralist and Serbian sympathies were a major factor in his fall.

The Croats also became restive. In 1971 a number of Croatian intellectuals began to demand more freedom for historical and national expressions in Croatia. In particular they wanted to establish the Croat language as being distinct from Serbian. The discontent, which came to be known as the Croatian Spring in an echo of the events in Czechoslovakia three years earlier, took the form of strikes and protests. After a student strike in December 1971 supporting these demands, Tito had the Croat party purged. He also acted against overt liberals and nationalists. Individuals from the Serbian minority in Croatia received positions of authority in the Croatian government.

Tito did not tolerate attacks on Communism. Although in his youth he was a true believer and later Tito's possible successor, the Montenegrin Partisan veteran Milovan Djilas wrote penetrating critiques of Communism and Stalinism during the 1950s.[7] For becoming the regime's gadfly, Djilas received terms of imprisonment in 1956 to 1961 and again from 1962 to 1966.

Yugoslavia also developed its own unique economic policies. By 1950 Tito had abandoned the collectivization effort. Many enterprises were run by Workers' Self Management. This concept allowed councils of managers and workers to make the major decisions of cost, labour and production. The regime permitted Yugoslav workers to seek employment outside the country. This not only helped with the problem of domestic unemployment, but it became an important source of income as Yugoslav *Gastarbeiter* (guest workers) in West Germany and Sweden sent home part of their income. Another important source of foreign income was the Yugoslav tourist industry. The regime promoted the scenic Dalmatian coast as a sunny respite for winter-weary northern Europeans. In 1972 alone Yugoslav *Gastarbeiter* sent home US$870 million while foreign tourists spent US$432 million in Yugoslavia.[8] This income was possible because Yugoslavia did not erect an Iron Curtain around its frontiers. Nevertheless the Yugoslavs continued to maintain a healthy trade with the COMECON countries.

In foreign affairs Tito followed a policy of neutrality. He accepted military aid from the United States, maintained correct relations with Soviet Russia and had observer status in COMECON. Tito wanted to develop Yugoslavia as a bridge between the West and the East. He became active in the non-aligned nations movement. During the 1960s Tito undertook many journeys to Asia, Africa and Latin America to emphasize Yugoslavia's status as a developing neutral nation.

In military matters the Yugoslavs pursued a strategy of National Self Defence. Yugoslavia's position astride the fault line of the Cold War caused a sense of great vulnerability among its inhabitants. National Self Defence was an attempt to replicate the Partisan successes of the Second World War. In case of an attack on Yugoslavia from the outside, possibly from Warsaw Pact forces, the Yugoslav National Army (JNA) would withdraw into the difficult terrain of the country, as in Bosnia and Montenegro, and harass the enemy with Partisan tactics. The JNA maintained stockpiles of arms and ammunition throughout the country. It also established arms and munitions factories in the centre of the country. It manufactured some of its own heavy weapons. All Yugoslav schoolchildren received civil defence training, and Yugoslav males had a two-year obligation of military service. Much of this military infrastructure was located in Bosnia. Bosnia's rugged terrain had been the location of many of Partisan successes during the Second World War.

After the ousting of Khrushchev in 1964, relations between the West and the Soviets again began to improve. There developed corresponding improvements for the Eastern European region. The West German *Ostpolitik* restored economic and political connections to Central Europe that had broken in 1945. Greater openings to the outside world developed, especially for Bulgaria and Romania.

The Helsinki Conference of 1975 was important for all of Southeastern Europe. This conference established the territorial settlement that resulted after the Second World War as permanent. On one hand this was reassuring to the Romanians in regard to Transylvania, but on the other it seemed to sanction loss of Bessarabia. This aspect of the Helsinki agreement had implications for the Bulgarians and the Yugoslavs with their border adjustments after the Second World War. It also accepted the Western definition of human rights in terms of freedoms.

By the late 1970s the process of development of separate identities within Communism had accelerated throughout the region. Bulgaria, Romania and Yugoslavia all benefited from détente. Albania rigorously maintained its isolationism. By the end of détente, however, economic and political problems had arisen everywhere.

Somewhat surprisingly, Enver Hoxha's dictatorship faced an apparent internal challenge. In 1981 Mehmet Shehu (1913–1981), the second most powerful man in the country and Hoxha's presumed successor, died in mysterious circumstances. Officially he committed suicide, but rumours suggested that he had lost a power struggle. In any event Albania began to emerge from its self-imposed isolation. Perhaps Shehu opposed this. In 1983 a ferry service between Albania and Italy began. In 1985, the year of Hoxha's death, a rail connection opened in the north linking Albania to the Yugoslav rail system and from there to all of Europe. Hoxha's successor, Ramiz Alia (1925–), continued the process of opening Albania in the face of opposition from Hoxha's widow Nexhmije (1921–). Driven by a need for foreign aid, Albania established diplomatic relations with West Germany and participated in a regional Balkan conference the next year. Nevertheless Alia maintained a firm grip on the internal situation in the country.

In Bulgaria the recovery of national identity began through the efforts of Todor Zhivkov's daughter, Lydmila (1942–1981). She had studied at Moscow State University and had spent some time at Oxford. In 1972 she joined the Committee for Art and Culture and rose from there to direct the cultural policy of Bulgaria. She initiated a series of cultural and educational exchanges with the West, including the Thracian Gold Exhibition, which travelled extensively outside the country. She developed archaeological and historical sites and produced movies and television series on important figures from Bulgarian history, including the nineteenth-century Russophobe Stefan Stambulov. In effect she engineered the revival of Bulgarian cultural nationalism. Her efforts culminated in the 1300 Years of Bulgarian Statehood campaign in 1981. This celebrated the continuity of the Bulgarian nation from the recognition of Bulgaria by the Byzantines in 618. She did not live to see the end of the campaign, however, as she died suddenly on 21 July 1981 of a cerebral haemorrhage. Her funeral was the occasion for an outpouring of national feeling not experienced in Sofia since the death of Tsar Boris in 1943. She was undoubtedly the most prominent dictator's daughter behind the Iron Curtain.

After Lydmila's death, her father reverted to his old ways. In 1983 Ali Ağca (1958–), a Turkish citizen who had attempted to assassinate Pope John Paul II (1920–2005) in May 1981, confessed to links to the Bulgarian Security service (DS). The involvement of the DS suggested the complicity of the KGB. The DS was probably more firmly under Soviet control than any other secret police in Eastern Europe. While these links were never legally proven, they brought the Zhivkov regime unwanted attention and animosity.

In an effort to arouse national support for his increasingly lacklustre regime, he began a campaign to 'Bulgarianize' the country's Islamic minorities. These included Turks and Bulgarian-speaking Muslims, the *Pomaks*. Zhivkov forced them to take Bulgarian names and closed Pomak and Turkish schools. This effort aroused little enthusiasm among the Bulgarians and much opposition among the Muslims. Over 300,000 Muslims migrated to Turkey, although some 100,000 later returned, complaining of discrimination there.

By the middle of the 1980s the Zhivkov regime, like its Soviet counterpart under Brezhnev, had stagnated. The country's economy was flat, its birth rate was in decline and its international reputation was sullied. Todor Zhivkov appeared to have no ideas on how to address these issues.

After becoming the darling of the West in the late 1960s, Nicolae Ceaușescu increasingly developed erratic and egomaniacal tendencies. A visit by him and his wife Elena (1916–1989) to North Korea in 1971 filled both of them with enthusiasm for the cult of personality modelled on that of the North Korean dictator Kim Il Sung (1912–1994). After their return from North Korea the Ceaușescus staged vast flag-waving pageants in imitation of the North Koreans and promoted themselves in numerous other self-serving ways. Elena, who had failed to graduate from high school, assumed a PhD in chemistry. They constructed luxurious palaces for their personal use throughout the country. They consolidated rural villages and levelled much of Bucharest in an effort to reconstruct the capital along grandiose lines. These efforts included a vast boulevard leading to the massive Palace of the Republic. This building, one of the largest in the world, was constructed exclusively from materials originating from Romania. It remains unfinished.

The Ceauşescus became increasingly self-centred and delusional, proclaiming Nicolae the 'Genius of the Carpathians' and their joint rule a 'Golden Age' of Romania. At the same time, the Romanian economy began to decline. Romania's oil reserves, located around the Ploeşti refining complex, became exhausted. Romania went from being an oil-producing state to an oil-processing state, to its economic disadvantage because of the cost of buying foreign oil. Many of the industries obtained with foreign credits in the late 1960s developed problems the Romanians did not know how to fix or needed updates they lacked the money to purchase. As a result these 'turn key' industries began to impede rather than propel the Romanian economy. The tourist trade declined because of the lack of reinvestment in the infrastructure. The state sent much agricultural production abroad to pay for Romania's foreign debts.

Another source of income for Ceauşescu's Romania was its German minority. Germans had lived in Transylvania and the Banat since the Middle Ages. Beginning in 1978 the West German government paid the Romanians DM10,000 for each German permitted to leave Romania.[9] As the Ceauşescu regime became increasingly despotic, large numbers of Germans availed themselves of the opportunity to leave Romania and emigrate to West Germany.

All of these things increased the economic misery of the population. In 1981 the state imposed food rationing. Commodities such as clothing were also rationed, as was gas and electricity. The state pursued policies intended to raise the birth rate. Since 1965 abortion had been outlawed. Oppression increased in order to make the population endure privations. This in turn greatly undercut Romania's international standing.

In Yugoslavia the system held together during the last years of Tito's life. The Partisan hero himself increasingly adopted a grandiose style, marked by opulent palaces and ornate uniforms. His position and presentation resembled that of the Habsburg monarchs he grew up under.

After his death, however, the Titoist system began to fray. A sense of desperation was apparent soon after his death on 4 May 1980. Signs appeared throughout the country with the slogan, 'Tito lived, Tito lives, Tito will live.' A complex collective leadership replaced Tito. Its main component was a rotating presidency among the leaders of the six republics, the two autonomous regions and the head of the Communist party. The presidency changed on a yearly basis. It could not replace Tito as a unifying factor, nor could it address Yugoslavia's growing difficulties.

The Yugoslav economy worsened during the 1980s. Foreign debt rose and inflation increased. Workers' Self Management proved to have limitations. Workers did not always act in their best interests. Even the influx of tourists for the 1984 Winter Olympics, held in Sarajevo, could not offset the economic decline, although it did help bring positive world attention to Yugoslavia.

After Tito's death, the problem of Kosovo emerged into Yugoslav politics. Since Serbian troops had occupied this region in 1912 during the First Balkan War, the Serbian population of this region had dominated it, except during the Italian- and German-sponsored regimes of the Second World War. Kosovo was central to the Serbian national mythos as the site of the 1389 battle against the Ottomans and as the location of several Serbian Orthodox monasteries founded during the Middle Ages. Nevertheless by the late 1970s the population was overwhelmingly Albanian, with only a small Serbian minority remaining. By 1980 the Albanian population of Kosovo had the highest birth rate in Europe. Yet Kosovo remained the poorest region of Yugoslavia. In 1981 students demanding that Kosovo achieve the status of a republic rioted. The Serbs and the Macedonians both opposed this because of the large Albanian minorities in their republics. The authorities suppressed the riots at a cost of hundreds of lives.[10] Anti-Albanian repression followed afterwards.

The Cold War isolated Greece from its Balkan and Orthodox neighbours. The victory over the Communist insurgents during the Civil War left Greece with a large military establishment and a pronounced dependence on American aid. This aid was especially important in reconstruction efforts in the war-damaged north of the country. Greece formally joined NATO in 1952. After King George's death in 1947, his brother Paul (1901–1964) succeeded him as king of the Hellenes. King Paul and his wife,

Queen Frederika (1917–1981), undermined their personal popularity and that of the institution of the monarchy through their interference in political issues. After Paul's death his son Constantine II (1940–) came to the throne. Generally the governments of the 1950s and early 1960s leaned to the right. However, in 1967 elections returned former prime minister George Papandreou and his Centre Union Party to power. His liberal policies brought him into conflict with the king and the military. In April 1967 the military ousted Papandreou from power. The rulers of the subsequent military regime, known as 'The Colonels' because of the rank of its many of participants, installed an authoritarian regime in Athens. In this respect Greece now joined the other Balkan governments in having an authoritarian-style government. The Colonels regime recalled the Metaxas dictatorship of the 1930s. They were no more willing to share power with the king than Metaxas had been. King Constantine made a feeble attempt in December 1967 to assert himself and overthrow the Colonels. After he failed, he fled the country. The Colonels maintained their repressive regime in the face of growing opposition.

In foreign policy, membership of NATO provided Greece with security. The dispute with fellow NATO member Turkey over the future of Cyprus, however, somewhat undermined this security. The British had ruled the island since taking it from the Ottomans in 1878. Greek support for a terrorist organization, EOKA (National Organization of Cypriot Fighters), which was dedicated to the union of Cyprus with Greece, exacerbated the hostility with the Turks. Georgios Grivas (1898–1974) led EOKA in its attacks on British, Greek and Turkish targets. In 1960 the British withdrew from Cyprus, although they continued to maintain military bases there. In a compromise settlement, the Greek archbishop Makarios III (1913–1977) led the government of independent Cyprus while the Turkish minority received the vice presidency and constitutional guarantees. The population of Cyprus was around 80 per cent Greek and 20 per cent Turkish at the time of its independence.

In 1974, in an effort to find some popular nationalist basis for their rule, the Colonels precipitated a crisis over Cyprus. A coup backed by the Colonels ousted the government of Archbishop Makarios and proclaimed union with Greece. The Turks responded with a massive military invasion. They occupied around 40 per cent of the island. The Colonels junta collapsed. A subsequent plebiscite abolished the monarchy and established the Hellenic Republic. At the same time, Greece withdrew its forces from the military command structure of NATO, but returned them to NATO command in 1980. After the trauma of the Cyprus debacle, the Greeks settled into a relatively stable democracy. The Greeks acted to normalize their relations with Western Europe. In 1981 Greece was admitted to the Common Market. Relations with Turkey remained problematic.

Overall the Balkan countries did derive some benefits from Communism. The Communist regimes facilitated economic and social development. Under the Communists, Albania, Bulgaria, Romania and Yugoslavia overcame the destruction of war, and made education, employment, housing and medical care available to the majority of their populations. The Communist regimes for the most part protected their minority populations and made the benefits of Communist society available to them. Above all, the Russians imposed a *Pax Sovietica* over the region. Despite the recent history of intra-Balkan conflict, no war broke out there between 1945 and 1991. This was a welcome respite considering that Southeastern Europe had been an area of nationalist conflict since the end of the *Pax Ottomanica* over a century earlier.

Changes introduced after 1955 enabled the Balkan Communist states to slowly rejoin the rest of Europe culturally and economically. In the case of Albania this process did not start until the 1980s.

These developments came at a heavy cost, however. Democracy and dissent were not possible. Travel opportunities, except for Yugoslavs, were limited. The secret police – whether called the *Sigurmi* in Albania, the DS in Bulgaria, the *Securtiate* in Romania or the UDBA in Yugoslavia – all acted without constraint.

Nevertheless each Balkan Communist regime adopted its own strategy for dealing with Communism and its Soviet purveyor. The Albanians maintained their precarious independence by seeking first Soviet and then Chinese protection. At the same time the Hoxha regime isolated Albania from its immediate neighbours. Bulgaria under Todor Zhivkov adopted a position of absolute loyalty to the Soviets. In return the Bulgarians received material and security benefits. Ceauşescu's Romania developed a Communist variant that presented a nationalist foreign policy abroad but sustained a strict Stalinist agenda at home. Tito's Yugoslavia was the most creative in its combination of federalism, neutrality and Workers' Self Management for a unique Communist regime. In each of the Balkan Communist countries the regimes to a considerable degree reflected the dictator's personality. The paranoid Hoxha isolated Albania, the obsequious Zhivkov tied Bulgaria firmly to Soviet Russia, the delusional Ceauşescu promoted Romania abroad and repressed it domestically and Tito created a grandiose version of the multinational Austro-Hungarian empire he grew up in. Each individual dictatorial pose provided some benefit for each country, at least for a while. By 1980, however, the year of Tito's death, all the Balkan Communist dictatorships were becoming politically and morally exhausted.

During this period Greece remained largely isolated politically and economically from the other Balkan states. Greece's membership of NATO and its eventual admission to the European Community oriented the country westward. Nevertheless the Greek government during much of the period continued the tradition of conservative rule begun at the beginning of the twentieth century. From 1967 to 1974 Greece had an overt military dictatorship. The Greek monarchy, never firmly established, disappeared for the last time. After 1974, however, democracy reappeared in Greece, although many would argue that it appeared then for the first time. With the normalization of Greek politics, Greece could rejoin the Western European community.

In the mid-1980s all of Southeastern Europe except for Greece seemed to slumber in stasis. Communist dictatorships remained in power in Albania, Bulgaria, Romania and Yugoslavia. Economies stagnated. The situation might have endured indefinitely. The regimes in Albania and Yugoslavia had made the transition to a new generation of leaders. Meanwhile in Bulgaria and Romania old Communists clung to power. Yet unperceived by most contemporaries, major changes for the entire region were on the horizon.

nine

An End and a Beginning, 1985–Present

During the 1980s no internal sources of opposition were strong enough to pose serious threats to the continued existence of the Balkan Communist regimes. Nor did there appear to be any discernible danger to their survival from Western Europe or anywhere else. Seemingly they would endure for the foreseeable future. Unbeknownst to most observers at the time, however, the real threat to the Balkan Communist governments came from a change of course in Soviet Russia.

Russian Communism, like Communism throughout Eastern Europe, had stagnated during the 1980s. Soviet leadership was elderly and lethargic, economic and social infrastructures lacked reinvestment, populations were cynical and the environment was distressed. The emergence of Mikhail Gorbachev (1931–) as the new Soviet leader in 1985 began a new era in the Balkans. Gorbachev assumed power with a certain mandate for reform. His effort to restructure the Soviet economy, *perestroika*, soon reverberated throughout the Balkans. Gorbachev's changes implied that the elderly Communist Eastern European leadership, especially in Bulgaria and Romania, would face challenges to their positions. Another implication was that the Soviets, with clear economic problems of their own, could not continue to subsidize their client states in Eastern Europe indefinitely. By the summer of 1989 events in Hungary and Poland, including the dismantling of the Iron Curtain and the election of non-Communist candidates, indicated that the Soviets were no longer able or willing to enforce their control of Eastern Europe by military means. This made the survival of Communist regimes there problematic.

In Bulgaria, the demise of Todor Zhivkov, whose mandate stretched back to 1954, had been anticipated for some time. As early as the autumn of 1983, when Soviet leader Yuri Andropov (1914–1984) was scheduled to visit Bulgaria, rumours abounded in Sofia that he would replace Zhivkov with a younger and more vibrant leader. Andropov's failure to appear due to his fatal illness created some disappointment there. When Gorbachev visited Bulgaria in 1985 he complained about the Bulgarian practice of exchanging shoddy goods for Soviet fuel, and then selling the fuel on the open market to obtain Western currency. Soviet oil deliveries began to dwindle after 1985, causing power shortages in Bulgaria. Zhivkov's assurances that Bulgaria had always maintained a policy of *preustroistvo* (reorganization) aroused little enthusiasm either at home or among Bulgaria's Soviet allies. His attempt to draw upon the lingering popularity of his late daughter Lydmila with his appointment of his son Vladimir Zhivkov (1952–) to the Department of Culture gained him contempt and ridicule.

Adding to Zhivkov's troubles, a number of unofficial opposition groups had emerged in Bulgaria during the late 1980s. Among these was a pro-reform organization called *Podkrepa* (Support) and the pro-environmental association *Ecoglasnost*. While these groups attracted some urban and youth support, they lacked the political strength to directly challenge the regime. In 1989 Zhivkov revived the anti-Turkish campaign. As it had earlier, this brought his government international opprobrium. The regime further embarrassed itself in October 1989 when it suppressed an *Ecoglasnost* demonstration during an international ecology conference held in Sofia.

Zhivkov lost his position on 10 November in a Communist party coup intended to preserve the party's power in the face of its collapse elsewhere in Eastern Europe. His ouster occurred without difficulty. The only casualty was the old man's pride. Zhivkov retired to a genteel house arrest at his granddaughter's home in Boyana, a suburb of Sofia. After the turn of the year, the new leaders changed the name of the Communists to the Bulgarian Socialist Party and began to make promises of the development of democracy and an open economy. In the face of massive demonstrations, they abandoned their monopoly of political power. They also ceased their anti-Turkish agitation. Yet given Bulgaria's close relations with the Soviets, any major change remained dependent on the developments in Moscow for the time being.

In contrast to Bulgaria's peaceful transition, the dissatisfaction and rage that had amassed over the past decade in Romania led to a violent conclusion for the Ceauşescu regime. Strong signs of discontent emerged in the late 1980s throughout the country. The police used massive force to suppress a major strike in Braşov in 1987. A large friendly crowd calling for *perestroika* in Romania came out to see Gorbachev when he visited Bucharest in July 1989. Enthusiasm for reform overcame the traditional Romanian nationalist suspicion of Russian leadership.

The Ceauşescus remained oblivious to the discontent around them as Communist regimes collapsed quickly and cleanly elsewhere in Eastern Europe. They travelled outside the country in the late autumn of 1989. In mid-December 1989 disorders erupted in Timişoara in western Romania. Attempts by the security forces known as *Securitate* to harass the Hungarian Reformed Church there resulted in a spontaneous anti-Ceauşescu demonstration in which both Hungarians and Romanians participated. The bloody suppression of these demonstrations only increased the mood of defiance throughout the country. When Ceauşescu attempted to address a staged rally in Bucharest on 20 December the crowd turned on him. He and Elena then attempted to flee to a secure location. The army soon captured them and on 25 December, after a brief and perfunctory trial, executed them both. Considerable doubt lingers over the rationale behind these executions.[1] The entire country was then in the grip of fear and confusion. Fighting occurred in Bucharest 22–5 December, apparently between regular army units who went over to the revolution and die-hard *Securitate* elements. The nature of this fighting, like the deaths of the Ceauşescus, remains somewhat obscure.[2] Undoubtedly friendly fire incidents occurred. The confusion may have been intentional on the part of Communist Party members who sought to rid themselves of the burden of the Ceauşescus. These same party elements might also have been behind the rapid trial and execution of the dictator and his wife. In any event, by the turn of the year, an inclusive political organization, the National Salvation Front (NSF), had assumed control. Many of its members were from the Communist Party, including Ion Iliescu (1930–), the leader of the NSF. For a time in the early 1970s Iliescu had pretensions to becoming Ceauşescu's successor. In any event, the end of Communism in Romania, like that in Bulgaria, did not mean the end of Communists.

Elections held in May 1990 confirmed the authority of the NSF. Iliescu and his supporters remained in power until 1996. As in Bulgaria, the party clung to power, but in the face of growing democratic opposition. The old regimes could not survive intact against the intrusion of open markets and open information.

During the dramatic events of 1989 Albania and Yugoslavia remained calm. Nevertheless the withdrawal of Soviet support for their Communist regimes in Eastern Europe undermined the legitimacy even of those two Communist regimes not under direct Soviet control. In Yugoslavia, Communist ideology and the Partisan mythology began to fade soon after the death of Tito in 1980. In their place long-suppressed nationalist sensibilities began to re-emerge. At the same time, the complex Yugoslav political system, with its annual rotating presidency, was unable to deal with mounting economic problems. No one individual could resolve the complex issues of economics within one year. Rising energy prices and growing foreign debts added to Yugoslavia's burdens. Inflation grew in the country. The Yugoslav *dinar* was rated 12.5 to US$1 in 1965. By 1985 it was over 300 to US$1 and in 1988 1,000 to US$1.[3]

One creative response to the economic problems was the marketing of a Yugoslav automobile, dubbed the *Yugo*, in the United States. The *Yugo* cost under $4,000 but was based on dated Fiat technology.[4] It was unreliable and the company lacked the American infrastructure to finish parts and repairs. Soon it became a byword for automotive junk. As such it failed to resolve the Yugoslav economic woes.

Beginning in 1981, the increased unrest in Kosovo contributed to the revival of Serbian nationalism in Yugoslavia. Rhetoric escalated considerably in 1986 when a memorandum issued by the Serbian Academy of Sciences asserted that the Serbian population in Kosovo was victimized by genocidal policies of the Albanian majority. The memorandum also contended that all Serbs had the right to live in a Serbian state, not necessarily with the same borders as the Serbian Federal Republic of Yugoslavia. This was a direct challenge to the territorial integrity of Bosnia-Hercegovina and Croatia, both of which had large Serbian populations. Furthermore it challenged the entire basis of the second Yugoslavia with the assertion that a strong Yugoslavia depended upon a weak Serbia.[5] The old Titoist strictures against overt nationalism clearly had lapsed.

The revival of Serbian nationalism provided political opportunity for a Serbian Communist banker and politician named Slobodan Milošević (1941–2006). In April 1987 Milošević travelled to the troubled autonomous region to address a Serbian crowd at the historic site of Kosovo Polje. There he gained considerable attention when he assured the crowd that the largely Kosovar Albanian police force there to provide order should not beat them. 'No one should dare to beat you', he proclaimed. Very likely he arranged the entire performance.[6] Thereafter Milošević, though still formally a Communist, became the leading Serbian nationalist figure.

The actual political disintegration of Yugoslavia resulted from an attempt by the Serbian leader Milošević to establish his power over the entire country. Milošević combined Communism with Serbian nationalism with some success. He had the strong support of his assertive wife, Mirjana Marković-Milošević (1942–). They worked together like the Ceauşescus, but without so much overt self-aggrandizement. On 28 June 1989 Milošević returned to Kosovo and made a nationalist speech on the 500th anniversary of the Battle of Kosovo Polje. This occasion marked his abandonment of Communism and acceptance of nationalism. That same year, he consolidated Serbian power in the two autonomous regions of Kosovo and Vojvodina, ousting the local leadership and installing nationalist Serbs. This gave Serbia three votes in the rotating Yugoslav presidency. Milošević also counted on the vote of allied Montenegro. With these votes, Serbia potentially could control Yugoslavia. The spectre of the Kingdom of Serbs, Croats and Slovenes loomed across the Federal Republic of Yugoslavia.

The other republics became alarmed at what they perceived to be Serbian aggression. Croatia and Slovenia especially resented that their taxes were indirectly funding Milošević's attempt to impose a Serbian nationalist regime on the country. The situation became especially tense in the two republics where Serbs constituted a distinct minority of the population, Bosnia and Croatia.

Nevertheless Slovenia became the first republic to make an open break with federal Yugoslavia. Slovenia was the most prosperous of the eight federal units. It developed an important light industrial economy and good trade relations with neighbouring Austria and Italy. Under Milan Kučan (1941–), a nominal Communist, it also had the most liberal regime within Yugoslavia. This government began to build up its territorial forces as the Serbian threat loomed. The Slovenes had prepared the defence of their territory thoroughly. On 25 June the Slovenes declared independence. In a brief campaign Slovene territorial forces defeated the attempt of the Yugoslav National Army (JNA) to hold the country together. After the rout of the JNA Milošević recognized that Slovenia, lacking a Serbian population, was not critical for his Serbian-dominated Yugoslavia. Slovenia became independent for the first time in its history. It oriented its policies towards Western Europe, especially Austria and Italy. Its connection to Yugoslavia and the Balkans lasted for slightly more than seventy years.

JNA conscripts had little motivation to fight to retain Slovenia for Yugoslavia. After this embarrassing defeat, the JNA disintegrated along national lines. What remained could not save Yugoslavia, but would actively participate in its destruction. The largely Serbian officer corps retained control of the JNA's equipment and infrastructure.

After the end of the fighting in Slovenia, Croatia became the scene of intense combat. The election in 1990 of the overtly nationalist Franjo Tudjman (1922–1999) as president of Croatia and the adoption by the new regime of symbols such as the red and white chequerboard shield (*šahovnica*) and the currency (*kuna*) associated with the Ustaša alarmed and alienated the Serbian minority, around 12 per cent of the population of Croatia. Tudjman's statement that, 'Serbs belong to the east. They are eastern peoples, like the Turks and Albanians. They belong to the Byzantine culture . . . Despite similarities in language we cannot be together',[7] did little to allay Serbian concerns. During 1990 and early 1991 the Serbian populations living in the Krajina region around Knin in western Croatia and in eastern Croatia armed themselves and prepared to resist Croatian authority. These areas were a part of the old Austrian Military Frontier that Serbs had settled at the end of the seventeenth century. Knin had been a Četnik stronghold during the Second World War.

Fighting between Serbian militias and Croatian government forces began in the spring of 1991 and escalated through the summer as the JNA withdrew from Slovenia and assigned many of its men and much of its equipment to assist the Serbian militias in Croatia. Particularly vicious fighting developed around the eastern Croatian town of Vukovar. It finally fell to the Serbs on 18 November 1991 after an 87-day siege. After entering the ruins of the city, the Serbian militias and the JNA murdered many wounded Croats and civilians. At the same time, Serbian and Montenegrin forces bombed the seaside tourist city of Dubrovnik, destroying many medieval buildings and tourist facilities. This Serbian behaviour alienated much of the international community. After the fall of Vukovar, both sides were exhausted. They agreed to an armistice monitored by the United Nations. UN personnel arrived to enforce the armistice. This armistice left the Serbs in control of about one-third of the territory of the former federal Yugoslav Republic of Croatia. The Croats received a boost in January 1992 when the European Community, led by Germany, recognized Croatian and Slovene independence.

Soon afterwards Bosnia-Hercegovina imploded. After the collapse of Communism, all three of the main nationalities in this most ethnically mixed Yugoslav republic – the Bosniaks (Bosnian Muslims) (43 per cent of the population), the Serbs (31 per cent) and the Croats (17 per cent) – sought protection in nationalist political parties. In a vote held on 1 March 1992 on the issue of independence, the Bosniaks and Croats voted for independence, while the Serbs boycotted the vote. The widely circulated aphorism at the time asked, 'Why should I be a minority in your country when you can be a minority in mine?' Soon afterwards, fighting between the Bosniaks and Croats against the Serbs broke out across the country. Initially some Croats and Serbs supported the multinational Bosnian government and served in its armed forces.

In the first phase of the war, which lasted from April 1992 to March 1993, the Serbs held all the advantages. With the help of the rump JNA, they fielded a well-armed force. They also had the support of Serbian nationalist militias from Serbia. The Bosnian government forces were poorly armed and disorganized. The Bosnian capital Sarajevo came under siege from Serbian forces in April. By the summer of 1992 the Serbs had seized control of two-thirds of the country. Much of their effort was concentrated in the north and east in order to maintain physical continuity between the Serbs in Krajina and those in Serbia proper. Everywhere the Serbs established control, they forced out the non-Serbian populations through murder, rape and other forms of intimidation. This brutal ethnic cleansing undermined the validity of the Serbian cause. UN forces arrived in Bosnia in November, but had little effect on the fighting. Attempts by outside mediators to find diplomatic solutions to the fighting in Bosnia also failed. The most important of these attempts was the Vance-Owen plan of January 1993, which would have divided Bosnia into ten cantons, three for each nationality with the tenth the capital, Sarajevo. Both sides rejected this idea.

In the second phase of the fighting, from March 1993 to March 1994, the Bosniak–Croat coalition collapsed. While the Bosnian government forces controlled territories only around Sarajevo and the northwestern enclave of Bihać, the Croats sought to establish themselves in regions contiguous to Croatia. Fighting developed between Bosnian government forces and Croats. Meanwhile the Serbs subjected Sarajevo to intense bombardments. Sarajevo was not only the location of the Bosnian government, but the centre of the concept of a cosmopolitan Bosnia. Thousands of civilians died in the shelling. During this phase the Bosnian government forces became more intensely Bosniak. One effect of the ethnic cleansing and the intense fighting was the destruction of the multiethnic character of Bosnia.

The third phase of the Bosnian war began in March 1994 and lasted until the end of the fighting in September 1995. The most important aspect of this phase was intervention on the side of the Bosnian government by NATO and America. Reports of Serbian atrocities and the carnage in Sarajevo led the American government to take action. Diplomatically it brought the Bosniaks and Croats together in a Bosnian federation, and secured the agreement of the Zagreb government for this undertaking. The incentive for this federation was the promise of American military aid in the form of arms and training. At the same time, NATO air forces took control of Bosnian skies. The Serbs initially reacted defiantly. On 11 July 1995 they took Srebrenica, an enclave of Bosnian government territory in the eastern part of the country. After gathering the population, the Serbs sent the women and children off to Bosnian territory. Serbian forces under the command of the former JNA officer Ratko Mladić (1943–) then massacred over five thousand men and boys over twelve. This was the largest atrocity in Europe since the Second World War.[8] Another Bosniak enclave, Žepa, fell to Serbian forces on 25 July. Most of the remaining population was able to escape to Bosnian government-controlled territory.

After a year of preparation and continued bloodshed, the Bosniak–Croat alliance took the initiative in the late summer of 1995. At the end of July, Croatian government forces intervened at Bihać against a Serbian attack. Then on 4 August a strong Croatian offensive dubbed Operation Storm swept the Serbs out of Krajina.[9] Most of the Serbian population abandoned their homes and fled to Serbian-controlled Bosnia and Serbia. The Croatian army forced out most of those who did not voluntarily leave. The three-hundred-year-old Serbian presence in Croatia in the Krajina region, a part of the old Austrian Military Frontier, was at an end. Simultaneously a combined Bosnian government and Croat offensive rapidly eliminated the Serbian presence in much of northern and western Bosnia. By the end of the summer Serbian control of Bosnia had receded to about 50 per cent.

By September both sides were weary of the fighting. They agreed to talks. These began in Geneva but on American initiative shifted in October to the United States at Dayton, Ohio. There Milošević, Tudjman and Bosnian government President Alija Izetbegović (1925–2003) agreed to a federal Bosnia consisting of a Bosniak–Croat federation and a Serbian republic. NATO troops entered Bosnia to stabilize the situation. Also as a result of the Dayton Accords, the Serbs returned the region around Vukovar, the scene of bloody fighting in 1992, to the Croats.

As a result of the war, Bosnia fragmented into distinct Bosniak, Croatian and Serbian segments. During the war, the Bosniaks attracted aid and volunteers from Islamic countries as well as assistance from NATO. The Croats also received help from NATO. The Serbs obtained similar aid and volunteers from Orthodox countries such as Greece and Russia. The old cosmopolitan Bosnia was a major casualty of the war.

After the Dayton agreements, the situation in Bosnia remained fragile. The Serbian Republic retained strong links to Serbia. The Croats remained connected to Bosnia and to the Balkans through the Bosniak–Croat federation. The Bosniaks, lacking a strong patron, depended on NATO to maintain their position in the federal Bosnian state. The war was extremely costly in terms of human suffering. The CIA estimated that 81,500 soldiers and 156,000 civilians died in the war.[10] The majority of both of these groups were Bosniaks. In addition over 900,000 people fled Bosnia and over 1.3 million were internal refugees. This amounts to about half of the pre-war population. In addition, huge numbers of rapes occurred.

As the fighting raged to the north, Macedonia made a comparatively peaceful exit from Yugoslavia. After a vote held on 8 September 1991 Macedonia declared its independence. The goal of IMRO at the beginning of the twentieth century was finally realized. A number of problems immediately confronted the new state. One issue concerned the Albanian minority. The Albanian population of Macedonia, consisting of up to 25 per cent of the total and concentrated in the northwest around Tetovo, boycotted the 1991 election. Unlike the Albanians in Kosovo, the Albanians in Macedonia perceived in federal Yugoslavia protection against the Slavic majority. This undermined the validity of the vote for independence. The Albanian minority was not reconciled to Macedonian independence.

Another problem was international. Neighbouring Greece, which controlled the new republic's main access to the outside world, refused to recognize it because of the use of the term 'Macedonia'. The Greeks claimed an historic right to this term. They feared that its use implied territorial claims on the northern Greek province of the same name. The Greek concerns at the time were far fetched, but they harkened back to the beginning of the twentieth century when Bulgaria and Serbia as well as Greece vied for control of Ottoman-ruled Macedonia. The Macedonians did not help their own situation by adopting the Star of Vergina – an artefact found in the ancient Macedonian King Philip II's burial site located within modern Greece – as a national symbol and initially on their flag. Nor did the pronouncements from a revived IMRO about 'Greater Macedonia' allay Greek concerns. Greece's position obstructed international recognition of the new state. The use of the expedient FYROM (Former Yugoslav Republic of Macedonia) by all concerned parties did not solve the problem.

A third problem became apparent soon after Macedonia's declaration of independence. Its economic situation was bleak. Its old markets in Yugoslavia were gone. Greece embargoed trade in 1993. No good transportation connections existed with Albania or Bulgaria. As a result the new state struggled financially. Nevertheless it avoided becoming involved in the fighting to the north. In particular Serbia's lack of interest in Macedonia meant that the claims of Serbian nationalists to 'South Serbia' from the time of the Balkan Wars were over.

Although Bulgaria had been the first nation to recognize Macedonian independence in 1992, relations between Macedonia and Bulgaria remained prickly. The Macedonians insisted on maintaining their newly realized identity. To the astonishment of the Bulgarians, Macedonians on occasion employed translators in official discussions with their eastern neighbour even though the languages are mutually comprehensible. Only in 1999 did the Bulgarians recognize the Macedonian language and culture as distinct from Bulgarian, in return for Macedonia's rejection of any claims to Bulgarian (Pirin) Macedonia.[11] Nevertheless, given the Yugoslav war, Greek hostility and Albanian minority problems, Bulgaria offered the most viable link to the outside world. All of these issues raised questions about Macedonia's viability. Could it exist as a multiethnic state? Could it survive in the face of economic and political isolation?

During the great changes of 1989 elsewhere, Albania remained quiet. The next year, however, the second Communist leader to rule Albania, Ramiz Alia, abandoned the party's monopoly on power. As in other Southeastern European states, the Albanian Communist Party repackaged itself as the Socialist Party of Albania. New political movements soon formed and in 1991 competed for parliamentary seats in what was the freest election in Albania's history. The next year Alia resigned after the overwhelming election victory of the main opposition organization, the Democratic Party. Alia deserves some credit for recognizing the circumstances and resisting the insistence of some die-hard Communists, like Hoxha's widow Nexhimija, on maintaining ideological rigour.

Despite the peaceful democratic transition Albania had many problems. Its industrial and agricultural infrastructures, never strong, had eroded during the years of isolation. Many young Albanians lacked jobs. After Alia loosened Communist control, Albanians fled the country seeking work, mainly across the Adriatic to Italy. United Nations officials in Albania found starvation in the countryside for the first time. Emigration and foreign aid helped to alleviate these problems. A major catastrophe occurred in December 1996 and January 1997 when several pyramid fund schemes collapsed. Investors who had little experience with capitalist-style financial dealings lost their entire savings. Some Albanians demanded that the government make good their losses. Mobs stormed government facilities and broke into military arsenals to seize weapons. By March anarchy prevailed in many areas and civil war threatened the country.[12] Many Albanians fled across the Adriatic. Only the arrival of an Italian-led international peacekeeping force in April 1997 restored order. Gradually Albania returned to political if not economic stability.

After the end of the fighting in Bosnia and Croatia and the near collapse of Albania, events in the Balkans came full circle in Kosovo. Milošević's takeover of this Albanian-inhabited region critical to the national identity of the Serbs in 1989 was a major step towards the dissolution of Yugoslavia. After the end of Kosovo's autonomy, the Serbian authorities shut down many Albanian institutions. The Albanian population boycotted most of those that remained, including schools. An underground movement established its own schools and even a shadow government under Ibrahim Rugova (1944–2006). This underground movement avoided conflict with the heavily armed Serbian security forces.

The Dayton Accords of 1995 shocked many Kosovo Albanians (Kosovars) by leaving Kosovo under Serbian control. The influx of Serbian settlers from Krajina also disturbed the Kosovo Albanians. Frustrated with Rugova's deliberate tactics, they organized the Kosovo Liberation Front (KLA) in 1993. Kosovars living abroad sent significant amounts of aid to the KLA. It became active in the more remote areas of Kosovo in 1996. The next year the influx of arms from looted Albanian arsenals expanded the KLA's membership and activities. These remained limited to terror attacks on Serbian police.

Serbian authorities responded to KLA attacks with brute force. Though both sides committed atrocities, those carried out by the Serbs received more widespread attention, probably because of the recent Serbian record in Bosnia and Croatia. The massacre of 45 Albanian civilians at Račak in January 1999 caused international diplomacy to act.

American, European and Russian pressure brought Kosovar and Serbian delegates to Rambouillet outside Paris in February 1999. There Milošević rejected a NATO proposal to restore Kosovo's autonomy and to permit NATO forces to enter. On 24 March NATO began systematic bombing of Serbian targets. Both Bulgaria and Romania granted NATO permission to fly over their airspace. In response, Serbian forces compelled much of the Kosovar population to leave the country, again committing some atrocities. These activities were the basis for the United Nations tribunal's

Yugoslavia after 1991.

indictment of Milošević as a war criminal. 848,100 of the Kosovars fled to Albania, 444,600 went to Macedonia, 69,000 went to Montenegro and 91,057 went to other countries.[13] Their welcome in most of these places was tepid at best.

Milošević 's motives remain obscure. Perhaps he thought that since the Croatian expulsion of the Serbs from Krajina aroused few objections, he could drive the Kosovars out of Kosovo without serious consequences. Possibly he also counted on help from Russia. In any event the Russians were unable to render meaningful assistance. On 10 June the United Nations reached a settlement. Serbian forces had to withdraw from Kosovo. The UN would govern the region with the help of a fifty thousand-man NATO force augmented by Russian units from Bosnia. The bombing stopped the same day. Refugees returned during the summer. After the bombing ended the Kosovar refugees returned. As many as twelve thousand people died in the fighting in Kosovo.[14] Much ethnic tension lingered between the Kosovars and the remaining Serbian population. The peace-keeping forces found much of their responsibility lay in protecting the remaining Serbian minority.

Kosovo remained under UN control until 2008. On 17 February of that year Kosovo declared its independence from Serbia. Albania, most of the European Union, Turkey and the United States recognized Kosovo's independence. A number of others, including three Orthodox countries – Greece, Russia and Serbia – have not. The NATO force remains in the country, although it will probably be reduced. Because of an anticipated veto from Russia, Kosovo did not apply to join the UN.

The influx of Kosovar Albanian refugees into Macedonia threatened to destabilize the Skopje regime's fragile independence. At the same time, the success of the KLA in Kosovo emboldened Albanian separatists in Macedonia. Fighting began in early 2001 between Macedonian government forces, which were commanded by mainly Slavic officers and manned by Slavic recruits, and Albanian separatists, known as the National Liberation Army (NLA). Sporadic fighting continued throughout the summer without either side achieving a pronounced success. Finally the two sides reached an agreement, signed on 13 August 2001 in Ohrid, which provided for the recognition of Albanian as an official language, an expansion of the numbers of ethnic Albanians in the police force and the entry into the country of a NATO force to maintain the peace.[15] Macedonia has since faced the challenge of becoming a viable multiethnic state in the Balkans.

After Yugoslavia began to collapse, Montenegro remained Serbia's most steadfast ally. Some Montenegrin troops participated in the fighting and looting around Dubrovnik. Nevertheless, going back to the beginning of the century there had remained a strong sense of separate identity in the smallest Yugoslav republic. The fighting in Croatia and Bosnia led some in Montenegro to distance themselves from their fellow Orthodox Serbian-speaking neighbour. EU and NATO officials encouraged the development of Montenegrin separatism with large economic incentives. After the Dayton Accords in 1995, the young Montenegrin prime minister, Milo Djukanović (1962–), increasingly sought contacts with Western Europe. In 1996 Montenegro adopted the Deutschmark as its currency. The Kosovo conflict increased the propensity of the Americans and Europeans to support separatism in Montenegro. Much European and Russian money streamed in to develop Montenegro's picturesque sea coast. Significantly in 1999–2000 Montenegro received more United States aid per capita than any other country in the world except for Israel.[16] After the NATO occupation of Kosovo, however, the Americans and Europeans sought to discourage Montenegrin separatism because of fears that this might encourage the Kosovars and Bosnian Serbs to seek their own independence and thus destroy the delicate stability that then existed in the Balkans. Nevertheless, in 2003, mainly on Montenegrin initiative, Montenegro and Serbia abandoned the framework of federal Yugoslavia and established a looser confederation of Serbia and Montenegro. The ideal of Yugoslavia, begun in the nineteenth century as a means of preserving Slavic culture in the Balkans, was finally dead. In 2006 a bare majority of 55 per cent approved Montenegrin independence. Subsequently Montenegro dissolved its remaining ties with Serbia. For the first time since 1918, the Montenegrin state was sovereign. To a considerable degree, however, the success of an independent Montenegro depends on its economic strength. An economic collapse could well propel the tiny state back towards its larger Serbian relative.

The defeats of 1995 and 1999 left rump Serbia exhausted. The country was also deeply divided between those who blamed outside forces for Serbia's catastrophe and those who blamed Serbia's leadership. Milošević's attempt to create a Greater Serbia had not only destroyed Yugoslavia, but lost areas Serbs had inhabited since the end of the seventeenth century. Serbia itself was reduced to its pre-1912 borders, except for the autonomous Vojvodina region and a sliver of the old Ottoman Sandjak of Novi Pazar. In 2000 Milošević lost his attempt at reelection as president of Yugoslavia to an opposition nationalist, Vojslav Kostunica (1944–). The next year the new prime minister of Serbia, Zoran Djindjić (1952–2003), extradited Milošević to The Hague to stand trial for war crimes. In 2003 individuals associated with the Serbian security forces assassinated Djindjić. In 2006, while his trial was ongoing, Milošević died. Serbia remains to some degree isolated from the European community. Strong ties with Russia remain and the economy continues to lag.

During the fall of the Southeastern European Communist regimes, Greece tightened its ties with Western Europe. In 1992 Greece became a charter member of the European Union. In 2001 Greece was among the initial members of the Eurozone. In addition relations with the United States improved after the Americans agreed to eliminate two of their military bases on Greek territory.

Nevertheless Greece's relations with the other regional powers remained troubled. The instability in Albania caused many refugees to join a number of Albanians already seeking work in Greece. This upset both the Greek public and the Greek government. The Cyprus issue, along with spats over potential oil and gas drilling locations in the Aegean, continued to plague Greek–Turkish relations. During the collapse of Yugoslavia, Thessalonika (Salonika) reprised its First World War role as a port of debarkation for NATO forces moving up the Vardar corridor to Kosovo and Macedonia. As in 1915, the Greek position on foreign intervention in Southeastern Europe was equivocal. The Greeks perceived the existence of an independent Macedonia as a threat to their control of their province of Macedonia. During the Bosnian War and the Kosovo crisis they evinced support for Serbia. The Greeks were receptive to Serbian propaganda on these issues, insisting that the Serbs were the defenders of Orthodoxy.

Albania, Bulgaria and Romania have had some similar post-Communist experiences. In all three of these states the former Communists have transformed themselves into socialist parties. As such they have competed in elections and participated in governments. During their times in power they have behaved more or less responsibly. They appear to have abandoned their previous authoritarian propensities. Nevertheless corruption plagues the political process everywhere in the region.

Another political phenomenon has been the return of former royalty. In 1997, 'King' Leka, accompanied by his mother Queen Geraldine, the widow of King Zog, visited Albania. A subsequent referendum rejected a restoration of the monarchy by a considerable majority. In Bulgaria the former Tsar Simeon returned in 1996 from exile in Spain to his former country to play a political role. While he remained coy about any intention to restore the monarchy, he did form a political party. His political organization, entitled, 'National Movement Simeon II', participated in the Bulgarian political arena. In 2001, after the success of his organization in the national elections, he became prime minister of the country where he as a child had been the hereditary ruler. Although he promised to end organized crime and corruption, Simeon made little headway against these huge problems. His main accomplishment was to secure Bulgaria's admission to NATO. In 2005 his party suffered defeat, and by 2009 had virtually ceased to have any public support. Since his exile in 1974 King Constantine has returned to Greece on several occasions, including the occasion of the 2004 Olympic Games in Athens. There is little interest in Greece in a restoration of the monarchy. After squabbling with the Iliescu government, King Michael returned to Romania in 1997, and resides there on a part-time basis. He has not advocated a restoration of the monarchy. Crown Prince Alexander Karadjeordjević (1945–) returned to Serbia after the fall of Milošević. His citizenship and some of his property was restored. He has remained largely apart from politics. Not even Montenegro escaped the Balkan royal nostalgia. A monument to the long-gone King Nikola was dedicated in Cetinje in 2005.

Since the beginning of the twenty-first century the Balkan countries overall have benefited from efforts to integrate them into the rest of Europe. The economic, defence and political systems of Greece had been integrated with those of Western Europe for some time. Bulgaria and Romania were admitted to NATO in 2004 and, despite concerns about corruption and financial responsibility, to the EU in 2007. Their entry into the Eurozone is pending. In 2009 Albania joined NATO, together with Croatia. Greece has vetoed Macedonia's application for membership of NATO, even though Macedonia has met the requirements. The Bosnian federation, Montenegro and Moldova had joined NATO's Partnership for Peace in order to gain consideration for membership. Serbia has recently indicated an interest in closer relations with NATO and the EU. In 2010 the Serbian parliament (*skupština*) passed a resolution condemning the Srebrenica massacre and apologizing for Serbia's failure to take action to prevent it. Nevertheless a major obstacle to Serbia's integration into Europe has been the inability or disinclination of the Serbian government to capture the indicted war criminal Ratko Mladić and turn him over to the international tribunal at the Hague. Mladić, commander of the Serbian forces responsible for the massacre at Srebrenica, remains at large somewhere in Serbia. For the other Eastern European countries admission to NATO has been a precursor to joining the EU.

Although peace returned to the Balkans during the first decade of the twenty-first century, several political issues remain unresolved. The most important of these concerns the continued viability of Bosnia. If Bosnia can hold together as the Muslim–Croat Federation and the Serbian Republic, it will demonstrate that a multiethnic state, even in this awkward circumstance, is possible in the Balkans. For it to become viable Bosnia must pursue European integration. In particular European money is critical to develop Bosnia's shattered economy. The possibility of admission to the EU would help to rein in the expectations of the more extreme nationalists on all sides.

If Bosnia fails, and its Croatian and Serbia components seek to join their respective national states, this could set off a chain reaction that would reverberate throughout the region. In addition to the augmentation of Croatia and Serbia, Kosovo would undoubtedly seek to unite with Albania. The Albanian regions of Macedonia would likely seek inclusion in this Greater Albania. The loss of the northwestern portion of its territory would call into question the continued existence of Macedonia. In such case, some kind of federal relationship with Bulgaria might not be out of the question. Already Macedonians have the privilege of travelling to EU countries on Bulgarian passports.

A crisis involving Kosovo could ignite the same scenario. Kosovo itself lacks a strong economy. Albania's economy, long the worst in Europe, has begun to expand. A move on the part of either Albania or Kosovo to unify with the other could well cause a crisis that would also undermine the viability of Bosnia and of Macedonia.

For Romania the issue of Moldova remains problematic. After its declaration of independence in 1991, Moldova faced a secessionist movement in Transnistria. With the help of the Soviet, later the Russian, Fourteenth Army, Transnistria established a separate although internationally unrecognized regime.[17] The Romanians did not want to become involved in this imbroglio. Nor did Romania, struggling economically itself, have much inclination to take on the economic problems of what is now Europe's poorest country. The integration of Romania into the European Union in 2007, however, offers hope for Moldova. In 2009 large demonstrations in Moldova's capital Chișinău (Kishniev) called for unification with Romania. Significantly, many of the participants were young people.

The end of Communism brought important benefits to the peoples of the Balkan Peninsula. Democracy prevailed everywhere. Western goods and services flooded into the region. Media of all kinds flourished. The heavy hand of the police lifted from the citizens of all Balkan countries. Properties lost to collectivization drives in the 1940s and '50s were restored to the owners. Other Europeans travelled throughout the region, while the peoples of Southeastern Europe were free to move away from home. Censorship of the media and the arts ended.

The Orthodox churches made a relatively smooth transition to the post-Communist era. The churches received back some of the property that the Communist governments had confiscated. Churches were restored and rebuilt. In some cases new churches were constructed. This religious revival was not limited to Orthodoxy. Often with foreign assistance, mosques were built or rebuilt in Albania, Bosnia and Bulgaria. In Transylvania the Uniate Church re-emerged after years of oppression by the Romanian Communist regime. It managed to recover some of the properties it had lost in the late 1940s, and to attract many old and some new congregants.

The end of Communism also had some drawbacks for the region. The extremes of wealth and poverty returned to the Balkans. Many retirees who only had Communist-era pensions as income found their lives difficult. Crime syndicates, which often had their origins in Communist-era organizations, operated more brazenly than under the previous regimes. Many Albanians, Bulgarians and Romanians, especially the educated and young, emigrated to Western Europe, Israel and North America in search of better economic opportunities. In Bulgaria, because of emigration and other factors, a serious demographic decline became apparent.

The end of the Communist regimes has left environmental damage throughout the region. Obsolete industrial enterprises closed but continued to blight the cities. The EU has finally succeeded in persuading Bulgaria to close the Kozludui nuclear reactor complex, which was built in 1970s to the same specifications as Chernobyl. It is slated to be shut down in 2013.

Above all, the excesses of nationalism reappeared. Nowhere was this more apparent than in Yugoslavia, where self-serving unscrupulous politicians used nationalist fears to incite ethnic hatred. In effect they figuratively murdered Yugoslavia.[18] In doing so they also literally murdered tens of thousands of Yugoslavs. Particularly susceptible to such blandishments were the Serbs, although the Bosniaks and Croats were not immune. Greek nationalism punished Macedonia and made the integration of Turkey into Europe problematic. Nationalist political movements appeared everywhere. In Romania the Greater Romania Party called for the rehabilitation of Marshal Antonescu. In Bulgaria the nationalist *Ataka* Party adopted a xenophobic attitude towards the country's Turkish minority. All such movements throughout the region are anti-Roma. The Roma themselves remain on the fringes of economic and political life throughout the region.

The process of integration of the Balkans into Europe has already begun. It holds great promise for the peaceful development of the entire region. Many of the old obstacles to development such as corruption and nationalism remain. Nevertheless the EU holds the promise for the Balkan countries of overcoming their ethnic differences and of developing the economies of the region as a whole.

Conclusion

The area of Southeastern Europe or the Balkans lacks precise geographic and cultural definition. Generally it lies south of the Danube River, southeast of the Carpathian Mountains and southwest of the Prut River. The dominant religious culture of the region has been Orthodox Christian since the early centuries of the Common Era. Other regions, such as Transylvania and Moldava, have at times in their history been linked to the Balkans through political rule or Orthodox Christian culture. These areas remain Balkan frontiers. Other cultures, Islam and Catholic Christianity, have established strong presences in parts of this region.

Civilization came to the region through the Greeks on the periphery and the Romans everywhere. After the success of Christianity in the Roman Empire, Roman rule eventually morphed into Byzantine power. After the death of Emperor Justinian I in 565 CE the Byzantine state was only able to maintain direct control of the Balkans for comparatively brief periods of time. However, it exercised a strong cultural, economic and political influence over the entire region. The resulting Byzantine Commonwealth had cultural unity but not necessarily political unity. The Orthodox culture emanating from the Byzantine Commonwealth served to impart to the region a distinct development separate from that of the rest of Europe.

The Ottoman conquest of the region over the course of a century and a half preserved this distinct development. The Orthodox hierarchy cooperated with the Ottoman rulers to preserve their cultural and religious authority over the Christian population. The Ottomans brought with them Islam, which gained some acceptance everywhere in the region. The inhabitants of Albania and Bosnia especially found Islam appealing, and over the course of several centuries converted in large numbers. The Balkans remained apart from Western European cultural, economic and political developments. Only at the beginning of the nineteenth century did Western European rationality and secularism intrude into the Balkans. This advent of new ideas caused convulsions that shook the region.

The most important of these Western ideas to gain attention in the Balkans was nationalism. The Orthodox peoples of the Balkans sought to define themselves in nationalist terms and then to implement these definitions to realize nationalist states. These efforts caused a tremendous amount of turmoil throughout the region. They shattered the *Pax Ottomanica* that had stabilized the region since the Ottoman conquest in the fifteenth century.

During the nineteenth century, first the Serbs, then the Greeks and the Romanians freed themselves from Ottoman rule. Later the Bulgarians revolted against Ottoman domination, and with Russian assistance established their own state. As the Ottoman Empire receded in the region, the Great Powers Austria and Russia sought to expand into the vacuum. By the beginning of the twentieth century a three-sided conflict had developed in Southeastern Europe. This positioned the Ottomans, attempting to preserve their empire, against the Austrians and Russians, attempting to expand theirs, and against the Balkan peoples, attempting to realize fully national states. Obviously these goals were mutually exclusive. The Austrian and Russian goals overlapped, as did the national claims of the Balkan states.

The conflict among the Ottomans, the Great Powers and the Balkan states resulted in the Balkan Wars of 1912–13, first between the Balkan states and the Ottomans, and then among the Balkan states themselves. These wars failed to resolve the ambitions of the Balkan states and the claims of the Great Powers. The conflict continued from 1914 to 1918. The resolution of these conflicts established four national states and one multinational state in the Balkans. The frontiers of the Balkans expanded into Croatia, Slovenia, Bessarabia and Transylvania. The dominant power of the previous five centuries, the Ottoman Empire, in its modernized form as the Turkish republic, retreated to the eastern end of Thrace, barely maintaining a presence in the Balkans. Austria ceased to exist as a Great Power. Russia, wracked by the convulsions of revolution and civil war, temporarily ceased to maintain a strong interest in the region.

During the 1920s the national states struggled economically and politically. Bulgaria and Greece contended with the consequences of military defeat. Romania and Yugoslavia faced the problems of integration of their territories and the issues of multiethnicity. The new Albanian national government attempted to overcome the traditions of tribal loyalties. During the 1930s the resurgent power of Germany attracted all of the Balkan economies. All of the Balkan countries oriented their economies if not their politics towards Germany. Albania was the exception. It barely had a national economy. Italy had dominated that country since the late 1920s.

Despite the overwhelming position of Germany in the Balkans, the region became the arena for fighting in 1940 and 1941. All of the Balkan states became involved in the Second World War. Albania, Greece and Yugoslavia underwent not only foreign occupation but civil war. Romanian forces mainly fought outside the Balkans, first alongside the Germans in the Russian campaign, and after August 1944 together with the Soviets in Hungary. Bulgaria avoided foreign occupation, civil war and the Russia campaign. Bulgarian troops occupied parts of Greece and Yugoslavia. After changing from the German to the Russian side in 1944, Bulgarian soldiers also fought alongside the Red Army in Hungary.

The victory of the Red Army over the Germans returned direct Russian interests to the Balkans. Not only did the Russians seek to realize their Great Power objects, but they also attempted to impose their economic, political and social systems on the region. After 1944 Moscow established a Communist Commonwealth on the Balkans. This was somewhat reminiscent of the old Byzantine Commonwealth. Russia dominated the region, but never was able to exercise direct and uniform control. Nevertheless the ensuing *Pax Sovietica* held to ease the national rivalries that had plagued the region for the previous 150 years.

Due to the victory in the Greek Civil War of the American-supported anti-Communist forces, Greece avoided coming under direct Russian control. Nevertheless, even Greece felt the Soviet Russian presence in the region. Direct pressure came from the Soviet-supported forces in the Greek Civil War. Indirect pressure thereafter resulted from the variety of Communist governments on Greece's northern borders. Under these circumstances, democracy struggled in Greece until at least 1975.

The erosion of Soviet power in the region resulted in the efforts of the Communist hierarchies in Bulgaria and Romania to save themselves by removing their leaders in 1989. Violence accompanied the second effort but not the first. The erosion of Soviet power and the decline of Communist ideology enabled nationalism to re-emerge in Yugoslavia. Ambitious and unscrupulous politicians utilized this situation to realize their own agendas at the expense of the unity of Yugoslavia. A decade of violence ensued. When it was over seven states replaced the single Yugoslav federation. The political situation in some areas remains precarious. The Bosnian Federation continues to face difficulties. Macedonia likewise is fragile. The viability of Kosovo and Moldova remain problematic. Can the Balkans sustain two Albanian states, two Romanian states and two or possibly three Serbian states?

By the beginning of the twenty-first century a new dynamic was emerging in the politics of the region. The Balkan states were gravitating again towards Western Europe. The forerunner of this European integration process was membership of NATO. Greece had joined back in 1952. Bulgaria and Romania joined in 2004. Albania joined in 2009. NATO functioned as the gateway to the European Union. Greece was a charter member of the organization; Bulgaria and Romania joined in 2007. All of the other Balkan states seek admission to both NATO and the EU. The European Union Commonwealth replaced the Communist Commonwealth. All the remaining former Yugoslav states and Albania are seeking membership. When this is accomplished the Balkans again will exist under a single domination. All people living there hope that prosperity will ensue and that a *Pax Europeana* will endure.

REFERENCES

Introduction

1 Ferdinand Schevill, *History of the Balkans from the Earliest Times to the Present Day* (New York, 1922).
2 Robert Lee Wolff, *The Balkans in Our Time* (New York, 1967).
3 L. S. Stavrianos, *The Balkans since 1453* (New York, 1958).
4 Mark Mazower, *The Balkans: A Short History* (New York, 2000).
5 John R. Lampe, *Balkans into Southeastern Europe* (New York, 2006); Andrew Baruch Wachtel, *The Balkans in World History* (Oxford, 2008).

one: Geography

1 A good discussion of the importance of the natural setting of the Balkans for the history and culture of the region is found in Traian Stoianovich, *A Study of Balkan Civilization* (New York, 1967).
2 Dennis P. Hupchick, *The Balkans from Constantinople to Communism* (New York, 2002), p. 8.
3 On the term Balkan, see Maria Todorova, *Imagining the Balkans* (Oxford, 1997), pp. 23–32.
4 Nicholas Kulash 'Grim Romanians Brighten over a German Connection', *New York Times*, 5 December 2009.
5 On the use of the terms Moldavia and Moldova see Charles King, *The Moldovans: Romania, Russia and the Politics of Culture* (Stanford, CA, 2000), pp. 1–7.
6 See for example, John R. Lampe, *Balkans into Southeastern Europe*

(New York, 2006) and Andrew Baruch Wachtel, *The Balkans in World History* (Oxford, 2008).

two: The Legacy of Empire: The Middle Ages to 1804

1 Andrew Baruch Wachtel, *The Balkans in World History* (Oxford, 2008), p. 19.
2 Kurt W. Treptow, ed., *A History of Romania* (Iaşi, 1996), pp. 46–7.
3 The Latinized form of the name of this location is Byzantium.
4 Edward N. Luttwak, *The Grand Strategy of the Byzantine Empire* (Cambridge, MA, 2009), pp. 67–77. There is a good pictorial overview of the city in Speros Vryonis, *Byzantium and Europe* (New York, 1967), pp. 28–9.
5 Jean W. Sedlar, *East Central Europe in the Middle Ages, 1000–1500* (Seattle, WA, 1994), pp. 59–60.
6 Plamen Tsvetkov, *A History of the Balkans: A Regional Overview from a Bulgarian Perspective* (New York, 1993), I, p. 96.
7 On this concept see Dimitri Obolensky, *The Byzantine Commonwealth: Eastern Europe 500–1453* (New York, 1971).
8 On the nature of this state see John V. A. Fine, *The Early Medieval Balkans* (Ann Arbor, MI, 1983), pp. 191–2.
9 The title 'Bulgar Slayer' is apparently anachronistic. The alleged atrocities committed by Basil II's forces against those of Samuel assumed an exaggerated importance in the nationalist conflicts between Greeks and Bulgarians in the nineteenth and twentieth centuries. See Paul Stephenson, *The Legend of Basil the Bulgar-Slayer* (Cambridge, 2003), pp. 110–34.
10 Tsvetkov, *A History of the Balkans*, I, p. 171.
11 See Stanford J. Shaw, *History of the Ottoman Empire and Modern Turkey* (Cambridge, 1976), I, p. 15.
12 John V. A. Fine, *The Late Medieval Balkans* (Ann Arbor, MI, 1987), pp. 379–80.
13 Contemporary Catholic sources accused the Bosnian Church of the heresy of Bogomilism. This was a medieval dualist heresy that originated in Asia Minor and spread to Bulgaria by the tenth century. These charges do not seem to be accurate. Dennis P.

Hupchick, *The Balkans from Constantinople to Communism* (New York, 2002), p. 154.

14 Dennis P. Hupchick, *The Bulgarians in the Seventeenth Century* (Jefferson, NC, 1993), p. 7.

15 See Elizabeth Roberts, *Realm of the Black Mountain: A History of Montenegro* (Ithaca, NY, 2007), p. 98.

16 Hupchick, *Balkans*, p. 132.

17 John R. Lampe, *Yugoslavia as History: Twice there was a Country* (Cambridge, 1996), p. 26.

18 See Barbara Jelavich, *History of the Balkans: Eighteenth and Nineteenth Centuries* (Cambridge, 1983), pp. 53–7.

19 John R. Lampe and Marvin R. Jackson, *Balkan Economic History 1550–1950* (Bloomington, IN, 1982), pp. 82–6.

three: The Intrusion of Modernity, 1804–78

1 Dennis P. Hupchick, *The Bulgarians in the Seventeenth Century* (Jefferson, NC, 1993), pp. 82–3. The appearance nearby of a Habsburg army was an important cause of this uprising.

2 Barbara Jelavich, *History of the Balkans: Eighteenth and Nineteenth Centuries* (Cambridge, 1983), pp. 155–6.

3 Kurt W. Treptow, ed., *A History of Romania* (Iaşi, 1996), pp. 215–17.

4 The written language was based on the western Serbian dialect word for what, *što*, as opposed to the use of the word *kaj* (kajka-vian) spoken in northwestern Croatia and the word *ča* (čakavian) spoken in northern Dalmatia and some Adriatic islands.

5 On this important political and literary figure see Milovan Djilas, *Njegoš, Poet Prince Bishop* (New York, 1966).

6 See Tatyana Nesterova, *American Missionaries among the Bulgarians (1858–1912)* (Boulder, CO, 1987).

7 Stanford J. Shaw and Ezel Kural Shaw, *History of the Ottoman Empire and Modern Turkey* (Cambridge, 1977), vol. II, pp. 55–171.

8 Douglas Dakin, *The Greek Struggle for Independence 1821–1833* (Berkeley, CA, 1973), pp. 214–17.

9 Stevan K. Pavlowitch, *A History of the Balkans 1804–1945* (London, 1999), p. 39.

10 Dennis P. Hupchick, *The Balkans from Constantinople to Communism* (New York, 2002), p. 266.

four: The National Wars, 1878–1918

1 Miranda Vickers, *The Albanians, a Modern History* (London, 1997), p. 30.
2 Stavro Skendi, *The Albanian National Awakening 1878–1912* (Princeton, NJ, 1967), p. 86.
3 Karel Durman, *Lost Illusions: Russian Policies Towards Bulgaria in 1877–1887* (Uppsala, 1988), p. 118.
4 Stephen Constant, *Foxy Ferdinand, Tsar of Bulgaria* (New York, 1979), pp. 13–14.
5 Duncan M. Perry, *Stefan Stambolov and the Emergence of Modern Bulgaria 1870–1895* (Durham, NC, 1993), p. 231.
6 L. S. Stavrianos, *The Balkans since 1453* (New York, 1958), p. 481.
7 Elizabeth Roberts, *Realm of the Black Mountain: A History of Montenegro* (Ithaca, NY, 2007) p. 269.
8 André Gerolymatos, *The Balkan Wars: Conquest, Revolution and Retribution from the Ottoman Era to the Twentieth Century and Beyond* (New York, 2002), p. 207.
9 F. R. Bridge, *From Sadowa to Sarajevo: The Foreign Policy of Austria-Hungary 1866–1914* (London, 1972), pp. 232–3. The principals were Austro-Hungarian foreign minister Agenor Goluchowski (1849–1921) and Russian foreign minister Michael A. Muraviev (1845–1900).
10 E. C. Helmreich, *The Diplomacy of the Balkan Wars 1912–1913* (New York, 1966) pp. 5–8.
11 Andrej Mitrović, *Serbia's Great War 1914–1918* (West Lafayette, IN, 2007), pp. 70–72.
12 See Richard C. Hall, *Balkan Breakthrough: The Battle of Dobro Pole 1918* (Bloomington, IN, 2010).
13 Charles King, *The Moldovans: Romania, Russia and the Politics of Culture* (Stanford, CA, 2000), pp. 32–5.
14 Richard C. Hall, *The Balkan Wars: Prelude to the First World War* (London, 2000), p. 135.

15 Spencer C. Tucker, ed., *The Encyclopedia of World War I* (Santa Barbara, CA, 2005), vol. I, p. 273.

16 James J. Sheehan, *Where Have All the Soldiers Gone? The Transformation of Modern Europe* (Boston, MA, 2008), p. 100.

five: The Interbellum, 1919–39

1 On Gaj see Elinor Murray Despalatović, *Ljudevit Gaj and the Illyrian Movement* (Boulder, CO, 1975).

2 Ivo Banac, *The National Question in Yugoslavia: Origins, History, Politics* (Ithaca, NY, 1984), p. 131.

3 Miranda Vickers, *Between Serb and Albanian: A History of Kosovo* (New York, 1998), pp. 99–102.

4 Ivan Ilchev, *The Rose of the Balkans: A Short History of Bulgaria* (Sofia, 2005), p. 317.

5 Bruce Clark, *Twice a Stranger: The Mass Expulsions that Forged Modern Greece and Turkey* (Cambridge, MA, 2006), pp. 87–107.

6 John R. Lampe and Marvin R. Jackson, *Balkan Economic History 1550–1950* (Bloomington, IN, 1982), pp. 464–9.

7 Noli wrote his senior thesis at Harvard on the subject of the fifteenth-century Albanian hero Skanderbeg.

8 His original name was the Turkish Zogolli. He adopted an Albanian form in Zogu.

9 John D. Bell, *Peasants in Power: Alexander Stamboliski and the Bulgarian Agrarian National Union, 1899–1923* (Princeton, NJ, 1977) pp. 154–83.

10 Ilchev, *The Rose of the Balkans*, p. 328.

11 The First Hellenic Republic was proclaimed in 1822 during the war for independence against the Ottomans. See chapter Three.

12 Hugh Seton-Watson, *Eastern Europe between the Wars 1918–1941* (New York, 1967), p. 204.

13 Dejan Djokić, *Elusive Compromise: A History of Interwar Yugoslavia* (New York, 2007), pp. 47–8.

14 Andrew Rossos, *Macedonia, and the Macedonians: A History* (Stanford, CA, 2008), p. 162.

References

six: Renewed War, 1939–45

1 As quoted in L. S. Stavrianos, *The Balkans since 1453* (New York, 1958), p. 725.
2 Kurt W. Treptow, ed., *A History of Romania* (Iași, 1996), p. 468.
3 In the First Vienna Award of 2 November 1938 German and Italian arbitration gave a strip of territory in southern Slovakia and Ruthenia to Hungary.
4 Mario Cervi, *The Hollow Legions: Mussolini's Blunder in Greece 1940–1941* (Garden City, NY, 1971), p. 153.
5 On German casualties see George E. Blau, *Invasion Balkans: The German Campaign in the Balkans, Spring 1941* (Shippensburg, PA, 1997), pp. 62, 108.
6 Bernd Fischer, *Albania at War 1939–1945* (West Lafayette, IN, 1999), p. 187.
7 A similar dispute had occurred in 1917 between the Bulgarians in Macedonia and the Austro-Hungarians in occupied Albania.
8 In the 1980s the Bulgarian Communist regime praised Second World War Bulgarian pilots who shot down American aircraft.
9 Stephane Groueff, *Crown of Thorns: The Reign of King Boris III of Bulgaria 1918–1943* (Lanham, MD, 1987), p. 383.
10 Mark Mazower, *Inside Hitler's Greece: The Experience of Occupation, 1941–44* (New Haven, CT, 1993), p. 41.
11 Mark Axworthy, Cornel Scafeș and Cristian Craciunoiu, *Third Axis Fourth Ally: Romanian Armed Forces in the European War 1941–1945* (London, 1995), p. 58.
12 Jozo Tomasevich, *War and Revolution in Yugoslavia, 1941–1945: Occupation and Collaboration* (Stanford, CA, 2001), pp. 233–4. Tomasevich tersely explained the situation, 'German bayonets kept the Ustasha regime in power.'
13 Stevan K. Pavlowitch, *Hitler's New Disorder: The Second World War in Yugoslavia* (New York, 2008), p. 49.
14 Ibid., p. 32.
15 Tito, a *nom de guerre*, possibly derived from the Serbo-Croat words *ti to*, you (do) that. This was Broz's verbal shorthand for issuing orders.

16 Stevan K. Pavlowitch, *A History of the Balkans 1904–1945* (London, 1999), p. 327. The degree to which the Partisans relied upon help from the Red Army became contentious after the Soviet–Yugoslav break.

17 Tomasevich, *War and Revolution*, p. 765.

18 Ibid., p. 738.

seven: The Establishment of Soviet Control, 1945–53

1 Barbara Jelavich, *History of the Balkans*, vol. II: *Twentieth Century* (Cambridge, 1983), p. 331.

2 Miranda Vickers, *The Albanians, a Modern History* (London, 1997), p. 165.

3 Milovan Djilas, *Conversations with Stalin* (New York, 1962), p. 143.

4 Hugh Seton-Watson, *The East European Revolution* (New York, 1951), p. 212.

5 Jozo Tomasevich, *The Chetniks* (Stanford, CA, 1975), pp. 460–61.

6 John R. Lampe, *Yugoslavia as History: Twice there was a Country* (Cambridge, 1996), p. 245.

7 R. J. Crampton, *Bulgaria* (Oxford, 2007), p. 339.

8 On the M.A.S.S.R. see Charles King, *The Moldovans: Romania, Russia and the Politics of Culture* (Stanford, CA, 2000), pp. 51–7.

9 Misha Glenny, *The Balkans: Nationalism, War and the Great Powers, 1804–1999* (New York, 2000), pp. 543–4.

10 John R. Lampe, *Balkans into Southeastern Europe* (New York, 2006), p. 195.

eight: Erosion of Soviet Control, 1953–85

1 John R. Lampe, *Yugoslavia as History: Twice there was a Country* (Cambridge, 1996), p. 263.

2 This ban did not apply to the Muslim-born Hoxha himself. His name means 'priest'.

3 R. J. Crampton, *A Concise History of Bulgaria*, 2nd edn (Cambridge, 2005), p. 195.

4 J. F. Brown, *Bulgaria under Communist Rule* (New York, 1970), pp. 173–87.

5 Hugh Poulton, *Who Are the Macedonians?* (Bloomington, IN, 1995), p. 116; Andrew Rossos, *Macedonia, and the Macedonians: A History* (Stanford, CA, 2008), pp. 251–2.

6 Robert J. Donia and John V. A. Fine, Jr, *Bosnia and Hercegovina: A Tradition Betrayed* (New York, 1994), p. 178.

7 See for example Milovan Djilas, *The New Class* (New York, 1957) and Milovan Djilas, *Conversations with Stalin* (New York, 1962).

8 Fred Singleton, *Twentieth-Century Yugoslavia* (New York, 1976), p. 181.

9 Tom Gallagher, *Modern Romania, the End of Communism, the Failure of Democratic Reform, and the Theft of a Nation* (New York, 2005), p. 81.

10 Tim Judah, *Kosovo: War and Revenge* (New Haven, CT, 2000), p. 40.

nine: An End and a Beginning, 1985–Present

1 See Peter Siani-Davies, *The Romanian Revolution of December 1989* (Ithaca, NY, 2005), pp. 136–43.

2 Tom Gallagher, *Modern Romania, the End of Communism, the Failure of Democratic Reform, and the Theft of a Nation* (New York, 2005), p. 72.

3 John R. Lampe, *Yugoslavia as History: Twice there was a Country* (Cambridge, 1996), p. 348.

4 On the Yugo see Jason Vuic, *The Yugo: The Rise and Fall of the Worst Car in History* (New York, 2010).

5 Louis Sell, *Slobodan Milosevic and the Destruction of Yugoslavia* (Durham, NC, 2002), pp. 45–6.

6 Central Intelligence Agency, *Balkan Battlefields* (Washington, DC, 2002), vol. I, p. 44; Tim Judah, *Kosovo: War and Revenge* (New Haven, CT, 2002), p. 53.

7 Lenard J. Cohen, *Broken Bonds: The Disintegration of Yugoslavia* (Boulder, CO, 1993), p. 208.

8 See Jan Willem Honig and Norbert Booth, *Srebrenica: Record of a War Crime* (London, 1996).

9 Central Intelligence Agency, *Balkan Battlefields*, vol. I, pp. 370–77.

10 Sell, *Slobodan Milosevic and the Destruction of Yugoslavia*, p. 360.

11 R. J. Crampton, *The Balkans since the Second World War* (London, 2002), p. 296.

12 Miranda Vickers, *The Albanians, a Modern History* (London, 1997), pp. 246–7.

13 Tim Judah, *Kosovo: What Everyone needs to Know* (Oxford, 2008), p. 88.

14 Ibid., p. 91.

15 John Phillips, *Macedonia: Warlords and Rebels in the Balkans* (New Haven, CT, 2004), p. 135.

16 Elizabeth Roberts, *Realm of the Black Mountain: A History of Montenegro* (Ithaca, NY, 2007), p. 457.

17 Charles King, *The Moldovans: Romania, Russia and the Politics of Culture* (Stanford, CA, 2000), pp. 191–6.

18 Laura Silber and Allan Little, *Yugoslavia: Death of a Nation* (New York, 1996), p. 25.

SELECT BIBLIOGRAPHY

Axworthy, Mark, Cornel Scafeş and Cristian Craciunoiu, *Third Axis Fourth Ally: Romanian Armed Forces in the European War 1941–1945* (London, 1995)

Banac, Ivo, *The National Question in Yugoslavia: Origins, History, Politics* (Ithaca, NY, 1984)

Bell, John D., *Peasants in Power: Alexander Stamboliski and the Bulgarian Agrarian National Union, 1899–1923* (Princeton, NJ, 1977)

Blau, George E., *Invasion Balkans: The German Campaign in the Balkans, Spring 1941* (Shippensburg, PA, 1997)

Bridge, F. R., *From Sadowa to Sarajevo: The Foreign Policy of Austria-Hungary 1866–1914* (London, 1972)

Brown, J. F., *Bulgaria under Communist Rule* (New York, 1970)

Central Intelligence Agency, *Balkan Battlefields* (Washington, DC, 2002)

Cervi, Mario, *The Hollow Legions: Mussolini's Blunder in Greece 1940–1941* (Garden City, NY, 1971)

Clark, Bruce, *Twice a Stranger: The Mass Expulsions that Forged Modern Greece and Turkey* (Cambridge, MA, 2006)

Cohen, Lenard J., *Broken Bonds: The Disintegration of Yugoslavia* (Boulder, CO, 1993)

Constant, Stephen, *Foxy Ferdinand, Tsar of Bulgaria* (New York, 1979)

Crampton, R. J., *The Balkans since the Second World War* (London, 2002)

——, *Bulgaria* (Oxford, 2007)

——, *A Concise History of Bulgaria*, 2nd edn (Cambridge, 2005)

Dakin, Douglas, *The Greek Struggle for Independence 1821–1833* (Berkeley, CA, 1973)

Despalatović, Elinor Murray, *Ljudevit Gaj and the Illyrian Movement*

(Boulder, CO, 1975)

Djilas, Milovan, *Conversations with Stalin* (New York, 1962)

——, *The New Class* (New York, 1957)

——, *Njegoš: Poet Prince Bishop* (New York, 1966)

Djokić, Dejan, *Elusive Compromise: A History of Interwar Yugoslavia* (New York, 2007)

Donia, Robert J., and John V. A. Fine, Jr, *Bosnia and Hercegovina, a Tradition Betrayed* (New York, 1994)

Durman, Karel, *Lost Illusions: Russian Policies Towards Bulgaria in 1877–1887* (Uppsala, 1988)

Fine, John V. A., *The Early Medieval Balkans* (Ann Arbor, MI, 1983)

——, *The Late Medieval Balkans* (Ann Arbor, MI, 1987)

Fischer, Bernd, *Albania at War 1939–1945* (West Lafayette, IN, 1999)

Gallagher, Tom, *Modern Romania, the End of Communism, the Failure of Democratic Reform, and the Theft of a Nation* (New York, 2005)

Gerolymatos, André, *The Balkan Wars: Conquest, Revolution and Retribution from the Ottoman Era to the Twentieth Century and Beyond* (New York, 2002)

Glenny, Misha, *The Balkans: Nationalism, War and the Great Powers, 1804–1999* (New York, 2000)

Groueff, Stephane, *Crown of Thorns: The Reign of King Boris III of Bulgaria 1918–1943* (Lanham, MD, 1987)

Hall, Richard C., *Balkan Breakthrough: The Battle of Dobro Pole 1918* (Bloomington, IN, 2010)

——, *The Balkan Wars: Prelude to the First World War* (London, 2000)

Helmreich, E. C., *The Diplomacy of the Balkan Wars 1912–1913* (New York, 1966)

Honig, Jan Willem and Norbert Booth, *Srebrenica: Record of a War Crime* (London, 1996)

Hupchick, Dennis P., *The Balkans from Constantinople to Communism* (New York, 2002)

——, *The Bulgarians in the Seventeenth Century* (Jefferson, NC, 1993)

Ilchev, Ivan, *The Rose of the Balkans: A Short History of Bulgaria* (Sofia, 2005)

Jelavich, Barbara, *History of the Balkans*, vol. I: *Eighteenth and Nineteenth Centuries* (Cambridge, 1983)

——, *History of the Balkans*, vol. II: *Twentieth Century* (Cambridge, 1983)

Judah, Tim, *Kosovo: War and Revenge* (New Haven, CT, 2000)

——, *Kosovo: What Everyone needs to Know* (Oxford, 2008)

King, Charles, *The Moldovans: Romania, Russia and the Politics of Culture* (Stanford, CA, 2000)

Kulash, Nicholas, 'Grim Romanians Brighten over a German Connection', *New York Times*, 5 December 2009

Lampe, John R., *Balkans into Southeastern Europe* (New York, 2006)

——, *Yugoslavia as History: Twice there was a Country* (Cambridge, 1996)

——, and Marvin R. Jackson, *Balkan Economic History 1550–1950* (Bloomington, IN, 1982)

Luttwak, Edward N., *The Grand Strategy of the Byzantine Empire* (Cambridge, MA, 2009)

Mazower, Mark, *The Balkans, a Short History* (New York, 2000)

——, *Inside Hitler's Greece: The Experience of Occupation, 1941–44* (New Haven, CT, 1993)

Mitrović, Andrej, *Serbia's Great War 1914–1918* (West Lafayette, IN, 2007)

Nesterova, Tatyana, *American Missionaries among the Bulgarians (1858–1912)* (Boulder, CO, 1987)

Obolensky, Dimitri, *The Byzantine Commonwealth, Eastern Europe 500–1453* (New York, 1971)

Pavlowitch, Stevan K., *A History of the Balkans 1804–1945* (London, 1999)

——, *Hitler's New Disorder: The Second World War in Yugoslavia* (New York, 2008)

Perry, Duncan M., *Stefan Stambolov and the Emergence of Modern Bulgaria 1870–1895* (Durham, NC, 1993)

Phillips, John, *Macedonia: Warlords and Rebels in the Balkans* (New Haven, CT, 2004)

Poulton, Hugh, *Who Are the Macedonians?* (Bloomington, IN, 1995)

Roberts, Elizabeth, *Realm of the Black Mountain: A History of Montenegro* (Ithaca, NY, 2007)

Rossos, Andrew, *Macedonia, and the Macedonians: A History* (Stanford, CA, 2008)

Schevill, Ferdinand, *History of the Balkans from the Earliest Times to the Present Day* (New York, 1922)

Sedlar, Jean W., *East Central Europe in the Middle Ages, 1000–1500* (Seattle, WA, 1994)

Sell, Louis, *Slobodan Milosevic and the Destruction of Yugoslavia* (Durham, NC, 2002)

Seton-Watson, Hugh, *Eastern Europe between the Wars 1918–1941* (New York, 1967)

——, *The East European Revolution* (New York, 1951)

Shaw, Stanford J., and Ezel Kural Shaw, *History of the Ottoman Empire and Modern Turkey*, 2 vols (Cambridge, 1976)

Sheehan, James J., *Where have all the Soldiers Gone? The Transformation of Modern Europe* (Boston MA, 2008)

Siani-Davies, Peter, *The Romanian Revolution of December 1989* (Ithaca, NY, 2005)

Silber, Laura, and Allan Little, *Yugoslavia: Death of a Nation* (New York, 1996)

Singleton, Fred, *Twentieth-Century Yugoslavia* (New York, 1976)

Skendi, Stavro, *The Albanian National Awakening 1878–1912* (Princeton, NJ, 1967)

Stavrianos, L. S., *The Balkans since 1453* (New York, 1958)

Stephenson, Paul, *The Legend of Basil the Bulgar-Slayer* (Cambridge, 2003)

Stoianovich, Traian, *A Study of Balkan Civilization* (New York, 1967)

Todorova, Maria, *Imagining the Balkans* (Oxford, 1997)

Tomasevich, Jozo, *The Chetniks* (Stanford, CA, 1975)

——, *War and Revolution in Yugoslavia, 1941–1945: Occupation and Collaboration* (Stanford, CA, 2001)

Treptow, Kurt W., ed., *A History of Romania* (Iași, 1996)

Tsvetkov, Plamen, *A History of the Balkans: A Regional Overview from a Bulgarian Perspective*, 2 vols (New York, 1993)

Tucker, Spencer C., ed., *The Encyclopedia of World War I* (Santa Barbara, CA, 2005), vol. I

Vickers, Miranda, *The Albanians, a Modern History* (London, 1997)

——, *Between Serb and Albanian: A History of Kosovo* (New York, 1998)

Vryonis, Speros, *Byzantium and Europe* (New York, 1967)

Vuic, Jason, *The Yugo: The Rise and Fall of the Worst Car in History* (New York, 2010)

Wachtel, Andrew Baruch, *The Balkans in World History* (Oxford, 2008)
Wolff, Robert Lee, *The Balkans in Our Time* (New York, 1967)

ACKNOWLEDGEMENTS

I wish to acknowledge the Toledo-Lucas County Library in Maumee Ohio, The Joint Universities Library (now Jean and Alexander Heard Library) in Nashville, Tennessee, and the Ohio State Library in Columbus, Ohio, where I began to read about Southeastern Europe. I note the impression Dr Carole Rogel's class on the History of the Balkans made on me. I also want to acknowledge the Central State Achieve and the Archive of the Bulgarian Academy of Sciences in Sofia, Bulgaria and the Hoover Institute Archive in Stanford, California, where I began to research into Southeastern Europe. Finally I would like to thank Mariyana Kostova for her help in producing the maps.

INDEX

LONGFORD LIBRARY

3 0015 00335597 3

949.6

LEABHARLANN CHONTAE LONGFOIRT